Postcommunism

Four Perspectives

Postcommunism

Four Perspectives

EDITED BY

MICHAEL MANDELBAUM

A COUNCIL ON FOREIGN RELATIONS BOOK

COUNCIL ON FOREIGN RELATIONS BOOKS

The Council on Foreign Relations, Inc., is a nonprofit and nonpartisan organization devoted to promoting improved understanding of international affairs through the free exchange of ideas. The Council does not take any position on questions of foreign policy and has no affiliation with, and receives no funding from, the United States government.

From time to time, books and monographs written by members of the Council's research staff or visiting fellows, or commissioned by the Council, or written by an independent author with critical review contributed by a Council study of working group are published with the designation "Council on Foreign Relations Book." Any book or monograph bearing that designation is, in the judgement of the Committee on Studies of the Council's Board of Directors, a responsible treatment of a significant international topic worthy of presentation to the public. All statements of fact and expressions of opinion contained in Council books are, however, the sole responsibility of the author.

If you would like more information on Council publications, please write the Council on Foreign Relations, 58 East 68th Street, New York, NY 10021, or call the Publications Office at (212)734-0400.

Library of Congress Cataloging-in-Publication Data

Postcommunism : four perspectives / Michael Mandelbuam, editor.
    p.   cm.
   "Council on Foreign Relations book."
   Includes bibliographical references and index.
   ISBN 087609-186-9
   1. Postcommunism.   I. Mandelbaum, Michael.
   HX44.5.P69   1996
   320.5--dc20
                                      96-3213
                                        CIP

96   97   98   PB   10   9   8   7   6   5   4   3   2   1

Contents

Acknowledgments

This volume is part of the Council on Foreign Relations Project on East-West Relations, which is supported by the Carnegie Corporation of New York. The chapters of this volume were presented as papers at the Henry A. Kissinger Symposium on Postcommunism held in Washington, D.C., on May 8 and 9, 1995. The views expressed are those of the authors alone.

The editor is grateful to all those involved in the production of this volume, especially Audrey McInerney, Xenia Iwasykiw, and Jay Cho, who helped organize the symposium, Anya Schmemann and Patricia Dorff, who supervised the publication of the book, and Anne Mandelbaum for her superb editing of the introduction.

Introduction

Michael Mandelbaum

The term "postcommunism" is backward-looking. It implies a world defined by what it used to be but no longer is. In fact, the 27 sovereign states that emerged from communist rule as a result of the upheavals of 1989 and 1991, which stretch from the center of Germany to the Pacific coast of Russia and, in Churchill's phrase, from Stettin in the Baltic to Varna on the Black Sea, share both a particular historical experience and a common set of hopes and plans. "Postcommunism" refers to both the past *and* the future.

The common experience of communism began with the Bolshevik seizure of power in St. Petersburg in 1917 and ended with the collapse of the communist regimes of central Europe in 1989 and the disintegration of the state the Bolsheviks built—the Soviet Union—in 1991.

It is clear enough in retrospect—indeed, it was clear during communism's heyday—just what communism was. It was a political system that was "totalitarian" in aspiration, aiming to control every aspect of social life. The instrument of control was the all-powerful, hierarchically organized, self-selected, and self-perpetuating Communist Party. The party claimed to be equipped for this ambitious task by its unique understanding of the laws of history, to which it had gained access through communism's sacred texts, the writings of Marx, Lenin, and, for a time, Stalin.

The Communist Party enjoyed a monopoly of power, which it maintained by force.

It was responsible for, among other things, managing the country's economy, which was "planned" in the sense that important decisions were made by administrative fiat. Party officials, not the ebb and flow of supply and demand, determined what would be produced and grown, in what quantities, and the prices at which what was produced would be sold.

The party sought to prevent any collective activity outside its control. All important social ties and transactions were supposed to be vertical, between the party and the society, rather than horizontal, among members of society independent of the regime. Private economic activity, organized religion, interest groups, clubs, associations of all kinds—all the elements of what has come to be called civil society—were suppressed.

That was communism. Or, at least, that was the ideal type of the communist system. The countries and provinces between Berlin and Vladivostok differed from one another in significant ways. In Poland the Catholic church achieved considerable autonomy. Hungary introduced market reforms in agriculture in the late 1960s. In the Central Asian republics of the Soviet Union effective power often resided with local clans. In the Caucasus, black market economic activity enjoyed wide tolerance. In Romania a nominally communist dictator tried to establish dynastic rule.

Still, all 27 countries are "postcommunist" in the sense that they left behind a political, economic, and social experience with recognizably distinct and common features.

As it is commonly used, the term "postcommunism" is forward-looking as well. It connotes both a clear direction and a fixed destination. It presumes a goal toward which the 27 countries are moving. That goal is, figuratively, the West: they are presumed to have embarked on a journey from totalitarianism to democratic politics and free market economics.

The presumption of a common destination is captured in another term that is often used in discussions of postcommunism: the transition. The term signifies the belief that the upheaval that is under way where communism once stood has a shape, a purpose, a theme. It is a transition westward. The idea of the transition is a common point of departure for the four chapters in this volume.

Used in the democratic, capitalist West, the idea of the transition is susceptible to the charge of "mirror-imaging," the reflexive assumption that others are like us—or at least that they *wish* to be like us. The idea of the postcommunist transition rests, however, on firmer foundations than that. It is grounded in recent history. The global conflict between communism and the West that dominated the four decades after World War II was an ideological struggle. It was a conflict of creeds, of political and economic systems. What Stalin said about World War II to Milovan Djilas and other Yugoslav communists was true as well of the Cold War: "This war is not as in the past. . . . Everybody imposes his own system as far as his army can reach."[1]

Like World War II, the Cold War had clear winners and losers. The armies of the winners did not, it is true, occupy the territory of the losers. Still, given the nature of the conflict and the way it ended, it was logical for the losers to adopt the institutions and beliefs of the winners.[2] It was logical in particular because the outcome represented a victory of the West's methods of political and economic organization rather than a triumph of its arms.

The West prevailed because its system was more durable and successful. Democracy secured popular allegiance, something the dictatorship of the Communist Party, for all its claims to represent the real interests of those it governed, failed to do. Market economics achieved prosperity in a way that the planned economies, despite their claim to being a more scientific method of channeling resources and producing goods, did not.[3]

Imitation is not only the sincerest form of flattery; where intense competition is the rule, it is the best formula for survival. This has always been true of military technology. It is true as well in market economies, where money-losing firms adopt the techniques of profitable ones. In the last part of the twentieth century, rivalry among sovereign states came to involve not only contests of arms but also competition in political cohesion and economic productivity; as with armaments, the most successful techniques for achieving these ends were bound to spread.

The most persuasive evidence for the relevance to postcommunist Eurasia of the idea of a "westward" transition, however, comes not from the academic vocabulary of the West or the logic of recent history, but from the 27 postcommunist states themselves. They have embraced the idea. Their governments profess their goals to be the construction of political democracy and the establishment of a market economy. They seek to become part of the Western-dominated international organizations, which require for membership the establishment of Western-style institutions and fidelity to Western norms: the Council of Europe, NATO, the International Monetary Fund, the World Bank.

After World War II Stalin refused to allow any of the countries under his control to participate in the American-sponsored Marshall Plan, which helped to underwrite the economic reconstruction of Europe. The Soviet dictator no doubt calculated, rightly, that participation would enmesh the communist-ruled countries in the coils of international capitalism. It is a sign of the revolutionary consequences of 1989 and 1991, as well as a mark of the Western orientation of the regimes that succeeded the communist ones, that in the wake of the Cold War the same countries, including Russia, clamored for a new Marshall Plan. They have received none, but since 1989 and 1991 the postcommunist governments have formed political parties, held elections, established stock markets, and turned previously communist-controlled economic assets over to private owners.

Still, while the end of communism is a matter of fact, the transition to democracy and free markets remains a work in progress. Each of the four chapters in this volume comments on both the idea and the fact of the transition, but each approaches it from a different perspective and arrives at different conclusions about its prospects for success.

THE CHAPTERS

The four essays divide into two groups of two. For Stephen Holmes and Robert Skidelsky, a successful transition—that is, safe passage to democracy and free markets in postcommunist

Eurasia—is contingent on the adoption of a particular set of policies. By contrast, both Charles Gati and John Mueller are ready to pronounce a verdict on the transition; but theirs are opposite verdicts.

For Stephen Holmes, the key to a successful transition throughout the postcommunist world is effective state-building. The troubles that plague the transition, he argues, are not what either local participants or foreign observers initially expected them to be. Postcommunist countries are not being paralyzed by divisive efforts to come to terms with the past. Nor are they weighed down by the heavy cultural burdens that the past imposes: the absence of the attitudes and values necessary for decent politics and efficient economics.

Instead, the postcommunist countries suffer from governments that are too weak to provide the elementary "public goods" on which tolerable social life depends, chief among which are law and order. The social pathologies that most trouble the inhabitants of postcommunist Eurasia—crime, corruption, and inflation—are the products of a state too weak to enact and enforce laws and control the government's budget. The epigraph for this chapter might be a quotation from an earlier Holmes, Oliver Wendell, who said that he paid his taxes happily, knowing that the check he sent to the government was purchasing "civilization." Civilization, in this sense, is something that most postcommunist governments have had difficulty putting in place.

An irony emerges from Holmes's argument: in the communist era the state was far too strong for the good of those it governed, so strong that it imposed a dismal kind of equality by stifling liberty, fraternity, and prosperity. Now, in the successor states of the Soviet Union and their neighbors, it is too weak. Where once it suppressed what in any normal society would be considered lawful behavior, now it cannot suppress what in every society qualifies as illegal conduct. Instead of enforcing the rules that are necessary for productive economic activity, postcommunist officials use their positions to enrich themselves. The postcommunist countries suffer not from oppressive but from unaccountable government. The chief problem they face is not tyranny but larceny, not autocracy but kleptocracy. The key to the success of the transition, by this analysis, is an honest, effective system of laws, courts, and police.

For Robert Skidelsky, a successful transition depends on solving a related but distinct problem: excessive government interference in the economy. Success requires reducing the proportion of economic output appropriated by the state. A state that is too large in Skidelsky's terms is not necessarily one that is too strong in the communist fashion: to the contrary, it is likelier to be too weak in the ways that Holmes describes. It is the toxic combination of the government's excessive economic and social aspirations with its administrative weakness that produces one of the most widespread and dangerous pathologies in the postcommunist world: inflation.

Inflation arises when a state's obligations exceed its revenues. Because it lacks the strength either to reduce the demands it tries to satisfy or to collect sufficient taxes to satisfy them, it must pay out more than it takes in. It fills the gap by printing money. The result is a rise in the level of prices: the larger the gap, the steeper the rise.[4]

Skidelsky is writing specifically about postcommunist Russia, but his argument extends across both time and space. He sees the "fiscal crisis of the state" as a chief cause of the implosion of the Soviet Union. The gap between income and obligations became so great that the Soviet machinery of government simply disintegrated: essentially, the central government in Moscow lost most of its revenue to the newly independent republics, the 89 autonomous republics and provinces that make up the Russian federation, and the informal economy, while retaining responsibility for the upkeep of the military-agrarian sector—the part of the economy that it still "owned." That is what is meant by the collapse of the Soviet Union.[5] The same problem that caused the collapse of the Soviet state has been responsible for the rampant inflation of the post-Soviet era in Russia.

Moreover, the collapse of communism is, in Skidelsky's view, merely the most extreme version of the contemporary worldwide fiscal crisis of the state, the crisis of collectivism. Communism was "a distorting mirror of ourselves."[6] Skidelsky sees the struggle to correct the chronic and virtually universal imbalance between the state and the private sector—the consequence of excessive obligations undertaken by the state—as perhaps the most important global trend of the last quarter of the twentieth century, a trend common to Margaret Thatcher's Britain, Ronald Reagan's United States, Deng Xiaoping's revolutionary market reforms in China that began in the late 1970s, and the more modest economic liberalization begun in India in the early 1990s. Each involved an effort to "restore profitability."

Holmes and Skidelsky enter the lists on one side of an ongoing debate about postcommunism, the debate about the feasibility of a successful transition to Western political and economic forms. They are in the camp of the optimists. What distinguishes this camp from the pessimists is a difference in emphasis in the interpretation of political and social life.[7]

The optimists emphasize the role of institutions. Institutions shape behavior by creating incentives. Establishing new institutions that change the structure of incentives that individuals confront thus will cause a shift in behavior. Once the institutions of a market economy are established—and this can be done in a few years, in some cases even months—people will master its rules and operate it successfully in short order.

The pessimists, by contrast, stress the role of culture in human affairs. For them it is habits, attitudes, and skills that determine the shape of social and political life. Because these must be learned, they can only accumulate very slowly, over decades. Thus, the changes in behavior that the shift from communist to Western politics and especially economics involves cannot take place immediately. Western rules of accounting, for example, can be promulgated overnight; but training an accountant takes years, and a generation, at the least, is required to produce the number of trained accountants necessary to constitute a full-fledged accounting profession.

These different assessments of the prospects for the transition are associated with different academic disciplines. Economists, whose professional worldview puts incentives and institutions at its core, tend to be optimists; historians and sociologists, who study long-term trends, gravitate toward pessimism.

Holmes and Skidelsky are unorthodox optimists in that they stress political rather than economic institutions. The institution that matters most is the properly designed state, which is one with a well-functioning government. It is not easy to establish such a state, however, particularly under the conditions of post-communism. Each author's analysis reveals an obstacle to doing so in the form of a circular problem. Holmes argues that in order to be legitimate, a government must be effective; but it is also the case that in order to be effective, it must be legitimate. People will not pay taxes unless they believe that what they pay will purchase services they deem important; but a government cannot provide these services if it cannot collect taxes.

A comparable circularity, involving the postcommunist relationship between politics and economics, emerges from Skidelsky's analysis: policies that are economically necessary may be politically impossible. Economic stability, meaning the taming of inflation, is a necessary condition for prosperity, and policies to promote stability require political support. But implementing policies of stabilization causes economic hardship—notably through unemployment—which is likely to undercut the political basis on which these policies must rest.

To break the vicious circle of ineffectiveness and illegitimacy, and of inflation and unemployment, the two authors prescribe political will and leadership; but these are, after all, easier to prescribe than to achieve.

Of the four authors, the one most optimistic about the transition in postcommunist Eurasia is John Mueller. In his view, it has already taken place. By the proper definition of democracy, according to Mueller—a political system in which the government can be overthrown nonviolently—the countries of post-communist Eurasia are already democracies. By the proper definition of capitalism—an economic system in which it is possible to make a profit legally—they are already capitalist. Democracies and market economies are not all alike in every particular, of course, and precisely what kinds of democratic political systems and capitalist economies these 27 countries will turn out to have remains to be seen; but democracies and market economies of *some* kind they will all, or almost all, turn out to be—indeed already *have* turned out to be.

The successful completion of the transition, Mueller further argues, demonstrates a broader truth: the establishment of both democracy and free markets is simple and straightforward, if not always easy. Both are natural in the sense that each will take root unless forcibly prevented from doing so. Neither requires elaborate cultural preconditions. Both spring from what is basic, almost biological, in human nature. Democracy is, in Mueller's view, a logical consequence of the universal tendency to complain. A capitalist economic system arises from another deep-rooted human impulse: the urge to acquire.

Societies will adopt democratic politics unless "thugs with guns" keep them from doing so. With the collapse of communism the thugs—that is, the security organs of the party—disappeared, or at least went into retreat.

The newly established political and economic systems of postcommunist Eurasia are not without problems; but these problems stem from the potential for popular misunderstanding of the character of democracy and free markets where they have recently arrived. Political expectations may be too high. The public may take to be pathological what are in fact part of the normal workings of democratic political systems. Apathetic, cynical, demagogic, money-riddled politics are not departures from the democratic norm: they *are* the norm in the practice if not the theory (or the mythology) of the West.

If democracy risks being discredited in the eyes of the citizens of postcommunist countries who are experiencing it for the first time because it is worse than they have (unrealistically) imagined, capitalism courts unpopularity because, in the form in which they will initially encounter it, it is shabbier and less efficient than what is normal in the West. If democracy is worse than they believe, capitalism is better.

In the minds of the citizens of the postcommunist world, capitalism is becoming associated not simply with greed but also with rampant dishonesty. In the long run, however, it is normal, Mueller argues, for capitalism to promote *honest* conduct. For the purpose of becoming rich, it is better to have a reputation for honesty than for dishonesty; to earn the desired reputation, it is better actually to *be* honest than dishonest.[8]

Mueller's chapter is similar to Skidelsky's in that the scope of its analysis is extremely broad, reaching far beyond the world of postcommunism. It is similar to that of Charles Gati in delivering a verdict on the transition. But Mueller's optimism stands in contrast with Gati's conclusion, which is bleaker than that of any of the other three authors.

Although the postcommunist countries may succeed in installing economies that partly incorporate market principles, Gati argues, many will not be democracies. In most of them it may be possible—although not easy, absent a position in or connections to the ruling oligarchy—to make a profit legally; but it will not be possible to overthrow the government nonviolently.

The differences between Mueller and Gati are partly matters of interpretation: what Gati sees as evidence of the failure to make the transition Mueller interprets as the inevitable costs of a transition already made. The opposed verdicts also stem from different perspectives. Mueller's is the bird's-eye view, a report of how things look from a distance, under the eyes of eternity—or the contemporary equivalent of eternity: the academic analyst. Gati's is what might be called the view from the trenches, an account of how the transition is being experienced at close range by those who are involved personally.

Still, Gati's chapter goes beyond the other three in challenging directly the premises implicit in the idea of the postcommunist transition: that all 27 postcommunist states are proceeding, albeit at varying speeds, in the same direction and will arrive, some sooner than others, at the same happy destination. Gati presents data that he believes suggest, to the contrary, that the various processions toward democracy and free markets may not all reach this destination.

While the first three chapters concern themselves with the requirements for (or the fact of) success in the transition, a scenario for failure can be deduced from each: for Holmes, it involves the failure to construct an effective state; for Skidelsky, the failure to reduce the state's role in the economy; for Mueller, the failure of the people of postcommunist Eurasia to appreciate what democracy and free markets do and do not involve. Gati is more pessimistic than any of them, and from his analysis a different theory of failure emerges.

The idea of the postcommunist transition, with its tacit presumption of a royal road to democracy and free markets, has a distinctly mixed pedigree. It is squarely in the tradition of the interpretation of history that considers the spread of liberty to be the principal political trend of the modern era. The idea of the transition also harbors, however, a Marxist component: the assumption that economics drives politics. Democracy will flourish, the idea of transition implies, because it will be accompanied by capitalism, which will produce prosperity, which will endow democracy with legitimacy and thus permanence. Democracy will take hold because it will, in Gati's phrase, "deliver the goods."

But Gati raises the possibility that the new states will *not* deliver the goods, at least not quickly or abundantly enough to anchor democratic government in popular approval. This failure, if it occurs, will stem from the uncommonly difficult economic and political legacies of the communist past. While the problems the postcommunist states face in building a market economy may in important ways resemble the pathologies of the noncommunist world, as Robert Skidelsky asserts, the damage that communism inflicted was far more severe than anything found in the West or the Third World. Communist damage will be harder, and take longer, to undo.

Communist economies were not, strictly speaking, *under*developed; they were *mis*developed. The transition from communism therefore involves not only building new structures but also destroying existing ones. This is bound to be a painful, protracted process. In its early stages it will produce more losers than winners. Unemployment will rise as old factories that produced what communist planners decreed but that consumers do not want to buy close down. Ultimately, as entrepreneurs respond to market demands, the workers cast loose will be reabsorbed into the workforce. But "ultimately" may turn out to be a painfully long time, and some workers may never be reemployed. For some period of time more people will have been made worse than better off by the collapse of communism. The result is the discontent registered by the poll data that Gati presents, which will lead to disillusionment not only with the sitting government, as would be true in the West, but also with the regime itself, with democracy.[9]

The failure of the transition, according to this scenario, stems from the deadly combination of discontent arising from economic hardship with the poisonous political legacy of the communist era. As Aurel Braun has put it: "The Marxist-Leninist baggage includes: an illiberalism that in key respects is more virulent than the pre-communist authoritarianism; a tendency against factionalism inherited from Lenin which makes it more difficult to form 'big tent' democratic parties; the absence or the dearth of the art of political compromise, which results in a kind of political autism; a cultural mistrust of authority yet a craving for statist economic security; a lack of (and enormous difficulty in constructing) a meaningful legal structure . . . and societies equating wealth with theft."[10] While the depth of what economists call the "transition recession" erodes the principal basis of support for democracy in postcommunist Eurasia—the economic benefits with which it is associated—the political legacy of communism inhibits the growth of democratic values: tolerance, fairness, belief in the importance of popular sovereignty, and the protection of individual rights.

The result could be the subversion of democracy through what is known as the "Pinochet solution," after Augusto Pinochet, the Chilean general who seized power in the 1970s and suppressed democracy while carrying out free market policies. The parallel between failed transitions in postcommunist Eurasia and military rule in Latin America is hardly exact. The military is not a likely candidate to seize power in most of the postcommunist countries. More plausible would be a dictatorship of parts of the old communist elite—the *nomenklatura*—and the security apparatus. (In some of the 27 countries such a combination does in fact hold power.) One feature common to both Pinochet's Chile and postcommunist autocracies, however, is likely to be a market economy of some sort. The communist economic system almost certainly cannot be restored, for this would require the restoration of the entire communist political apparatus, with its ideological underpinnings, which is simply not feasible. Thus, even in the scenario of transition failure, it will be possible, although not necessarily easy, to make a profit legally; but it will not be possible to overthrow the government peacefully.

If the results of the opinion polls in central and southeastern Europe that Gati cites suggest a way in which the transition could fail, the figures he supplies that rank all 27 postcommunist countries on several political and economic scales suggest, by the variations in the scores, that some countries will succeed and others will not—or at least that some are better placed than others to establish stable democracies and working free markets.[11]

The scores are, of course, estimates—crude, imprecise, and based on subjective judgments. Still, they are in keeping with what seems intuitively plausible. They correspond roughly to the conclusion to which observers of the trends in postcommunist Eurasia have generally come: that progress toward Western institutions is uneven across the region and varies, again very roughly and with exceptions and overlaps, according to geography.

REGIONAL DIFFERENCES

The 27 countries may be usefully divided into three broad categories: the postcommunist West, which includes central and eastern Europe reaching into the northern part of the Balkans; the East, consisting of the two great Slavic states, Russia and Ukraine, and Belarus, effectively an adjunct of Russia; and the South—the central and southern Balkans, the Caucasus, and Central Asia. (See table 1.)

What accounts for these regional variations? One obvious source is what Holmes calls "preconditions": specifically, three distinct but closely related forces—geography itself, history, and culture.

The most successful postcommunist countries are those closest to the part of the world from which the definition of success comes. Central and eastern Europe is the most promising sector of postcommunism because it is closest, both culturally

TABLE 1—PROGRESS IN TRANSITION IN EASTERN EUROPE AND
THE FORMER SOVIET UNION

West	Score	South	Score	East	Score
Bulgaria	21	Albania	19	Belarus	13
Czech Rep.	27	Armenia	15	Russian Fed.	20
Estonia	25	Azerbaijan	NA	Ukraine	12
Hungary	26	Georgia	10		
Latvia	NA	Kazakhstan	12		
Lithuania	24	Kyrgyzstan	21		
Poland	26	Moldova	16		
Romania	20	Tajikistan	10		
Slovakia	25	Turkmenistan	7		
		Uzbekistan	12		
AVERAGE	24	AVERAGE	14	AVERAGE	15

Source: The number for each country comes from combining the Freedom House political rights and civil liberties scores (cited in Charles Gati's chapter, pp. 173, 174)
with the economic scores of the European Bank for Reconstruction and
Development. [*Nations in Transit: Civil Society, Democracy and Markets in East
Central Europe and the Newly Independent States* (New York: Freedom House,
1995) and *Transition Report* (Washington, D.C.: EBRD, 1994).]

Notes: The EBRD scores include large-scale and small-scale enterprise privatization, restructuring, price liberalization and competition, trade and foreign exchange system reform, and banking reform. The Freedom House scores cover political rights
and civil liberties. A higher number here signifies greater progress toward democracy and free markets, and a lower number means lesser progress in the transition process.

    The countries have been grouped into three general categories—West (central
and east Europe and the north Balkans), South (central and south Balkans,
Caucasus, Central Asia), and East (the Slavic nations)—and the average score for
each group has been supplied. The former Yugoslav republics are not included
because of a lack of data. As noted, these scores are rough estimates and not precise measurements.

and geographically, to western Europe. This should not be surprising: cultural diffusion, after all, is among the oldest of all social patterns. Ideas and institutions are invariably carried beyond
their points of origin. They tend to take root earliest where the
distance they have to travel is shortest.

    Ideas and institutions, like democracy and capitalism, spread
by example, as well. The example of Western freedom and prosperity was most potent for the people who could observe it at
closest range, the people of the postcommunist West. Ideas and
institutions can spread not only through this "demonstration effect" but also by what might be called the "membership effect."

The postcommunist countries aspire to belong to Western-dominated international organizations. Membership requires adopting Western institutions and procedures. The closer a country is to the West, the likelier it is to be admitted to these Western associations, and thus the greater are its incentives to remake its political and economic structures according to Western standards. With a fully functioning market economy, the Czech Republic can expect to gain admission to the European Union. No matter how pristine its capitalism, this will not be possible, at least not in the near future, for Kyrgyzstan.

The three regions, as it happens, have distinctive histories. For most of the early modern period, each was under the control of a particular dynasty: the "West" was Habsburg, the "East" Romanov, and the "South" Ottoman. All were multinational empires ruled autocratically; but the impact of political and economic liberalism, and of their historical precursors, the Enlightenment and the Reformation, varied among the three. The impact was more pronounced in the West—the Habsburg Empire was part of the Western Christian world—than in the East, a stronghold of Eastern Christianity. And although the influence of the liberal tradition was faint in the Romanov world, it was fainter still where the Ottoman Turks ruled.[12]

While these 27 countries may share a recent past, their precommunist legacies vary in ways that may account for, by contributing to, their varying degrees of success at making the changes the transition involves, which Gati's scales illustrate.

A different source of regional variation within postcommunist Eurasia has to do with what Holmes and Skidelsky place at the center of their respective analyses: the state. It is arguable that what distinguishes successful from failed transitions is not the *effectiveness* of the state but rather its *legitimacy*, meaning the broad acceptance not of the regime's ideological character but of its geographic scope. Legitimacy here involves not who governs but who *is* governed.

The absence of legitimacy of this kind and the resulting disputes about where the borders of the state should be drawn and which groups should be included in it are responsible for what is perhaps the most glaring, and is certainly the most troubling, feature of postcommunism: large-scale violence between ethnic groups. Economics aside, some inhabitants of postcommunist Eurasia are worse off than they were under communism (at least during its final three decades), in that they are now more likely to be killed. The wars of postcommunism have been waged over the issue of legitimacy; and they have been waged in the "South": in the Balkans in Bosnia, in the Caucasus over Nagorno-Karabakh, and in Central Asia in Tajikistan.

It is these wars that most sharply distinguish the postcommunist South from the West; and they also distinguish the South, although less sharply, from the East. War is not raging everywhere along the southern tier of postcommunist Eurasia. But even where there is peace, order often is maintained, in the absence of a consensus on legitimacy, by autocratic rule. Dictatorship is one alternative to civil war, a way of preventing fundamental disputes about sovereignty from bursting violently into the open.

What accounts for the presence or absence of a consensus about legitimacy? The most obvious factor, although one that has limited explanatory and predictive force, is nationalism. The most powerful modern political sentiment, nationalism is the conviction that the national unit and the political unit should be congruent, that each nation should have its own sovereign state.[13] The lack of consensus about the legitimate borders of a state often stems from the absence of such congruence.

What, then, defines a nation? The only foolproof definition is tautological: a nation is a group that considers itself a nation and is willing and able to act as one; the best evidence that a group can act as a nation is that it is trying to secure its own state. Self-conscious nations tend to be groups that speak the same language or that are ethnically homogeneous or both; but there are exceptions to the first condition, and the second is not at all clear-cut.

Moreover, it is now accepted that nations are not primordial entities, born in the mists of time, straining at the leash of imperial rule and ready, once the leash is snapped, to emerge as full-fledged nation-states. To the contrary, they are communities that are imagined, constructed, devised—called into being by political and cultural entrepreneurs, although on the basis of some preexisting sense of collective identity.[14]

One instrument by which nations are created is the state. To the question of where coherent nations are to be found, the answer often is: where a state has forged one. The modern state can impose a common language through its bureaucracy and system of mass education. The state machinery also can create ethnic homogeneity by evicting those who do not belong to the core group. Ethnic cleansing in Europe did not begin in 1992 in the former Yugoslavia. It is an all-too-familiar feature of the modern era. Ironically, the ethnic cleansing of the past seems to have contributed to stability in the postcommunist present precisely by producing, by gruesome means, ethnic homogeneity, thus eliminating one potential cause of strife. Poland is predominantly Catholic and Polish because its sizable Jewish population was killed by the Germans during the war and the many Germans living in what became Poland after the war were evicted. Similar annihilations and evictions took place in the Czech Republic and the Baltic states.

The most peaceful part of postcommunist Eurasia—the West—is, on the whole, more ethnically homogeneous than the least peaceful part—the South. Not coincidentally, the states of the West have, on the whole, histories of sovereignty stretching back to the end of World War I; their counterparts in the South have been sovereign only since the end of the Cold War. E. J. Hobsbawm has referred to the aftermath of 1989 and 1991 as the unfinished business of 1919: "The eggs of Versailles and Brest-Litovsk are still hatching."[15] The South is in some ways repeating the history of the West, struggling to form viable states and in some cases seeking to make them ethnically homogeneous by the familiar, terrible, but proven methods. The pattern is not confined to the Balkans. Armenia and Azerbaijan have engaged in forcible exchanges of population. Russians are being encouraged to leave Central Asia.[16]

The presence of an ethnically heterogeneous population has not led to conflict or repression in every postcommunist state. Bulgaria's treatment of its Turkish minority actually improved after 1989. The long rivalry between Poles and Lithuanians now seems extinct. Vilnius, the Lithuanian capital, was historically a Polish (and Jewish) city; but Warsaw has made no claims on it. These happy outcomes, provisional though they are, may be due to what Mueller identifies as one of the basic features of democracy, properly practiced: the protection of minorities.[17] The absence of both war and repression may be the result of the existence of an ethnic majority that is credibly committed to observing the rules of democratic politics and a minority that recognizes that this provides enough political space to safeguard its interests.

The largest postcommunist minority consists of the 25 million Russians who, with the breakup of the Soviet Union, suddenly found themselves living as minorities in independent Estonia, Latvia, Ukraine, Kazakhstan, and other former Soviet republics. All things considered, the Russian minorities have thus far engendered remarkably little strife.[18] The reason may lie in the size and proximity of their historic homeland and protector. If a commitment to democratic norms is one basis for the fair treatment of national and ethnic minorities, the fear of a powerful neighbor where the minority is a majority may well be another. The military and political power of the Russian Federation is perhaps at least as effective a guarantor of the rights of Russians outside the federation as the moral power of democratic ideas.

In the political geography of postcommunist Eurasia, therefore, the countries of the West are struggling to establish effective states while those of the South face the task of creating legitimate ones. The pathology that besets the first group is crime and corruption; the second is plagued by civil war.

The three large post-Soviet Slavic states, the postcommunist "East," are situated, in cultural and political terms, between the West and the South. Russia and Ukraine confront both rampant crime and corruption and the threat of secession: the first is more acute than in the West, the second less pressing than in the South. Russia and Ukraine are less ethnically homogeneous than the countries of central and eastern Europe, but more so than the newly independent states of the Balkans, the Caucasus, and Central Asia. Both Slavic states contain numerically large minorities, but because the states themselves are so populous—numbering 150 million and 52 million people, respectively—

minorities form smaller proportions of their total populations than they do in the postcommunist South. The Slavic countries have less experience of independent statehood than the countries of the postcommunist West: Ukraine was never an independent state in the modern era and Russia was always a multinational empire rather than a nation-state within its present borders. But they emerged from the communist period with more relevant experience than the new states of the South: there was always a Russian-*dominated* state, in the management of which the Ukrainians were junior partners.

From a geopolitical point of view, the fate of the Slavic East is of monumental importance. Russia is the largest and most heavily armed state in Europe. Together Russia and Ukraine contain 200 million of the 325 million people in the 27 postcommunist states. The Russian-Ukrainian relationship will have a decisive impact on the security policies of all the countries to the west, including the United States. The political and economic futures of Russia and Ukraine are uncertain. They may move in the direction of the West, or the South, or they may chart a separate course.

If they are drawn in the direction of either the West or the South, and if the two flanking regions continue the trajectories that the data cited by Gati imply, the ultimate result will be a new global political and economic configuration. What was known, during the Cold War, as the Second World will have been partitioned between, and absorbed by, the First and the Third.

The international system will have been divided between states for which the central issue is the one on which Skidelsky concentrates—striking the proper balance between the public and private domain in economic affairs—and those for which the overriding preoccupation is the question of the legitimate borders of the state. The problem with which the first group will have to cope is inflation (or in the case of the United States, debt). The problem for the second will be civil war or its suppression by dictatorship.

Whether or when such a clear global line of division will become apparent cannot, of course, be known in advance. What is clear, however, is that if and when it comes into being, the world will have crossed a threshold into a new historical epoch. It will have entered the *post*-postcommunist era.

NOTES

1. Milovan Djilas, *Conversation with Stalin* (New York: Harcourt, Brace and World, 1962), p. 114.
2. Among the losers was not only orthodox communism but also the idea on which Mikhail Gorbachev staked his career—the idea of reform communism, of a "third way" between Stalin (or Brezhnev) on the one hand and John Locke and Adam Smith on the other.
3. The familiar phrase "goods and services" does not apply. Communist economics did not allow for services, which was one (but only one) of the reasons that it failed.
4. Skidelsky notes that inflation is actually a tax—hidden and unacknowledged, perhaps, but a tax all the same in that it gives the state control over resources it would not otherwise have.
5. See Skidelsky's chapter in this book, p. 91–92.
6. Ibid., p. 82.
7. For Skidelsky's version of this debate see pp. 77–101.
8. Here Mueller implicitly disagrees with Holmes, who argues that an effective state must actively promote honesty because in the absence of the apparatus for doing so—an effective legal and judicial system—people will find it rational and profitable to be dishonest. Mueller argues the contrary position. Over time, he says, like Gresham's Law in reverse, good conduct will drive out bad.
9. See Gati's chapter in this book, pp. 168–98. Here Gati disagrees with Mueller, who argues that the polls express attitudes that are normal for democratic capitalism, since they are common in the West. Gati, however, implies that the same responses have different implications in the East, where the political consequences are likely to be more dire.
10. Aurel Braun, personal communication.
11. See Gati's chapter in this book, pp. 179, 183, and 185. The data in the *Eurobarometer* polls, it should be noted, come from the western-most postcommunist countries, the ones *most* likely in Gati's view to make a successful transition to democracy and free markets.
12. The Ottomans ruled directly in two of the three areas that comprise the "South" of postcommunism: the Balkans and the Caucasus. The third area, Central Asia, although not formally part of the Ottoman Empire, resembles it in that its people are ethnically Turkic and the primary faith is Islam.
13. Ronald G. Suny, *The Revenge of the Past: Nationalism, Revolution, and the Collapse of the Soviet Union* (Stanford, CA: Stanford University Press, 1993), p. 14.
14. The best-known statement of this point of view is Benedict Anderson, *Imagined Communities: Reflections on the Origin and Spread of Nationalism* (London: Verso, 1983).
15. E. J. Hobsbawm, *Nations and Nationalism Since 1780: Programme, Myth, Reality* (Cambridge: Cambridge University Press, Canto Edition, 1992), p. 64.

16. Ronald Suny has noted that the nationalisms of the Caucasus and Central Asia, such as they are, were created largely during the Soviet period: the Soviet Union was a hothouse as well as a prison house of nations. The Soviet experience may have left these new states with the worst of both worlds: a sufficient concentration of the population of the titular nationality in what was designated its "home" republic to give that group a proprietary sense there, leading to the desire to accomplish what it proceeded to attempt upon independence—the expulsion of minorities—without a strong enough commitment to democratic norms to forgo "ethnic cleansing." See Suny, *The Revenge of the Past*, ch. 3.
17. See Mueller's chapter in this book, pp. 102–67.
18. There has been some strife. The civic status of ethnic Russians in the Baltic states is an ongoing subject of dispute; but in none of the three states has that dispute turned violent.

CHAPTER ONE

Cultural Legacies or State Collapse? Probing the Postcommunist Dilemma

Stephen Holmes

In one vertiginous decade, the term "postcommunism" has gone from being virtually inconceivable to being shockingly self-evident, only to revert to being flatly unintelligible once again. To a limited extent, we comprehend the postwar period, but not even a coherent disagreement about what cluster of factors triggered the earthquakes of 1989 and 1991 has taken shape, and informed observers readily acknowledge that the shattered and ceaselessly evolving ex–East bloc still lies beyond our powers of classification. Indeed, the future seems more unknowable than ever, which is why the overused term "transition" should probably be junked, implying, as the noncommittal "postcommunism" does not, that we somehow know where we are headed. Optimists and pessimists will no doubt continue to sneer at each other in the journals, but their exchanges probably tell us more about their own moods than about the future of the region. While seven years have elapsed since the old systems began to dissolve and the military division of Europe was ended, Western politicians and political scientists continue to stumble forward, groping in the dark.

True, essayists opine about the upsurge of nationalism and a return of the communists. And a farfetched analogy with the 1930s (Chicago or Weimar) is currently in vogue. But our wholly unforeseeable *fin d'époque* still awaits its convincing interpreter.

In the meantime, frequent references to "chaos" accurately express a general lack of confidence about emerging patterns and long-term trends. All we know for sure is that the multiple processes under way are unscripted and unsteered and that there is no guarantee of a happy end. One unfortunate consequence of our interpretive failure, so far, is that policymakers too proceed blindfolded, without a global account of the new world disorder, without a simple map to help them distinguish minor nuisances from lethal threats or to decide when an incident is a portent.

Admittedly, to sketch a "simple map" is a formidable task. There is not one postcommunism, after all, but many postcommunisms, strewn across a fifth of the globe, comprising 27 countries with over 400 million inhabitants. One-size-fits-all theories are obviously useless in such a sprawling context. The sheer miscellaneousness of the states and quasi-states in question is made even harder to bring into focus by the roller coaster of political, social, and economic developments throughout the region. Although some exceedingly interesting scholarly works have begun to appear, the basic inscrutability of the swiftly changing scene is undeniable. Even a well-researched journal article is likely to have a painfully ephemeral shelf life. Inundated by an unmasterable flood of half-reliable and arbitrarily selected facts, anecdotal or statistical, specialists speculate and surmise. They extrapolate trends from crumbs of information and are quickly overtaken by unfathomable events. Surface conflicts are brightly lit, but deeper changes remain shrouded in darkness. Electoral percentages are duly reported, but their wider implications are not well explained.

The situation in Russia has been particularly fluid and difficult to interpret.[1] No one has any idea what will happen when Boris Yeltsin passes from the scene. Even if CIA spymasters could infiltrate the innermost Kremlin and secret police circles, they would still be clueless about what was happening in the rest of the vast Russian Federation or even, for that matter, elsewhere in Moscow. What forces may counteract or accelerate territorial unraveling? How reliable is the chain of command? Will privatization hit a snag once unwieldy state enterprises contain nothing more worth stealing? Will the wholesale larceny of state assets by public officials and "red directors" eventually produce a popular backlash? Was the war in Chechnya a turning point, or just another bump in the road? What do seemingly endless contract murders of bankers, businessmen, deputies, and TV personalities mean for the country's future? And how will generational conflicts, which are increasing with time, play out politically? To watch Russian politics is to observe a football game through a soupy fog where you can make out the teams only faintly and in outline, where you are unsure who has the ball or which way he is running, and where you strongly suspect there are some other strange players on the field whose intentions are perhaps sinister but in any case unknown.

The variety, complexity, and pauseless revamping of postcommunist systems baffle students and practitioners alike. But part of the difficulty for onlookers, domestic as well as foreign, stems from the fact that embezzlers and asset-strippers dislike being observed. Many important actors in these societies are waist deep in clandestine operations where millions of dollars are at stake. With immensely valuable state assets and raw materials waiting to be carted off or acquired semilegally at dirt-cheap prices, "cherry pickers" have learned to organize their lives in order to deceive the eye. Official statistics, as is well known, are useless indicators of activity in the unrecorded shadow economy. Off-the-books transactions, kickbacks, cash-filled envelopes, and forged invoices are ubiquitous, as is natural when newly prosperous individuals strive to present a moving target to tax collectors and ruthless extortionists, as well as to stockholders and bureaucratic overseers. Skills of duplicity and disinformation, not to mention cloakroom "connections" and techniques for ducking public responsibility, all honed under the old regime, have proved unexpectedly useful, and not only to privileged groups, in the new conditions.

CULTURAL LEGACIES?

These and other factors obstruct or blur the vision of the student of postcommunism. Yet some of the problems lie not there but here, not in the thing itself but in our approach, in our own concepts, presuppositions, and biases. Many of our fondest categories are simply inapplicable. "Left" and "right," it is now universally recognized, when applied to partisan rivalries in the 27 new postcommunist states, conceal more than they reveal. Similarly, 1989 in eastern Europe was not a "revolution," as its earliest commentators claimed.[2] (It was not even a jailbreak; the demoralized jailer simply left the prison door unlatched.)

So some of our basic categories fit awkwardly, or not at all. The Western scholars with the deepest historical knowledge of the region, whether they have been crippled by what they know or not, remain untutored novices when it comes to the new realities: imperial breakup and unstable borders, deindustrialization and capital flight, decolonization and the stranded diaspora, kleptocracy and gangland slayings, Manchester capitalism without rules and the inflationary consequences of lobbying by self-appointed representatives of unstable interest groups, pluralistic politics without real parties and self-identified "communists" who own sleazy casinos but nevertheless promise to turn back the clock.

All of this requires a new vocabulary and a new approach. But the problem of inappropriate categories, not to mention scholarly unpreparedness, is most clearly visible in attempts to answer the great questions of the day: Why has democratic and market reform turned out to be such an arduous process? Why has Western-style liberalism, embraced almost everywhere in theory, proved difficult even to approximate in practice? Why has freedom not yet been established, even though the totalitarian state has been torn down?

"Not enough time has passed" is a standard but vacuous response. It is vacuous because it leaves unanswered some crucial questions: What are the necessary preconditions for the consolidation of a well-functioning market democracy? And what are the existing obstacles, which presumably vary from country to country, to the creation of these preconditions? To answer these more precise but still highly general questions, some commentators invoke the famous absence of a middle class. Others emphasize the special difficulties involved in making a simultaneous transition to political democracy and market economics (for those hurt by economic change will presumably use the franchise to block necessary reforms). But by far the most widely diffused theory, if we want to call it that, about the yet unsuccessful or still incomplete liberalization of postcommunist states refers to *cultural legacies*, habits acquired in the past, which are difficult to shake and which purportedly obstruct the successful creation and function of democratic and market institutions. Habits die hard and mentalities change slowly, so no wonder the shocking disappearance of the Communist Party's monopoly on power has failed to produce a full-blown liberal society.

This cultural-legacy theory of abortive or half-baked liberalization comes in two distinct, and perhaps mutually inconsistent, versions. The first locates the main obstacle to reform in the revival, under conditions of extreme social stress, of nationalism or identity politics. The second emphasizes the subversive role of "learned helplessness" and psychological passivity inherited from totalitarian times. In both cases, inherited or resurrected values and attitudes, proclivities and norms, have purportedly derailed an otherwise natural process of Westernization.

We can put aside, as unworthy of refutation, teleological pictures of historical development that assume that the whole world is destined to become like the West. What deserves careful thought, by contrast, is the reform-hampering role of inherited attitudes and patterns of behavior. People do more easily what they are used to doing than what they have never done; of this there can be no doubt. Habits and expectations, which perversely constrict freedom of choice, can be handed down from generation to generation and survive for centuries by sheer inertia. But does not the deeply pessimistic notion that "endowment is fate" also exaggerate our predictive powers? Although people often, perhaps inevitably, underestimate their own capacity to adapt, do they not frequently learn to do new things? In many cases, dishabituation proves easier than it appears. The revolutionary transformation of journalism throughout the region, for all its shortcomings, suggests that mind-sets are actually much easier to change than, say, the location of military bases and oil pipelines. (To be sure, legacy-less developments, innovations with absolutely no cultural roots, are more likely to occur among the young than among the old.[3])

Perhaps the commonplace that "the best indicator of the future is the past" has loomed so large in post-Soviet studies because it is a stubborn cultural legacy of Soviet studies itself. Perhaps it is a Western habit of thought that we have yet to rinse out of our systems.[4] Brilliant analysts from Berdyaev to Jowitt, it is worth recalling, "explained" communism as an unintentional replication of pre-revolutionary Russian patterns. They analyzed the Soviet Union, for instance, as an almost inevitable "relapse" into a traditional Russian arrangement where passive masses were governed by a privileged elite.[5] Similarly, peasant envy was said to have been "repackaged" as an antiegalitarian ideology, while the old ruling class was "replaced" by the *partdvoryanstvo*. Messianic illusions about a Third Rome were thought to have "resurfaced" as proletarian internationalism, while Lenin "reoccupied" the place of the tsar. You cannot understand Stalin if you have not studied Ivan the Terrible, or Gorbachev if you are unacquainted with Peter the Great.

In other words, some important schools, at least, within Soviet studies were purveyors or victims of the same fallacy that afflicts much contemporary social science: *they confused analogy with causality*. Put crudely, their thesis was that the world is the way it is because it reminds us of the way it used to be. Being admirably knowledgeable about pre-revolutionary Russia, for instance, they naturally tended to exaggerate the current importance of what they worked so hard to learn. Formulated diagnostically, they mistook the false pleasure of pattern recognition for the genuine pleasure of causal explanation. The past is such a wonderful predictor of the future, in truth, because the past is almost infinitely rich. Genetic stories with a determinist hue usually result from an unspoken sifting of the evidence. If you examine the past closely, you can find foreshadowings of just about anything that comes to pass. (If communism was such a "natural fit," incidentally, why did it require so much violence to impose?)

Not that inherited expectations and especially skills can be simply ignored. Far from it. Russian authorities still lie shamelessly about how much oil has been spilled into Arctic rivers, no doubt. But what does this imply about the future? Does it mean that Russia is doomed to neo-annexationist adventures? The cultural-legacy thesis cannot simply be tossed aside, but it needs to be handled carefully, so that we can extract its element of truth while discarding its exaggerations. Take the first version of the thesis. The iron lid is off, so what stands in the way of successful reform? Should not blame be laid on the sudden resurgence of age-old nationalisms that festered just beneath the surface during the Soviet era?

RIP VAN WINKLE

In periods of dizzyingly rapid social change, exactly as in wartime, scholars and policy analysts are exceptionally dependent on journalists while journalists, in turn, rely intuitively on metaphors to knead and color "typical" anecdotes, making them chime with popular expectations and apprehensions. In the past few years, two of the most common metaphors used to frame the postcommunist experience and identify its leading dangers are Rip van Winkle and Pandora's box.[6] After a long interruption, we are told, buried ethnic tribalisms and nationalist xenophobias have been rudely disinterred. This purported outcropping of virulent atavisms is brought home to readers by a variety of images. If you remove the straitjacket, the lunatic will start acting as he was always inclined to act. Alternatively, the river of hatred flowed underground earlier in the century only to resurface with a vengeance today. Thermal analogies, such as cryogenesis and hibernation, also are used. Smoldering resentments were kept on ice during the subzero weather of the Cold War, but now, after the meltdown, they are boiling up. Speaking abstractly of eastern Europe and the former Soviet Union, Isaiah Berlin has compared injured nationalism to a bent twig, "forced down so severely that when released, it lashes back with fury."[7] If we are to believe many commentators, then, the entire region is pullulating with "unleashed" furies, "reopened" wounds, and interwar fascisms "reborn."

How persuasive is this "ancient hatreds" argument? Surveying postcommunist societies (putting Yugoslavia and

Transcaucasia aside for the moment), we can admittedly observe intercommunal acrimony, racist hooliganism, cemetery and synagogue desecrations, xenophobic graffiti, antiforeigner rhetoric, skinheads sporting Nazi symbols and chanting anti-Romany slogans, calls for the restoration of lost national greatness, the moral rehabilitation of unsavory former leaders (such as Ion Antonescu, Josef Tiso, Ante Pavelic), and paranoia about foreign plots to dismember the fatherland. The observable facts are these. Old prejudices have been dredged up. Hotheaded politicians talk a lot of rot. But what does it all add up to? Are we faced with marginal disturbances or harbingers of a new barbarism? Do these *fleurs du mal* have deep roots? And will they grow? Is eastern Europe pregnant with dozens of Bosnias? Is Russia about to ignite into a Yugoslavia with nukes? Do population transfers, land seizures, ethnic internment camps, drunken plunderers, war profiteering, and fascist psychopaths reveal the true face of postcommunism? Put more personally: Zhirinovsky exists, but does he epitomize Russia's future?

The prediction or fear that he does is based, in part, on a vague and unproved postulate about the relation between economic distress and extremist politics. Why do postcommunist societies provide "fertile ground" for national-populism or even fascism? Purportedly because people lost what they had but did not get what they wanted. Psychological disorientation and disappointed hopes are said to provide the soil in which populist paranoia can grow. Economic decline, combined with a lifting of communist restraints, ostensibly dooms many of the nations exiting from communism to some kind of nationalist frenzy. Communitarian hatred, authoritarian politics, and punitive aggression toward neighbors will surge up from subterranean depths. It will be a return of the repressed. What will be regurgitated is not healthy patriotism, to be sure, but wounded national pride in search of someone to blame.

An amazing number of articles about the aftermath of 1989 give scapegoating center stage. Václav Havel typifies the genre: "In a situation where one system has collapsed and a new one does not yet exist, many people feel empty and frustrated. This condition is fertile ground for radicalism of all kinds, for the hunt for scapegoats, and for the need to hide behind the anonymity of a group, be it socially or ethnically based."[8] Distinguished scholars concur: "life has become uncertain, often incomprehensible and threatening. Hence the need for scapegoats,"[9] or "Political leaders searching for popular support in the midst of often severe social and economic disruption may seek to capitalize on nationalist feelings and exploit the presence of minority scapegoats."[10]

The pop-psychological premise behind this sort of analysis runs as follows. Faced with unexpected hardship and destitution, people will manage their latent self-reproach by turning their aggressions outward. When life becomes dangerous and confusing, people look for a guilty party in order to overcome their sense of shame and helplessness. Under such conditions, aggressive feelings can be discharged most readily upon vulnerable cultural minorities who are stigmatized in national memory as enemies, as infiltrators or humiliators of the now-dominant ethnic group. When young adult males can no longer live under the protective wing of state enterprises, for instance, governments will be tempted to "play the anti-Semitic card." In this context, imaginary or real injuries to ethnic kinfolk abroad can perhaps be used to fuel a politics of resentment and mobilize constituencies at home. As mammoth industries go extinct, charismatic demagogues with a sense of mission, who inevitably emerge in times of crisis, will lather up a mass following among the frustrated and the frightened. Unable to provide social services, leaders can at least help mentally tortured citizens reinterpret their pain as a result of treachery. Since it is much easier to unify people around a negative than a positive, crude-minded but skillful political entrepreneurs, capitalizing on mass distress will lure their peoples into a replay of Weimar 1933. And so on.

This nightmare scenario, while not to be flippantly dismissed, has the feel of boilerplate. Postcommunist states are repeatedly, not to say repetitiously, described as providing "textbook conditions" for the rise of aggressive mass intolerance (as if every schoolteacher perfectly understood what factors contributed to such developments). But how useful are the categories of scapegoating and irrational blame for interpreting the murky events of the past seven years? If the straw is as dry as many observers assume, we should be astounded by this simple fact: it has yet to catch fire.

THE END OF DECOMMUNIZATION

That public demand for scapegoats is relatively low in eastern Europe, not to mention Russia, is suggested, first of all, by the near-universal failure of decommunization campaigns. In eastern and central Europe, just three years ago, decommunization was a burning issue. But it has now almost everywhere guttered to a quiet end. The unexpected but increasingly obvious tendency is to close the books on the crimes of the past. Far from being roasted on a spit, former communists have been elected to govern, ousting fiercely anticommunist cabinets, in Poland, Hungary, and Lithuania. Even in the Czech Republic, a partial counterexample, documented misbehavior has seriously affected the careers of a few hundred people at most. Many communist judges with compromised records, for instance, have acquired tenure under the Klaus government.[11] In Bulgaria, the doddering Todor Zhivkov was sentenced to seven years for embezzlement, but for reasons of health he never served a day. In 1993, the last two Romanian communist officials imprisoned for involvement in the December 1989 massacres were released. The Russian coup plotters of 1991 got out of jail, even before the amnesty, and even ran for seats in the Duma. Prime Minister Jan Olszewski's 1992 attempt to use secret police dossiers against Lech Walesa was a spectacular failure.[12] And so on. The only real exception to this trend is the former East Germany, where tens of thousands of petty informers have been fired from their jobs as schoolteachers and so on, an exception that supports the hypothesis that decommunization is not a process that a sovereign nation willingly inflicts upon itself. (Something similar could be said of denazification.)

Important differences are visible in this matter among the countries of eastern Europe, needless to say. But it is nevertheless generally true that the search for communist scapegoats has petered out. A few party bosses have been rusticated, and one or two criminal trials have taken place, but the dreaded witch-hunts have completely failed to materialize. Many presumably guilty people walk free, some have become wealthy, and some have even acceded to power. On the face of it, this lack of anticommunist animus is difficult to understand. The opportunists and stooges of the old regime turned a profit (sometimes handsome, sometimes paltry) off popular suffering. The party elite lived well by squeezing the people, occupying relatively decent apartments, for example, while most people were crammed together in uncomfortable conditions, and so forth. This is probably why some commentators initially expected a witch-hunt against former elites and their lackeys. By quarantining a few, the majority of citizens (whose hands were not exactly spotless) would metaphorically cleanse themselves. It sounded logical, but if it happened to a limited extent in the Czech Republic, it occurred virtually nowhere else. Why not? Why have voters been sweeping former communists into office rather than shunning and purging them? Why no inquisition in eastern Europe?

This is a typical example, it seems to me, of a question *mal posée* (based on an unjustified expectation of irrational patterns of mass behavior in the postcommunist world). In fact, there are some very good reasons why, contrary to expectations, militant decommunization has failed to materialize. Historical justice turns out to be a highly specialized concern, holding little interest for either those who look forward or those who look back. The former are devoted to making the most of the possibilities they have, while the latter, far from wishing to right past wrongs, feel that life was, yes, duller, but still "cozier" and more secure under the old regime. But the public disinterest in purges does not necessarily represent a flight into golden-age delusions or a turning away from reality. Arguably, at least, quiescence and inaction in this domain is rational, even commonsensical, or at least perfectly natural. We can hardly claim certainty at this early stage. But here are five perfectly respectable considerations that may have helped mute the politics of anticommunist resentment.

1. People are rightly of two minds about the moral question. Collective guilt is an incoherent idea and retroactive pun-

ishment is wrong. It is impossible to undo tragedy by legal means. How will symbolically stomping on a few perpetrators compensate the victims or make them whole? After 45 years of state socialism, moreover, many families had at least one member involved in some compromising activity. It would be unbelievably perverse, therefore, for most people to unload all guilt on some discrete and insular "other." [13] In the Czech Republic, while the ex-dissident Havel is extremely popular, the most popular politician of all is Vladimir Dlouhy, minister of industry and trade and a man who, like most Czechs, was never a dissident and who quit the Communist Party only after November 1989. Contrary to the irrational logic of scapegoating, a socially diffuse sense of complicity with the former system may make it extremely difficult to galvanize citizens to "root out the reds."

2. The urgency of current problems pushes concern for temporally remote crimes off the front pages of the popular press. Ordinary citizens understandably care more about personal security and day-to-day survival, fighting the mafia and fixing the economy, than about historical justice. They also have lost patience with clumsy attempts, by politically bankrupt parties, to distract popular attention from practical problems with hollow promises of moral purity.

3. People understand that decommunization is basically an elite power game. Most Hungarians knew what was really at stake, for instance, when Joszef Antall accused Istvan Csurka and Joszef Torgyan of having been informers. Lustration was a stick with which one group of would-be leaders was attempting to beat another. Popular skepticism about the politicization of morality, moreover, may be a sign not of amnesia but of indelible memory. After all, when the communists seized power after World War II, they cynically used the charge of collaboration with the Germans to discredit and deport noncommunists, even executing opponents after trumping up fake charges. Such tactics do not necessarily go over well when used a second time.

4. The older generation also knows, from bitter experience, what it takes to dislodge an entrenched social elite from its privileged perch. Only a terrorist state or perhaps a war could make a tabula rasa and exterminate the last germ of communism in

these systems. And many people not only share a strong aversion to replicating the political style of the Stalin regime, with its paranoid purges of revisionists, deviationists, and the enemy within, but also feel a stronger desire for normalcy than for retributive justice: "This is not what is done in normal countries and we are not going to do it here."

5. Those who exercised no important functions under the old regime believe, with some justification, that their country's ministries, bureaucracies, and factories desperately need the skills, contacts, and self-confidence of the old-regime elite and their educationally privileged children. Very few individuals with impeccably clean pasts or pedigrees are available to fill leading positions in the polity and economy. Moreover, seeing old elites (however despised) cling to positions of political and economic influence may actually provide psychological reassurance to those who are disoriented by the devastating discontinuities in their lives.

These are some of the factors that may help explain both the startling absence of retributive politics in the region (and, to a lesser extent, the electoral triumphs of communist successor parties). The list could easily be modified, qualified, and expanded. In some cases, it should be said, the counteroffensive by former communists, waged in their own media, was skillful and effective. But if they won the propaganda war, they did so only because considerations such as the ones mentioned "subsidized clemency" in the face of past misdeeds. If this analysis is at all plausible, then the driving force behind the tendency we now observe is not solely an attenuation of historical memory, but partly a reasonable assessment of the unprecedented moral and practical dilemmas of the present. While some diehards will condemn the unexpected demise of decommunization as a deplorable evasion of moral responsibility, it is just as plausible to see it as a predictable reassertion of human nature, if not a victory for common sense. But however we judge this unexpected and still understudied trend, we should now recognize it for what it is and try to think through its further implications. Does it not suggest, for instance, that the politics of rage and irrational scapegoating, even in its nationalist versions, have dimmer chances of success in postcommunist societies than many pessimistic commentators have assumed?

THE UNEXPECTED WEAKNESS OF ILLIBERALISM

Indeed, the most underreported event of the past years may be the *failed emergence* of extremist politics in almost all of eastern Europe and the former Soviet Union (the bloody exceptions duly noted). There are no grounds for complacency here. Paramilitary groups of alienated youths armed with Kalashnikovs can raise havoc and set unpredictable processes in motion. And an ethnic definition of citizenship can definitely have disastrous consequences in multinational states. But an excellent collection of articles on xenophobic nationalism in the region published in 1994 inadvertently made it clear that, for some reason, the politics of resentment has not become a major political problem so far.[14] This may explain why the former communists elected to power in Poland and Hungary, unable to solve their countries' biggest problems, have nevertheless made no significant effort to forge red-brown alliances. Political entrepreneurs—Istvan Csurka, Corneliu Vadim Tudor, Miroslav Sladek, Jan Slota, and others— have striven valiantly to stoke popular animosities and frustrations.[15] But they have gained scant electoral support. They apparently cannot generate the groundswell of "enthusiastic hopefulness" that fascism requires.[16] Postcommunist societies, for some reason, are largely bereft of zeal. Postcommunist man has not been, so far, mobilized in extremist movements because he has not been, so far, mobilized for anything at all. He remains politically inert. He is "cocooning."[17] Hence, until now, populist paranoia has not been a major force. Vladimir Meciar, it is true, has returned to power. But it is generally admitted that the breakup of the Czechoslovak federation was due to Klaus's perception that the road to Brussels does not run through Bratislava (and his decision to call Meciar's bluff), not to an irresistible outpouring of Slovak nationalism or a desire "to be ourselves at last."[18] And while sabers rattled, the Russians finally did pull out of the Baltic states, seemingly oblivious to a nationalist backlash.

So far, then, extremist parties have proved to be trees without roots. The leaders of these fringe groups, in turn, are sound-bite fascists, without spellbinding magnetism, with a bark worse than their bite, who talk rubbish but fortunately have no more plebiscitary appeal than, say, their counterparts in western Europe. Indeed, "no Polish leader espousing nationalist or racist rhetoric has had anything like the success of, say, Jean-Marie Le Pen in France."[19] This is a genuine anomaly. Despite the acknowledged incapacity of postcommunist parliaments to represent the interests and aspirations of suffering citizens, extraparliamentary extremist movements remain tiny, fragmented, kaleidosopically unstable, and politically marginal. The "politics of the street," orchestrated by charismatic demagogues, is not an observable trend. Like Gorbachev, some years back, Zhirinovsky is more popular in the West than in Russia.

It is difficult or perhaps impossible to explain a nonevent, the shoe that did not drop, the time bomb that failed to go off. And tomorrow's news may force the would-be explainer to eat his words. Prediction is futile, and the worst could still be ahead. But given the tremendous strains put on the population of the region, even the temporary nonappearance of political extremism, on a mass scale, should catch our eye. One reason this nonevent, the nonappearance of mass leaders able to turn mass resentment into a politically exploitable resource, has attracted less attention than it deserves may be understandable Western guilt about our failure to have foreseen the Yugoslav tragedy, a failure partly due to our unwise reliance on subjective reports from all sides that ethnic warfare would be impossible among peoples who intermarried, intermingled, and played volleyball together. This is not the sort of rosy optimism anyone wants to repeat.

As many commentators have remarked, various weighty and well-positioned actors have a stake in exaggerating the nationalist threat. Not only east European diplomats in pursuit of fast-track admission to NATO and the European Union (EU), but Russian leaders themselves have helped swell Zhirinovsky's reputation. Kozyrev knew that one of the most effective ploys in any bargaining situation was to claim that a failure to strike a deal with him would result in his being replaced by someone even more intractable or bloody-minded. And Gaidar was not above using the highly questionable economic-growth-absorbs-the-frustrations-that-would-otherwise-lead-to-fascism theory in pleading for Western aid. But, in my view, the real reason we are so attracted to the idea of déjà-vu nationalism, despite the paucity of evidence that it poses any immediate or substantial threat, is not that we have been duped. We are drawn to predictions of "fascism reborn" because they allow us to give a familiar name to a situation that we basically cannot understand.

Rip van Winkle metaphors and pop-psychological speculations about scapegoating, however, provide little guidance to the genuine problems of postcommunism. True, they echo the old literature on the crisis of modernization, where insecurities produced by the destruction of traditional patterns of life were "worked out" in attacking imaginary enemies.[20] But the "Westernization" of postcommunist societies did not begin from the traditional basis that most modernization theory presumes. We are not witnessing, for instance, a shift away from patrimonial or patriarchal to impersonal relations of production. Weberian "disenchantment" is not causing eyes to roll and heads to spin. The iron grip of tradition is not now, for the first time, being cruelly shattered. Age-old kinship ties and village solidarities are not being suddenly replaced by national labor markets and rationalized bureaucracies. The consequences of these simple facts are enormous. Communism had already deeply reshaped these societies, although in differing ways and degrees, before the most recent wave of "Westernization" began. As George Schöpflin has pointed out, east European peasants now have wristwatches and no longer believe in werewolves.[21] Stalinist modernization brought industrialization, urbanization, secularization, mass education, mass communications, and the integration of women into the workforce. These innovations do not make xenophobic nationalism politically untenable, of course. Rip van Winkle may not have died in his sleep. But the peoples of the region have very different outlooks, expectations, and behavioral patterns than the extremist generations earlier this century. Today's footloose youths, for instance, surely prefer porno videos to torchlight parades, new cars to leather boots. And is hostility toward symbols of uprooted modernity (such as Jews, where they still exist) likely to flare up among people who have no memory of village life and who dream longingly about foreign travel, prefer dollars and deutsche marks to national currencies, and may even hope to emigrate to the West?

After the killing of three million Jews and a westward shift of its borders, Poland's population is now 95 percent Polish. The postwar homogenization of some east European societies, in other words, makes the normally dangerous "nationality principle" somewhat less explosive there. And while interwar East European regimes imitated their Western neighbors by flirting with fascism, the "demonstration effect" now favors liberal developments. But the most elementary point to make here is that xenophobic nationalism does not "pop up" and that "the return of the repressed" is a metaphor, not an explanation.

Ernest Gellner, among others, persuasively argued that modern nationalism, far from being an atavistic upsurge of latent tribalism, is actually a complicated political achievement, built on complex and wholly modern social preconditions.[22] But a perhaps simpler version of the same argument notes that most people in most societies live comfortably with multiple loyalties and multiple membership. Extremist nationalism cannot simply "pop up" because it must first *kill the multiple loyalties* with which most people live. To explain how such a war against multiple loyalties is conducted and won is no easy matter, and requires us to put atavisms and primordialisms out of our minds. It is certainly not sufficient to say that the present is caused by the past or that nationalism must be here now *because* it was here before. (This sort of thinking would also predict the reemergence in eastern Europe of royalist dictatorships and who knows what else.)

One question to ask, then, is why scapegoating or the political revival of ancient hatreds under conditions of social stress is not as easily set in motion as many observers initially assumed.[23] The Milosevic route to popular success has proved difficult to reproduce elsewhere. Survey research, the reliability of which I cannot fully judge, suggests that most people throughout the region are looking for moderate solutions and yearning for some sort of normality. As the German term *Ostalgie* suggests, even the most frustrated groups regret lifetime job security under the old regime. They are not combat-ready or burning for adventure. Storm troopers cannot be recruited easily from people who are nostalgic for Brezhnev-style stagnation and a low-stress lifestyle and who advocate a go-slow approach to reform. And since society is changing unbelievably fast, there is no pent-up need to escape life's tedious routine. Almost no one is raging to smash the status quo, for there practically is no status quo. As for the old *nomenklatura*, with no ideology or combat mission, very few of them would favor mass shootings simply to start living again in the subsidized but shut-off-from-the-world manner to which they had become accustomed.

But there are many other factors that help explain why scapegoating has proved less fashionable than Havel and others predicted. Antifascist and antiracist indoctrination has presumably had very little effect. A more plausible reason why the politics of resentment has fallen so unexpectedly flat is that for mass frustrations to lead to mass aggression, an intermediate element is required. This intermediate element is a *narrative of injustice, victimization, or betrayal*. Despair must be theorized if it is to have political consequences. The causal narratives that finger culprits, organizing the world into a sinning "they" versus a sinned-against "us," magnify lived frustrations, turning them into resentful solidarities and targeted aggressions. Milosevic had it easy in this regard. He had a ready-made traditional enemy whom it was (at least vaguely) plausible to blame and fear. That the Croatians were perceived as looking down on the Serbs, viewing them contemptuously as not-quite-Europeans tainted by the Orient, simply added fuel to the fire. In any case, only when current suffering can be interpreted plausibly through narratives of injustice, victimization, betrayal, and arrogant disrespect does it serve as the viable basis for an extremist and violent politics of resentment.[24]

But stab-in-the-back narratives cannot simply be invented out of whole cloth and imposed by clever orators on brainless masses. For instance, "that the USSR was not destroyed by foreign invaders means the persecutionist interpretation lacks any tangible link to the personal experience of ordinary Russians."[25] This is an extremely important point and should be taken into account by those who claim that "Russia is indeed suffering from textbook conditions for the rise of extremist parties."[26] The emotional aftershock of the mass killing of a whole generation of young men surely contributed to the spectacular failure of East European democracies after World War I. The breakup of the Eastern bloc and the Soviet Union, by contrast, resulted from a domestic implosion. It was not the product of *military defeat*. In most places, almost no one was killed, and no territories were brutally occupied by foreign troops. Hence, the new borders in the region, however questionable or weakly legitimate, are not now widely perceived as running wounds. However shocked Russians are or claim to be when contemplating their amputated territories, opportunity for paranoid interpretations would be infinitely greater if millions of young men had died in establishing the new borders. (Analogously, Jeffrey Sachs too is exaggerating when he suggests that International Monetary Fund conditions are as humiliating to Russia as the Versailles Treaty was to Germany.)

A key to the nonreappearance (so far) of interwar fascisms in the region, then, is the amazing and perhaps insufficiently appreciated bloodlessness of communism's collapse. The change of regime simply fell from the sky. One result is that people may like the sound of nationalist rhetoric, but they are not eager to pay taxes to beef up the army or willing to accept a reimposition of censorship and travel restrictions for the sake of national greatness.[27] For the same reason, irredentist fantasies about a Greater Hungary or a Greater Bulgaria are not politically serious. And even the Russian-Ukrainian quasi-border, as I said, although it is bitterly resented in some circles, is not soaked in blood or widely interpreted as the product of *force majeur* hypocritically presented as "justice." Most people live locally and do not identify emotionally with distant peoples whose names end in the same vowels. Thus, many of them, to Solzhenitsyn's great dismay, would be perfectly content to shed the remote and shadowy periphery, stranded diaspora and all.

There are two further and somewhat different reasons why blame narratives hawked by power-hungry political entrepreneurs have not found many purchasers among postcommunist populations at large. First, broad swaths of the citizenry in almost every country of the region despise politicians and think that they are all liars and cheats. (Milosevic, again, had a tremendous advantage here, for he was able, already in 1988, convincingly to present Serbian authorities as the voice of truth by broadcasting documentaries about Ustashi killings that had been unviewable under the old regime.) Elsewhere citizens do not believe it when they are told whom to blame, and they are very unlikely to trust a self-proclaimed political savior. Second, no nationwide collective self-interpretation has so far been able to take hold in these disillusioned and distracted, or perhaps postideological, societies. There seems to be no demand for grand mobilizing narratives of any sort, including narratives of blame.[28]

Russia's future may be grim and even bloody, therefore, but it will not follow the terrible Yugoslav path. The two federations are simply incomparable. The cynical landgrab of a small loser nation, dressed in historical costume, holds no clues for the behavior of its giant neighbor to the east. Waggish references to the double-headed eagle as a "Chernobyl mutant" do not prove the inherent weakness of Russian nationalism, of course. But flickering nostalgia for a multinational empire in which Russians made up 51 percent of the population, by contrast with their current 82 percent, should not be equated with the (apparent) Serbian longing to live in an ethnically homogeneous land. (Inculcated Serbian doubts about a multiethnic empire have no parallel in Russia, for obvious reasons.[29]) While some prominent Russians seem to view the Ukraine as "essential" to Russian identity, there seems to be no public feeling of urgency about the matter. What Russian politician would dare declare all-out war on the ethnic intermingling bequeathed to his country by history? There is no "national state" in Russia's past to which the country could return, for the tsars did not build their state on the principle of ethnic homogeneity. The proponents of a strong state (*gosudarstvenniki*) cannot consistently favor national purity.

And the desire to live in an imperial Russia conflicts with the desire to live in an ethnically undifferentiated Russia. Slavophilia, on the other hand, which *does* exclude "the other" on ascriptive grounds, is "not nationalism in the usual sense of the word," because Orthodoxy and the Slavonic languages constitute "a spiritual and intellectual identity rather than a political one."[30] None of this is meant to belittle the episodic role, say, of elite anti-Semitism (as in the Vladimir Gusinsky affair), or the harassment of Chechens by big-city police.[31] But such events and patterns do not amount to extreme nationalism on a mass scale.

But what about the beached diaspora? Will not Russian neo-imperialism, a new gathering of the Russian lands, be provoked by the mistreatment of ethnic Russians in the contiguous republics? This is such a sensitive issue because here lies one of the few areas in which plausible narratives of victimization and injustice can arise *in the present*, not requiring long historical memory (which exists almost nowhere), just television coverage on the evening news. The undeniable fact, however, is that Moscow has done absolutely nothing for the extraterritorial Russians. Its "constitutional annihilation" of the Russian inhabitants of Grozny does not suggest that humanitarian concern for kith and kin will be dominating Russian foreign policy in the near future. It is nevertheless true that televised massacres of Russians in the near abroad could trigger some kind of a nationalist outburst.

HOW GREAT A SHOCK?

While some commentators assert that ancient hatreds resurface under conditions of severe economic stress, others direct our attention to noneconomic catalysts of xenophobic resurgence. That the unexpected end of communism, apart from its strictly economic consequences, delivered an enormous cultural shock is something on which many commentators agree.[32] What occurred, it is commonly assumed, was an unthinkable rupture in the continuity of lives. It is this personal trauma, even more than any material deprivation, that ostensibly makes postcommunist man such an easy target for nationalist ideologues. The basic argument runs like this.

After 1989 and 1991, much of the known world went up in smoke. Once-powerful men became nonentities. Dissident intellectuals and samizdat poets lost their awkward cultural prestige. The changes involved were unsurveyably immense, from the shattering of a belief structure to the loss of great power status. (And if the seemingly permanent can vanish so quickly, what are people to expect from the flimsy arrangements of today?) The humiliation of it all is undeniable. Warehouses stacked to the ceiling with unmarketable goods suggest that the least fortunate of these societies are long-term losers, plummeting headlong toward Third World conditions, condemned to a lingering death. Despite their earlier we-will-bury-you pretenses, they have failed spectacularly in their attempt to become modern economies and have little useful to contribute to the rest of the world. One lesson seems to be that postcommunist societies can become, at best, low-quality carbon copies of the West. Democratic politics and market economics are utopian ideals and, as such, represent a grim cultural defeat. Today, streets are rampant with crime, pornography, prostitution, refugees, and crass "businessmen" flaunting their dubious gains. It is not an easy situation for proud peoples to accept.

The Czech commentator Jirina Siklová has written some of the most subtle, or if not wholly persuasive, essays on the moral psychology of postcommunism. She begins one article with a discussion of adaptation problems faced elsewhere by adult immigrants, often condemned to sterility and inaction by the unknown contours of their newly adopted homelands. Given the flood of Western products, visitors, values, images, English-language graffiti, movies, and advisors currently inundating eastern Europe, Siklová concludes that the inhabitants of postcommunist societies have psychologically immigrated en masse, even without moving.[33] They have awoken abruptly in a new and unknown country. They are freer politically and economically than before, but they are also dispossessed. There is no road back, moreover, for they come from Atlantis, a land now irretrievably engulfed in high seas, and they suffer from all the most wrenching adaptation problems faced by adult immigrants. People over 50, especially, are too old to be resocialized. Indeed, they feel personally "phased out" along with inefficient socialist enterprises. Parents have lost moral authority over their children. The terrible pauperization of the elderly is just another sign of lost continuity among generations.

These may or may not be additional "textbook conditions" for the rise of fascism. But is the diagnosis correct? Was the psychological shock really so great? Notice that savagery broke out in Yugoslavia, where the challenge of an economic transition to Western-style capitalism was considerably *smaller* than elsewhere in the region. This suggests that the psychological trauma of adaptation may not be the root cause of the problem. Another important clue here is the common remark, heard repeatedly throughout the region, that "everything has changed, and nothing has changed." What this paradox suggests, quite simply, is that we should be careful not to exaggerate the extent of experiential discontinuity and thus the debilitating consequences of "the shock." The most obvious continuity, of course, is the recycled elite.

The nameplates on the doors have changed, but the people inside are the same. The survival and in some cases flourishing of the old elite may at first seem annoying and unjust. But would postcommunist societies be more stable politically if *none* of the old *nomenklatura* were included among the new rich? Would they all resemble the former German Democratic Republic, by all accounts the most anomic and psychologically distraught of all the postcommunist populations, but deprived of the apparently stabilizing influence of an occupying power? The continuities of leadership and social status between the old regime and the new, then, may have muffled the psychological trauma of system collapse. If the whole country has emigrated, as Siklová imagines, at least the despised privileged classes have come along. (In the 1994 Hungarian elections, according to Gaspar Miklos Tamas, the communists ran as "old money.") Such continuity serves as a shock absorber. On the one hand, the Brezhnev-era *nomenklatura,* traditionally accused of consumerism and acquisitiveness, does not necessarily feel alienated under the new conditions. On the other hand, their continued grip on power and privilege allows citizens to complain publicly about the same remote and indifferent officials they have always complained about privately.

Similarly, various coping strategies allow people to get by and survive the status loss, disorientation, and insecurity of the new situation. Multiple economies within the same household, as Richard Rose has convincingly argued, mean that GOSKOM-STAT calculations, such as, for example, that 45 million Russians now live below the poverty line, are somewhat off the mark.[34] Russians "have become proficient in learning how to get by in a society under stress."[35] Rose cites data suggesting strongly that Russians do not, in fact, blame "others," such as foreigners and Jews, for their economic woes.[36] Factors that reduce the shock of change, such as extraordinary survival skills, also obviate the need for scapegoats. In his view, "low expectations," in particular, help "prevent frustration and the acts of aggression that may follow."[37] Expectation is the mother of frustration, this is the idea, and most people in eastern Europe and the former Soviet Union have very modest hopes.

The *ideological* crisis caused by communism's collapse is another alleged trigger for the outbreak of virulent nationalism. For similar reasons, it too should not be overstressed. The toppling of the old icons was relatively noiseless, perhaps because they had already been rusted out by time, because the post-Stalinist system had created something like a nonideological personality, ready to accept mandatory hypocrisy but inwardly indifferent to publicly authorized beliefs. Respect for authority and commitment to collective duties had already been decaying for four decades before the collapse. As a result, no passionately held worldview, no utopian vision, was shattered in 1989. While the common notion that "people have to believe in something" has never been proved, its truth is presupposed by those who claim that wounded nationalism in search of an enemy "fills the gap" left by the disappearance of communist beliefs. This gap-filling theory, in my view, mistakes a threadbare ideology mouthed by opportunists for genuine belief, the collapse of which, if it had actually existed, would indeed have left people pained and in search of anesthesia.

Finally, one of the most important but unappreciated shock absorbers has been Marxism itself. Luckily, the inhabitants of postcommunist societies were not mentally debilitated by Chicago economics, which does not have a single word to say about how capitalism begins. Instead, they were blessed with schoolboy Marxism, which teaches, as a law of history, that capitalism begins with unjust seizures, slave labor, and brutal exploitation. The only people who are deeply shocked by (rather than merely angry at or disgusted by) the profiteers and swindlers, con men and shysters, robber-baron capitalists and ruthless pirates, are the American Peace Corps workers, who had never before heard wealth equated with theft. (The average Russian may not be able to define "primitive accumulation," but he or she understands the general idea.) As everyone knows, Marx never explained in any detail how communist society was to be organized. But he did give a vivid and believable description of Manchester capitalism without rules. For the first time, therefore, the inhabitants of Russia and eastern Europe can be actors in a Marxist play. For the first time they can be Marxists.[38]

LEARNED HELPLESSNESS?

Failed or incomplete economic and political reform also can be explained, needless to say, without any reference to anything so headline-grabbing as atavistic ethnic hatreds. Unsurprisingly, therefore, a second cultural-legacies theory is also in vogue. Habits of dependency, craving for job security, lack of initiative, intolerance for income inequality, disrespect for the law, and so forth are all said to play a role in stalling or perverting postcommunist reform.

Samuel Huntington's nightmare, a feverish and hypermobilized society making excessive and unfeasible demands on a weak state, has not come to pass in any postcommunist society. The labor movement, for instance, has been startlingly quiescent almost everywhere.[39] The great majority of citizens are nowhere even players in the political game. Most people are passive and privatized. One reason is that many Russians, for instance, spend every weekend, from spring through fall, cultivating their countryside vegetable plots and therefore cannot be easily recruited into a "politics of the street." How long these populations will remain unmobilized or ungalvanizable is anyone's guess. But we still need to explain the political inertness that has afflicted or blessed them so far. To explain the low political temperature of postcommunist societies, a second cultural-legacies theory has been invoked, one that ignores the shock of change and focuses our attention on a wholly different set of inherited attitudes and predispositions.

Under the old regime, this theory goes, all initiative was interpreted as criticism and was therefore discouraged. That is, autocratic government created a passive or submissive personality, indelibly marked by habits of dependency and unjustifiable patience. People still expect to be taken care of but cannot yet protest or rise up to claim their rights to dignified treatment. Why not? One frequently proposed answer is a profound sense of worthlessness or lack of self-esteem. Old adages such as "God is in heaven and the tsar is far away" or "Suffering makes us pure" reflect adaptive fatalism among peoples who seem never to have controlled their own destinies. Prisoners who have lived many years in jail and victims of harshly punitive surveillance systems apparently lose affect and creativity, becoming unable to see or seize possibilities that lie at their feet.[40] According to Elemér Hankiss, "the communist oligarchy relieved its prisoners of all real duties and responsibilities, keeping them anesthetized with childish irresponsibility."[41] Such infantalized citizens naturally suffer without protesting. Scapegoating, in particular, is incompatible with their profound fatalism and culturally transmitted glorification of suffering. Alexander Herzen's great novel, *Who Is to Blame?*, answers its own question not by finger-pointing (which would unleash aggression against a presumably guilty party) but by observing that failure is simply the nature of life. Our hopes are unfulfilled and the promises we receive are never kept because of the milieu, the time, the place.[42] No one in particular is to blame. To the extent that this attitude (which infuriated Nikolai Chernyshevsky) is culturally ingrained, we might speculate, scapegoating is difficult to sell.

This "childhood polio" explanation for political patience and the failure of scapegoating may seem plausible at first. But does it hold up methodologically and does it fit the facts? Not necessarily. The coping strategies described by Rose, for one thing, make Russians seems extraordinarily inventive and resourceful, as does almost every story one hears about organized crime. And anyway, is it really helpful to explain political inertness by invoking, to paraphrase Molière, an inherited tendency to political inertness? Russian immigrants to the United States do not find it impossible to adapt to a rule-of-law environment in which job security is minimal. What does such turn-on-a-dime adaptability, which is not particularly unusual, suggest about the second cultural-legacy hypothesis?

It suggests that the reform-inhibiting "baggage" that Russians carry with them is more situational than psychological. Russians are psychologically prepared to obey the law, provided the law is enforced. Why should I pay taxes if my neighbor can evade payment with a wink and a nod from corrupt tax inspectors? Why should I deny that wealth is based on theft when wealth *is* based on theft? Lack of labor unrest, along the same lines, is not necessarily a sign of inherent passivity, for workers may simply be calculating that their protests, directed to insolvent and incompetent governments, will do no good.

Invocations of cultural disabilities nevertheless loom large in commentaries on postcommunism. Why do postcommunist workers perform poorly? Because they have inherited a weak work ethic. Why are constitutions in the region treated so frivolously? Because political elites have a poorly developed constitutional culture. Why is capitalism still subject to pejorative commentary? Because the public has preserved its disapproval of income inequality from the old regime. It is undeniable, of course, that postcommunist society nowhere began as a tabula rasa. Skills and expectations acquired in the past continue to influence events in the present. The question is merely how much explanatory weight we can place on this truism. In my opinion, attempts to explain the shortcomings of liberalization have placed excessive emphasis on a *purported lack of receptivity to Western values*, ostensibly due to habit formation under communism. Not enough emphasis, by contrast, has been placed on the crumbling of the state.

POLITICAL DISARRAY AND ADMINISTRATIVE DECAY

The focus on cultural legacies, as I have presented it, results from an attempt to answer the question: Why has reform stumbled and liberalization been excruciatingly slow even after the totalitarian dragon has been slain? The two answers that have suggested themselves are resurgent nationalism and inherited values (such as anti-individualism) and attitudes (such as lack of initiative) incompatible with the normal functioning of democratic politics and market economics. Both of these answers are flawed, methodologically and empirically. The shortcomings discussed earlier suggest that we should look for answers not in the past but in the present (such as in the overnight drop in military procurement orders or the even more sudden collapse of markets caused by the breakup of the old trading partnerships within Comecon and the Soviet Union). Even more radically, they suggest that there is something wrong with the underlying premise of the question itself.

What if reform has stumbled and liberalization been slowed *because* the totalitarian state has been dismantled? This sounds wildly paradoxical, of course, and cannot be true in its crudest form. But formulated more soberly, it amounts to common sense. Liberalization cannot succeed under conditions of state collapse, for the democratization of state authority is pointless if no state authority exists. (Why participate in making the laws if no one obeys the laws?) Similarly, no modern market system can flourish outside a coercively enforced legal system. Private property is not an object but a social relation, a bundle of enforceable rules of access and exclusion that function properly only if public authorities use coercion to exclude nonowners and maintain owner control over resources, predictably penalizing force and fraud and other infractions of the basic rules of the game.

While postcommunist political and administrative institutions have not "collapsed" in a literal sense, the occupants of public office are unable to produce the most elementary public goods, such as reliable electrical power. Liberalism has no need of a land-grabbing police state, but it does need an effective government that can extract resources and apply them intelligently to the provision of basic public services.[43] While removing price controls and state subsidies may be economically beneficial, the lack of an enforceable, intelligible, and coherent law of contract, for instance, is not.

The universal problem of postcommunism, which cuts across the enormous variety of countries involved, is the crisis of governability. In the Russian case, which is admittedly extreme, its symptoms include: railroad banditism and an epidemic of prison breakouts, commercial assassinations (freedom of contract killing) and journalists and FSK (counterintelligence) agents blown to bits, rolling brownouts; ever fouler-smelling tap water, an inability of governments to monitor food handlers for cholera, packs of howling dogs wandering the streets in major cities, a high percentage of draftees who do not show up when called, Moscow authorities who learn about Komi oil spills from *The New York Times*, and an inability to prevent transit migration or monitor the influx of Chinese into Siberia. The problem is that Moscow's old governing techniques—which emphasized border sealing, censorship, and travel restrictions—are no longer workable, and new techniques have not yet been developed.

(Weak states typically rely on customs duties for extraction purposes, because monitoring borders is much easier than getting into the pockets of citizens, which may actually require cooperation and consent. This suggests that the Soviet Union, while repressive, was also administratively weak. Those who now worry about a return of Russia to authoritarian rule should ask if today's successful ex-*nomenklatura* would be willing or able to seal their countries' borders. If they did this, one wonders, would they still be able to vacation so easily with their families or reach their second homes and bank accounts?)

Many of the events and trends that have been routinely interpreted as symptoms of a reemergent extremism (such as skinheads beating up skinheads) are not cultural legacies but rather products of state weakness. Similarly, the Russian decision to keep bases in the near abroad may reflect not an appetite for neo-imperialist adventures and a desire to restore lost greatness but rather a lack of sufficient resources to pay for base relocation, an inability to defend Russia's present borders, and of sufficient resources to house the ethnic Russians who might be forced to immigrate if conditions in the contiguous republics become even more unstable. Similarly, tax evasion and general disrespect for the law is better explained by corrupt and incompetent law enforcement than by a culturally transmitted incapacity to follow rules. When J. F. Brown says that, under conditions of postcommunism, the open society has a sickening resemblance to an open sewer, he means that civil society is always society civilized by relatively honest agents of the state. In short, postcommunist studies should shift its investigative agenda away from contemplating cultural traditions toward discovering the way these countries are now being governed.

That some crazy right-wingers also long for a strong state should not throw us off the track. The *effectiveness* of the state, after all, does not depend on the trouble it causes its neighbors or the ironness of its fist but, on the contrary, on its capacity to elicit voluntary public cooperation for the solution of collective problems. For liberalization to occur, the postcommunist state must be effective enough to rebuild the nation's infrastructure (its educational, health, judicial, energy, and transportation systems) and repair or mitigate the country's ecological catastrophe. It also must be able to push the mafia back into its "normal" spheres of influence (narcotics, gambling, pornography, and prostitution) and out of banking, the stock market, and the export of raw materials. Among the other public goods that any liberal state must provide to make liberal pluralism, as distinct from illiberal pluralism, possible are a well-organized and easily accessible system of recordation (titles, deeds, and land surveys), a clear and enforceable condominium law (so that someone fixes the elevators), a legally stable definition of collateral, enforced auditing of private enterprises to give meaning to stockholders' rights, and a permit system designed to inhibit the poisoning of public water supplies. And the government must produce public confidence that contracts will be enforced and that infractions of patent law and trespass law will be punished.

Civil society also presupposes a relatively consistent government that does not erratically alter tax, banking, customs, and investment regulations. Property is meaningless if the future is radically uncertain. Few people will invest time, effort, and resources to improve their assets without some degree of faith in tomorrow. Similarly, potential partners will not trust each other, and will therefore refrain from mutually beneficial deals, if contract law cannot be reliably enforced. A liberal postcommunist state, then, must not only guarantee personal security and social stability, but must also strive to lengthen the short time horizon of the average property owner if it is to make privatization bear fruit. To improve the business climate, the regulatory and legal system will have to become predictable and transparent. The same achievements will be necessary in order to reverse the debilitating trend toward capital flight (some economists estimate that there is more than $50 billion of private Russian capital invested in western Europe today) and increase the intake of foreign investment. (Annual foreign investment in Russia is around four percent of annual foreign investment in China.)

Indeed, "short time horizons" is another name for the real dilemma facing weak-state postcommunist systems today. Short time horizons, for one thing, favor myopic coping strategies over bold system reforms, inhibiting party formation ("What will you and I have in common a year from now?") as well as property improvement. Russia's impulsive but self-destructive resort to retroactive taxation of foreign firms implies that hungry authorities can see today's goose more clearly than tomorrow's golden eggs. The decision to sell nuclear know-how to Iran, a fundamentalist state close to Russia's own borders, also suggests that the future plays a distressingly small role in Russian foreign policy.[44] Cultural-legacy theorists might point out that ecocidal behavior under communism supports the claim that short time horizons themselves are traditional in this part of the world. But currently instability, associated with a deep crisis of governance, is probably sufficient to explain the survival of short time horizons today.

If consistency is a form of state strength, in any case, then liberal pluralism requires a strong state. Postcommunist states have to have stature and authority if they are going to broker ongoing agreements between labor and capital with the aim of preventing a destabilizing wage-price spiral. Typically, a weak state taxes inefficiently and spends incontinently.[45] While a shaky and dysfunctional government with a tenuous social basis takes demands sequentially and caves in to pressures for decides rationally which are the most important according to some clear conception of the public interest, and delivers a package to satisfy, at least partly, the most powerful supplicants. In line with this model, it takes a "strong" state to produce the public good most hotly debated everywhere in the postcommunist world, that is, currency stability. Weak states typically use inflation to reconcile conflicting demands on the state treasury. Only a state that is strong in the specified sense can insulate budgets from the forces of lobbying and inertia and can resist the temptation to print money to fulfill its reckless promises.

If the government can provide these services, the population is likely to view it with a friendly eye and be more willing to bear the burdens of citizenship, especially taxation. We can call this "performance legitimacy." If the government cannot or does not provide these services, citizens have an even greater incentive than they would ordinarily have to conceal their income and engage exclusively in under-the-counter cash transactions. The illegitimacy of taxing power, needless to say, starves the public treasury and forces the government to rely disproportionately on other sources of money (such as taxes on foreign investors, currency speculation, and the direct sale of raw materials and gold). Because taxed groups of citizens have no incentive to monitor the expenditures of a government that draws its revenues from other sources, such governments tend to behave irresponsibly, as if they were not being watched (which they are not). Under such conditions, it is no surprise that those who manage the direct sale of raw materials, for instance, prove fonder of their personal Swiss bank accounts than of antibiotics earmarked for public hospitals. What we have, in this case, is a vicious circle: the resource-strapped state cannot provide public goods and is therefore less and less able to extract resources through either voluntary compliance or threats of coercion. (And the revenues it does grab are especially vulnerable to being siphoned off into private hands.) Here we see the source of the fiscal crisis of the postcommunist extractive state. Political and administrative elites have a very hard time providing public goods that will, in turn, help elicit further popular cooperation. One important moral and psychological basis of any functioning liberal democracy is an exchange of popular cooperation for the provision of elementary public goods. The basic challenge facing every postcommunist state is to work out such a social compact, or rather to build political and administrative institutions on its basis.

A slowness to recognize state weakness as the principal problem in the region may be due to our own cultural legacies, to our antitotalitarian hangover, or to our current rage against taxation, regulation, and bureaucracy and our belief that state power is the source of all evil, reflected in a widespread fear of resurgent authoritarianism in the region, especially in Russia. Strangely enough, international relations theorists and neoclassical economists conspire to obscure the real problem here, the former assuming that it does not have much to do, that market society flourishes naturally when the state is "unable to interfere." These are unfortunate biases, however, since the most immediate dangers faced by the West all stem from state weakness, especially in the successor nations of the former Soviet Union.

The Geiger counters that German police in Frankfurt airport point at passengers arriving from Russia are a reminder of the potential hazards of a society full of costly weapons and impoverished guards and suddenly deprived of effective authority. The full military alert triggered by the launching of a Norwegian weather reconnaissance missile, of which Yeltsin foolishly bragged in 1994, suggests that the inability of the Russian Foreign Ministry (which had been repeatedly notified of the launch) to communicate with the Defense Ministry is no longer just a domestic problem. Old anxieties about the command and control system and civilian control of the military are growing. Western diplomats, comfortable only when dealing with "counterparts" abroad, become frustrated and disoriented when the man across the table has the right title but no effective authority in his designated area of responsibility. The fiasco of Western involvement in the former Yugoslavia has been caused not only by disarray among the allies, but also by diplomatic cluelessness in dealing with violent quasi-states where the command and control structures are highly precarious. In the Russian case, a decaying state not only makes for an unreliable diplomatic partner. An unraveling Russia is also impossible to "balance" (or deter) in a realpolitical fashion. (Has anyone ever tried to balance Africa?)

Furthermore, the experience of postcommunism suggests that ethnic tensions themselves are most likely to get out of hand in breakup states, such as the former Yugoslavia, or in very rickety states, pasted together artificially at the end of World War I, frozen in place by Soviet occupation, and plagued by fears of succession, where borders are now up for grabs and the country's very survival is, or seems to be, at stake. "Ethnic tensions" are more likely to escalate into "ethnic conflicts" when irredentist or secessionist rhetoric accompanies serious state-building or state-dismantling action. (Consider Nagorno-Karabakh, South Ossetia, Iranian Azerbaijan, Crimea, and perhaps the problem of Albanians in Macedonia. Such examples lend support to the claim that ethnic problems are also political and institutional, not simply cultural or psychological.)

The task here is not merely to notice, along with others, the problem of postcommunist state weakness but to think through its consequences. Keeping it constantly in view, as economists and international relations theorists, say, seldom do can save us from many common misperceptions of the postcommunist dilemma. For instance, it allows us understand the nature of widespread discontent with economic liberalization without resorting to flimsy speculations about culturally transmitted biases against private property and individualism. According to Wojciech Jaruzelski, "the rising disparities between rich and poor are offensive in a society where everyone once lived equally. In the West, people respect success. Here it arouses suspicion."[46] We were raised on socialist principles and we therefore scorn money-making and income inequality. This is the cultural-legacy thesis applied to the spirit of anticapitalism. It is popular, but is it true? Why would people object to an entrepreneur who buys one ton of cat food at dirt-cheap prices, relabels it as tunafish, and resells it to unsuspecting consumers, some of whose children become deathly ill while the "entrepreneur" vacations in Cyprus? Where antifraud legislation is ineffective and enforcement bodies underfunded and understaffed, "capitalist" exchanges will appear to many people as scams, as the immoral exploitation of informational asymmetries. But we do not need to posit any *residual socialism* to explain public discontent with unregulated markets in such a case.

In the anarcholiberalism of postcommunist societies, as already mentioned, wealth commonly *is* theft, and moneymakers often are con men. As a result, property rights are associated by many ordinary people, who perhaps expected as much, not with elementary justice but with the shady deals of scoundrels and crooks. This line of thought has important policy implications. What postcommunist states need most in order to increase public acceptance of the new market economy is *enforceable antifraud legislation*. This may be extremely difficult to obtain, but it is a matter of institution-building, not of counteracting an alleged socialist ideology by preaching the virtues of unregulated markets or of making social-democratic concessions to allegedly inherited habits of dependency.

Enforceable and publicly acceptable property rights are not the only rights that depend on state authority. The same can be said of all liberal rights. Indeed, the principal lesson of the end of communism is not that state power endangers liberal rights, but exactly the contrary, that liberal rights are wholly unrealizable without effective extractive, administrative, regulative, and adjudicative authorities. Rights protection and enforcement depend on state capacities. Statelessness, therefore, means rightlessness. People without states, such as Vietnamese or Caribbean boat people, or those who live in societies where state authority has collapsed or gone into steep decline, have few or no effective rights. The problem does not lie in inherited attitudes or a lack of psychological receptivity to Western values. Instead, the obstacles should be sought in empty treasuries and decomposed administrations. The legal codification of prisoners' rights, for instance, has little meaning when political authorities lack supervisory powers or the financial wherewithal to purchase medicines for prison hospitals. As a consequence, a constitution that does not organize effective government, capable of taxing and spending, will wholly fail to protect rights. This has been a lesson long in learning, and not only for libertarian economists, but also for some human rights advocates who have devoted their careers to a militant campaign against brutal and overmighty states. Rights, quite obviously, are an enforced uniformity. Equality before the law cannot be secured over a vast territory without a relatively effective, honest, centralized bureaucratic organization.

The resource-dependency of a liberal rights regime becomes undeniably clear when we inspect the weakness of rights enforcement in a financially strapped state. Even negative rights will not be protected in an insolvent country, as is shown by the case of a Polish criminal court that was sued for failing to pay its rent.[47] Less frivolously, we can all imagine how well protected rights are likely to be in a society—such as Russia today—where local police departments are monitored only erratically from above.[48] (The procuracy, which once fulfilled this function under party supervision, is apparently no longer doing its job.) An inspection of pretrial detention cells and state psychiatric hospitals in any postcommunist state would quickly reveal that rights protection is a problem of complex institutional design and resource allocation, and of maintaining an effective chain of command, not merely building judicially tended "limits" around the government and its agents. To create an institutionally independent subunit within each local police department, immune to bribes and threats and responsible for monitoring the illegal and corrupt behavior of fellow policemen, is no easy matter and cannot be achieved without the coercive extraction and intelligent reallocation of considerable resources, neither of which, unfortunately, is likely to occur in, say, Russia today.

Rights will not be protected if, to take a hypothetical case, German firms can truck dangerous industrial waste into Poland

and bury it there by night without either the German or the Polish government knowing that it happened. Here again, state weakness (in this case, state ignorance or blindness) makes rights enforcement impossible. One of the main lessons political theory can learn from the postcommunist experience, in fact, is the tenuousness of the distinction, common in Western discussions, between welfare rights and classical liberal rights. The distinction seems commonsensical in the West largely because our societies are so fabulously wealthy and the earmarking of social resources for the guarantee of negative rights is politically uncontested. In resource-poor societies with ambitions to imitate the West, the distinction between welfare rights and classical liberal rights seems much less obvious. Both types of rights depend on scarce resources, first of all. Rights cannot be trumps, in fact, because they depend *essentially* on scarce resources, extracted from society by state authorities and strategically applied where most needed. A whole array of liberal rights cost money and therefore involve distributional choices. All this implies that we cannot improve human rights conditions in insolvent and administratively disorganized countries simply by preaching and threatening trade sanctions (although such techniques can admittedly yield token gestures, such as the release of a few unrepresentative dissidents from jail, acts that are pleasing to the West).[49]

Legal defense for the poor, for instance, presupposes complicated fiscal and bureaucratic arrangements (such as tax breaks for lawyers who engage in pro bono work). Refugee rights are similarly meaningless unless registration offices are established, funded, staffed, and made easily accessible. Freedom of movement in Russia, which presupposes effective abolition of the residency permit system, requires the availability of housing in big cities. Obviously enough, constitutional guarantees of "good health" are derisory when the state cannot afford to clean up the water and air, or when public hospitals have no gasoline for their ambulances (as happened in 1993 in Vilnius), and where the best doctors leave the country to practice their profession under minimally decent conditions. But the right to litigate (a classical liberal right, not a welfare right) is similarly degraded by a lack of resources. Take the case of liability for medical malpractice. There are laws on the books in postcommunist societies—Hungary is an example—that make it possible to sue doctors for compensatory damages. But these laws are next to useless where judicial dockets are impossibly crowded, where there is no service for reliably hand-delivering written judgments (normal overworked postmen are given the job), where hospitals do not have funds even for buying antibiotics, much less for paying compensation, and where there is no insurance system ready and able to pay. Injured patients win court cases but receive nothing. In this way, they learn to despise the hypocritical currency of liberal rights.

A final way in which rights-enforcement hinges upon administrative competence and the artful allocation of scarce social resources should be mentioned here. The problem of criminality, especially gang warfare and extortion by threats of violence, is growing everywhere in the postcommunist world. It is already clear that, psychologically, the majority of citizens quickly lose interest in legal restrictions on the discretion of lethally armed policemen in crime-intensive environments. To put this in bookish but pertinent terms, the Hobbesian problem has to be solved before the Lockean solution looks attractive. If citizens will tolerate police brutality so long as the crime rate is high, then a full-fledged rights regime will emerge only in those societies where the crime rate (that is, the ordinary citizen's fear of bodily harm) is kept below a certain level. Or, to formulate the same point the other way around, rampant criminality is one of the central obstacles to the rise of rights consciousness under postcommunism. It may prove additionally dangerous if skillful demagogues manage to use popular frustration with anarchical conditions to mobilize political support in the streets. Here again, rights are a matter of institutional architecture and resource allocation. In postcommunist societies, even if they had been blessed with the most perfect historical traditions, rights consciousness will never emerge unless the police achieve a minimal level of effective control. And this is a question of scarce social resources effectively applied.

A Russian proverb says, "The law is like a horse cart: it will go whichever way you turn it." Those who cite this saying usually mean to lament the low level of respect for law in Russian history and the tendency to see law as a mere tool. They often go on to attribute the fast and loose attitude of Russian politicians toward their own constitution to this same inherent anarchism in the Russian soul. But is it not just as plausible to explain the casualness with which constitutions sometimes are treated under postcommunist conditions by referring not to inherited psychological habits but, once again, to unavoidable present problems? First of all, postcommunist constitutions have yet to make decent and effective governance possible. So what claim can they make on public loyalty or respect? Constitutional cynicism, to the extent that it exists, does not result from a lack of legal culture, to be remedied by preaching and propaganda, but from a realistic assessment of the situation. To repeat: Why should people pretend that they can succeed by following the rules when they cannot?

But may not paper constitutions have disappointing results because political elites themselves have been wrongly socialized and therefore do not "work" the institutions in the proper way? There is something to this idea, I believe, but it is not the whole story. When societies are in tremendous flux, it is very unlikely that bargains struck one day will seem reasonable the next. The problem here is not debilitating cultural baggage but a wholly new social instability. Institutional rigidity in times of rapid change will produce unpredictability, not predictability, as Juan Linz has explained, because unforeseen social pressures will force political actors to abandon an obsolete framework entirely. This is a good reason for even well-meaning politicians to take constitutional rules with a grain of salt. And anyway, how can they respect a bargain made yesterday, when they know that it was designed to trick their political opponents who, it so happens, have now utterly vanished from the scene? Could we really expect Lech Walesa or Arpad Göncz to rest satisfied with presidencies strategically designed for Wojciech Jaruzelski and Imre Pozsgay? Why would anyone (whatever his cultural endowment) treat myopic political bargains made under turbulent circumstances as beyond the reach of renegotiation? More generally, it is very difficult to formulate clear rules for distributing resources and settling conflicts without violence among important groups, when the groups in question are dissolving and re-forming kalei-doscopically every few months. This is true even if all actors are looking desperately for elements of stability in a hyperfluid world. As social interests are being constantly redefined, the rules governing their interaction are naturally going to be repeatedly recast.

STATE-BUILDING IN THE CZECH REPUBLIC

The most formidable challenge facing postcommunist societies is the creation of effective and accountable instruments of government, able to extract resources efficiently and fairly and to channel them not into private pockets but toward the provision of elementary public goods—such as security, sanitation, electricity, education, transportation, currency stability, and the legal preconditions of a functioning market economy, including enforceable contract law. Those who say that postcommunist societies are burdened by "state decay," then, are not being nostalgic for an iron fist but are simply looking forward to the creation of, among other things, a coherent legal framework and an effective and nonpredatory civil service. After decades of agitating to loosen the noose, Russian and east European liberals must make a 180-degree turn and begin *building* extractive, administrative, regulatory, and adjudicative institutions on a rule-of-law basis. But how can we say that state dysfunction or disorganization is the principal problem of postcommunist societies if the greatest achievements of the much-praised Czech Republic have been deregulation, pulling down political barriers, preventing administrative interference, and allowing the market to flourish?

The answer is that Prime Minister Václav Klaus, far from being the antistatist he pretends to be, is the most talented statebuilder of postcommunist Europe. His neoliberal rhetoric conceals a neostatist practice. Despite Klaus's Chicago School self-presentation, the relatively successful liberalization process in the Czech Republic has been painstakingly planned and managed from the top down. A certain sequence of reforms has been orchestrated in Prague (for instance, financial stabilization was pursued before price liberalization) and a cushion provided to absorb the economic shock, so that marketization has been anything but the spontaneous outcome of decentralized choices by millions of private actors. The "transition," in this its (so far) most successful version, therefore, has not been simply a matter of applied economics. It has required political savvy and leadership. Above all, it has required careful attention to legitimacy as well as efficiency. Klaus did not have Konrad Adenauer's good fortune. The West has not handed him the resources with which to provide public goods and thereby win popular support and cooperation. Indeed, he can gather the resources he needs only by first winning popularity at home and abroad. At this difficult bootstrap operation, he has, so far, excelled.

Klaus's team (20 or so well-trained economists who make decisions while sitting around a table), not the "miraculous" market, has been in charge. Thus, the Czech example confirms, *a contrario*, that political weakness, ineptitude, inconsistency, and venality are the fundamental problems plaguing postcommunist regimes. The shedding of Slovakia, essential to Klaus's aim of quick entry into the EU, is a case in point. This was the achievement not of a master economist but of a master state-builder.

The same can be said about Klaus's creation of local party chapters for the Civic Democratic Party, the most successful example of liberal party-building in the postcommunist world. (Ironists refer to the CDP unfairly as "a liberal party of the Leninist type.") As a result of Klaus's organizational strategy, in any case, his party garnered a formidable 25 percent in the 1994 local elections, while recent polls show popular support for the party fluctuating between 27 and 32 percent. Klaus also has managed to keep a firm grip on power by a deft use of the committee system in parliament. And he has brilliantly played the issue of the missing senate, going neither forward to elections nor backward to a constitutional amendment. In this way he has strengthened his own government, despite coalition tensions, by depriving the president of his normal right of dissolution. His

push for a referendum on membership in the EU, when juxta-
posed with his avoidance of a referendum on the breakup of the
federation, reveals his skillful opportunism in the service of an
institution-building cause.

Klaus's unrivaled mastery of the capitalist buzzwords probably has contributed significantly to the republic's exceptional
attractiveness to foreign investors. But constant professions of
the free market creed also help him throw dust into the eyes of
adversaries and potential critics. Chicago economics is very useful in this regard. He says publicly that all he is doing is "lifting
restrictions" and letting the market work. Those who do not
look too closely criticize him for being heartless, then, because
he purportedly refuses to intervene in the economy. This criticism, although inaccurate, is welcome because it diverts attention from the important ways his government *does* strategically
intervene in the economy, keeping down the value of the koruna
to boost exports, for instance, or refusing to deregulate wages.
(Some wage hikes remain tied to inflation regardless of company performance.) His political style is hands-on, not hands-
off. Coupon privatization itself was a political decision, of
course, and a stage-managed process. (The proof is that the head
of the National Property Fund was dismissed for *mismanage-
ment*.) In short, Klaus does not broadcast it openly, but he knows
perfectly well that an energetic centralized state has an essential
role to play in economic reform. That is why his party has consistently and fiercely opposed administrative decentralization.[50]

The Europe into which Klaus seeks admission is a system
of economies all of which operate within highly complex, and
increasingly integrated, legal frameworks. The pursuit of entry,
therefore, requires both the dismantling of the totalitarian state
and the building of the liberal state (in line with EU standards).
Only an effective state can enforce the law and extract sufficient
taxes to protect basic rights, including property rights. The legislative task facing all postcommunist regimes is therefore immense, including the creation not only of contract law but also
of trespass law, bankruptcy law, patent law, condominium law,
environmental law, and so forth. And the state being built also
has to have sufficient strength to repel demands for budget-

swelling subsidies and to prevent the formation of noncompetitive monopolies. From bitter experience, the Czech government has learned the need for more stringent licensing procedures for, and greater Central Bank supervision of, private banks, reliable depositor's insurance, and so forth. All this is a matter of state-building. In general, private property is meaningless (will not elicit investment or improvement) if owners do not feel relatively secure about the future. Hence, in west European language, the state must be powerful enough to provide *securité juridique* or *Vertrauensschutz*, the protection of legitimate expectations. For the sake of foreign investment, presumably, the government also will have to be able to prevent Czech policemen from shooting to death German motorists who have a taste for speed.

Even the most brilliant economic policy will fail, under conditions of electoral democracy, if it does not gain the support of the public. Since daily life in the Czech Republic remains hard for many people, Klaus cannot neglect legitimacy in a one-sided Chicago-style pursuit of efficiency. The basically untouched social safety net, an extremely cautious housing policy (rents remain below building maintenance costs), the 3.1 percent unemployment rate (the lowest in Europe), output-per-worker statistics that place the Czech Republic behind Poland, and the tiny number of bankruptcies in the country all reflect governmental worries about public responses to marketization. (If the banks that supervise the funds that, in turn, own the "privatized" enterprises expect government bailouts, it should be noticed, then they are purely private actors in name only, which might explain some politically welcome unemployment-reducing delays in restructuring even after privatization.) Since his government first took office, Klaus's principal challenge has been to lead the Czechs to perceive market-oriented reforms as harbingers of a better future. If he succeeds in this attempt, he will be able to use his government's stored-up popularity (along with foreign investment) to keep reforms on track even when unemployment begins to mount.

Given his lack of material resources, Klaus is compelled to pursue legitimacy by symbolic means. He is postcommunism's greatest Machiavellian, for as Machiavelli remarked, if you want to make a successful revolution, call it a restoration. Instead of allowing people to think they are being colonized by the West, which implies the worthlessness of everything the Czechs have been, Klaus spreads the message that the old businesslike Bohemia, full of hardworking Czechs, is back where it belongs, awoken from a long slumber, released from a Soviet detention camp. This is not a wholly accurate message of course. (Many of the bourgeois Bohemians about whom he boasts were actually Germans and Jews, for instance, which is only to say that the old Bohemia was brutally destroyed and that there is simply no chance of picking up where the country left off; moreover, the idea of a "return" to the capitalist past should be measured against the fact that Eastern Europe's largest communist vote in a semifair election, 38 percent, occurred in the Czech part of Czechoslovakia in 1946.) But the slogan "back to Europe" has proved immensely popular. It may even, as Klaus hopes, turn into a self-fulfilling fiction. For similar reasons, Klaus is coaxing the Czech public to speak and think about integration into the EU, to prevent it from contemplating the unappetizing prospect of annexation to a Greater Germany.

An aggressively reformist state requires not merely acquiescence but also cooperation. Postcommunist citizens are being asked to adapt their behavior to new and complicated rules of the game. This increases the government's need for legitimacy. But by what means can this legitimacy be attained by a state that is strapped for carrots as well as short on sticks? Once again, symbolism turns out to be an important, and relatively cheap, element in the legitimation of Czech reforms. Although President Havel, when thundering against the spiritual emptiness of television commercials, probably irks the impatient and professorial Klaus, he may add to the global legitimacy of the regime, lessening the political alienation of those who have lost most from the transformation, and preventing them from voting communist or looking for extraparliamentary representation. If this is true, then the new Czech system resembles the nineteenth-century British regime memorably described by Walter Bagehot: the queen is the moral and emotional symbol of the nation, while the prime minister is an effective technocrat who gets the job done. In the Czech case, Klaus's policies are probably strengthened, rather than weakened, by Havel's wholly impractical and apolitical criticisms of the shortcomings of market society.

Legitimation problems are especially acute when it comes to first property rights. An economist will tell you that it does not matter how first property rights are assigned. So long as free exchange is guaranteed, an efficient outcome will result. But most human beings are not economists, so the palpable injustice of private holdings presents a political problem. Western countries never faced this problem, since they democratized under conditions of historical amnesia, having long forgotten the acts of piracy and fraud by which private property was originally acquired. The Czechs cannot forget because, unlike some of their neighbors, they had absolutely no private property before 1989, and they continue to be reminded of the injustice of initial appropriation by the country's politically necessary but morally questionable refusal to restore the property expropriated from 3.5 million Sudeten Germans after 1945.[51] The consequences of a palpably unjust distribution of first property rights for postcommunist marketization are difficult to calculate. But one thing is certain. Private property, in the Czech Republic today, cannot be justified by its origins but only by its result. Unable to "sacralize" property in the deceptive Western manner, the government must show people that marketization pays off. While the postcommunist liberal state cannot be "based on justice," then, it can at least make possible a minimally decent life. Klaus has been successful, relatively speaking, because Czechs believe (as the latest *Eurobarometer* public opinion survey suggests) that he is on the way of leading them to a better life.

All methods of privatizing state assets while the public is watching have their characteristic defects. Consider the five basic methods: restitution, domestic auctioning, direct sale to wellheeled citizens, direct sale to foreigners, and voucher privatization. Restitution is problematic for several moral reasons (why should those who lost their lives or careers not be compensated as well?); but its main shortcoming is that it cannot bear enough of the real burden, which involves putting hundreds of state enterprises into private hands. Domestic auctioning and direct sale to citizens are also questionable because money stashed away by domestic groups in the last years of communism or the early years of democratic exhilaration probably was stolen. (*Nomenklatura* privatization, by this route, does not take scads of money, incidentally, since dirt-cheap prices can be "arranged" by contacts.) For obvious reasons, direct sale to foreigners will sound fine to a Chicago economist but not to a state-builder like Klaus. The political costs of such a "sellout" would be intolerably great. To solve some of the legitimacy problems, to dilute, or divert attention from, foreign and *nomenklatura* buyouts, voucher privatization was introduced into Czechoslovakia. Its purpose was first political, then economic.

Unfortunately, voucher privatization has problems of its own. These problems were nicely illustrated by the October 1994 arrest of Jaroslav Linzer, chairman of the Center for Voucher Privatization, who was found with $300,000 in his briefcase, provided by a police anticorruption squad in a sting operation.[52] In other words, the coupon system itself can be manipulated to the benefit of inside traders. But even a public that knows about primitive accumulation eventually will become disaffected if exposed schemes for the self-enrichment of government officials are regularly swept under the carpet.

The exploitation of public office for private benefit is widespread throughout the postcommunist world. The most pathological example of pervasive privatistic attitudes and the weak sense of public property is the furtive sale of weapons by Russian draftees to Chechen fighters. But the private use of public office is ubiquitous, from customs officers to tax collectors, from privatization ministers to policemen working hand-in-glove with organized crime. Corruption on such a scale necessarily generates cynicism and antipolitical attitudes among the public, independent of culturally inherited attitudes. The crying need for political legitimacy, then, suggests the wisdom of serious conflict-of-interest legislation.[53] So why has such legislation been so slow in coming, if it can help solve the postcommunist state-builder's acute need for public acceptance and cooperation?

One reason there has been no effective "clean hands" move-ment in any postcommunist society may be that there are so many assets being divvied up that even the opposition gets its cut. A sec-ondary reason may be that conflict-of-interest legislation, if it were genuinely and fairly enforced, might exacerbate the recruitment problems of postcommunist state-builders. How can an east European government recruit talented and well-trained young peo-ple into government service when it has to compete with the pri-vate sector but can supplement the glamour of office only with noncompetitive salaries? (The need to recruit talented young peo-ple is pressing, for government officials must be at least as bright and innovative as the average tax evader.) The most widely cho-sen technique for solving this problem throughout the region is to write vague and toothless conflict-of-interest laws, allowing gov-ernment officials to hold second jobs, even in the industries they monitor, in order to keep their salaries at a normal level. This re-cruitment-corruption dilemma remains important in all postcom-munist societies, including to some extent in the Czech Republic.

A concluding note about the Czech Republic's struggle to join the EU is warranted. Every inclusion is an exclusion. When Slovenia snuggled up to Austria, it left Croatia behind to a diffi-cult fate. The analogy with the Czecho-Slovak breakup is too ob-vious to mention. But the Milan Kundera fantasy, that Bohemia was on the wrong side of a political borderline that should sim-ply be shifted to the east, is unrealistic. Advocates of a selective treatment of postcommunist countries by the West may gracefully draw our attention to ancient spiritual frontiers. But there will be no second Yalta. The back door will not be slammed shut out of respect for age-old religious and cultural divides. For one thing, Russia is now too weak to seal its own borders. Hence, the Czech accession to the EU, if it happens, will not resemble West Germany's entry into Western Europe after the war. And the now-uncloseable roadway to the East presents problems (such as the wholly unregulated market in ground-to-air missiles) that cannot be solved by Chicago economics. Such problems can be con-fronted only by determined political actors, struggling to build ef-fective states with few material resources, and who succeed in bringing collective efforts to bear on common problems.

CONCLUSION

Any attempt to explain the current setbacks or shortcomings of postcommunist economic and political reform must face not only the problem of enormous regional variation but also the prior difficulty of making clear what exactly is being explained. At this early stage, for one thing, we cannot be sure if what we are looking at are temporary aberrations or long-term trends. Explanatory efforts will not be inhibited by such considerations, however, and since scholarly thinking in this area affects policy-making as well as social science, it is presumably not useless to examine skeptically the various approaches that now dominate the field.

The central thesis of this chapter has been that a cultural-legacies approach to unsuccessful or incomplete democratic and market reform is faulty both methodologically and empirically. A more promising focal point for postcommunist studies, by contrast, is the crisis of governance that afflicts every country of the region. This problem is intensely practical but also philosophical. Today's Russia is not exactly a "state of nature," for instance, but it does raise the fundamental questions of political theory: How can a government impose order on a disorderly society if the government's own agents are themselves infected with disorder—if they will neither obey instructions nor follow the law? How can a stable legal framework, essential for functioning markets, be established in a country where all things, including public officials, are for sale?

Public fatigue at the side effects of state weakness (such as, in many cases, no electricity or running water) is noticeable everywhere. But so far, at least, diffuse frustration has not found a serious political expression. What form will the politics of popular discontent take when it finally emerges on the scene? Phrased differently, how liberal or illiberal will the postcommunist state-building process turn out to be? Conceivably, political entrepreneurs could invoke an illiberal legitimacy formula (such as a promise to seek revenge for past ethnic humiliations) in an effort to build public support for current or proposed territorial borders and to mobilize cooperation with extractive, administrative, regulative, and adjudicative institutions. Alternatively, they could attempt to generate support by organizing fair elections, conceding freedoms and influence to important social groups, and delivering generally useful public services in exchange for popular support. Since neither solution has proved workable so far, weakly legitimate governments have become the rule under postcommunism.

Predictions are out of the question, as I said at the outset. But it is safe to say that the future of these societies will be profoundly marked by the relatively liberal or illiberal course of the state-building processes now tentatively under way. In the proximate future, it should be reemphasized, illiberal processes will be characterized less by a return to authoritarian or totalitarian rule than by a tendency toward unaccountable government. While Russian authorities have harassed and threatened the press on various occasions, for instance, they have not attempted to impose a party line. Their only interest, apparently, is to prevent exposure of scandals and theft of public assets. Officials seem more intent on enjoying their ill-gotten gains, in an undetected manner, than on controlling or brainwashing their societies. For elites to walk off with big chunks of public wealth, secrecy is required, but not autocracy or social regimentation.[54]

A relatively liberal solution to the frustrations of state weakness or ungovernability requires that political elites forgo the short-term advantages of clandestine plundering for the long-term advantages of presiding over a prosperous society. It is so hard to get from here to there because transparency of government presupposes not merely personally honest civil servants but also functioning institutions. In postcommunist systems, so far, parliaments remain poorly informed about decisions made within the central ministries. Their ability to control or influence these decisions is vanishingly small. Similarly, the absence of party consolidation means that voters have little information about and less control over their elected representatives. Such snapped connections between assemblies and both the ministries above and the voters below mean that parliaments cannot function effectively as arenas where conflicting social interests are articulated and reconciled and where national goals are defined. (Until the "who speaks for whom?" problem is solved, it seems, political battles will remain eerily unrelated to underlying social tensions.)

But why not see state weakness itself as a cultural legacy? After all, the least successful of the 27 postcommunist regimes are those, such as Ukraine, having no history of statehood upon which to fall back. And can we not say that the distressingly short time horizons and deplorable privatistic attitudes of public officials throughout the region are psychological residues of Soviet times? In the case of governing elites, then, do not psychological and cultural factors regain their decisive importance?

Some taxpayers evade taxes because they can get away with it. Some tax collectors accept bribes for the same reason. Perhaps traditions are decisive only when reinforced by incentives (or lack of disincentives). One of the main purposes of democracy, in any case, is to give public officials an incentive to decrease the percentage of extracted resources they personally engross for themselves and thereby to increase the percentage they spend on providing public services. If fair elections really determine who holds power, the behavior of officials may well change, not totally of course, but somewhat.

Cynicism about pseudodemocracy, at any rate, probably is misplaced even where democratic or semidemocratic elections have produced nothing resembling accountable government so far. Even in such cases, elections may have already had an unnoticed salutary effect. For example, elections publicly display the relative weakness of radical factions, which are partly cured by universal suffrage of any illusions about their ability to speak for the nation as a whole. Absenteeism, opportunism, and incompetence may blemish parliamentary life everywhere in the region, but even a clownish and powerless parliament may serve a prophylactic function, giving losers a sense that their voices are heard, however faintly, and preventing the rise of extraparliamentary demagogues. Moreover, national elections, as Linz and Stepan have stressed, provide an instrument of state-building more palatable than the war-making by which so many states in the past have been created.[55] The slowly developing sense of a procedural community, where the millions of members of a large nation vote together, on the same day, for political representatives, gives some modest experiential legitimacy to civic-territorial definitions of citizenship. In weak multinational states, the temptation for political leaders to fall back on an ethnic definition of citizenship as a source of legitimacy should not be ignored. So the uses of elections for heading off the worst, even in countries where parliaments cannot effectively monitor their ministries, should not be underestimated, especially by those observers of postcommunism who are anxious about the future of nationalism and skeptical about the future of democracy.

NOTES

1. Students of postcommunist societies share an embarrassing dilemma with NATO: we cannot leave Russia out of the picture, but if we bring it in, Russia will naturally tend to overwhelm the others, absorbing all of our attention, denying us the benefits of a genuinely evenhanded approach.

2. Theda Skocpol argues in *States and Social Revolutions* (Cambridge, England: Cambridge University Press, 1979) that social revolutions invariably strengthen the powers of the state. This thesis, if we accept it, reinforces the perception that the end of communism, although it affected all aspects of life, was not a revolution in the classical sense.

3. As is suggested by Sabrina Petra Ramet, ed., *Rocking the State: Rock Music and Politics in Eastern Europe and Russia* (Boulder, CO: Westview Press, 1994).

4. See, for instance, Norman Stone, "The Hungarians: History Makes a Comeback," *The National Interest*, no. 36 (Summer 1994), pp. 58–64.

5. A classic instance is Reinhard Bendix, *Kings or People* (Berkeley: University of California Press, 1978), pp. 88–127, 491–581.

6. Representative examples, among scholarly writers, are Bogdan Denitch, *Ethnic Nationalism: The Tragic Death of Yugoslavia* (Minneapolis: University of Minnesota Press, 1994), p. 128; and Paul Hockenos, *Free to Hate: The Rise of the Right in Postcommunist Eastern Europe* (New York: Routledge, 1993), p. 4. For a journalistic variation on the same theme, see William Pfaff, "Ancient Hatreds May End the New World Order before It Begins," *Chicago Tribune*, August 2, 1992, p. C3.

7. Nathan Gardels, "Two Concepts of Nationalism: An Interview with Isaiah Berlin," *The New York Review of Books*, November 21, 1991, p. 19.

8. Václav Havel, "The Post-Communist Nightmare," *The New York Review of Books*, May 27, 1993, p. 6.

9. J. F. Brown, *Hopes and Shadows* (Durham, NC: Duke University Press, 1994), p. 224.

10. Janusz Bugajski, *Ethnic Politics in Eastern Europe* (Armonk, NY: Sharpe, 1994), p. xix. See also Dieter Frey, "The Unification of Germany from the Standpoint of a Social Psychologist," in Heinz Kunz, ed., *United Germany and the New Europe* (Aldershot, Hants, England: Bookfield, Vt.: Edward Elgar, 1993), p. 67. In my opinion, our expectations of mass scapegoating in postcommunist societies are due in part to misinformation provided by ex-dissidents, one of the groups that lost most from the collapse of the old regime. Human beings naturally interpret neglect as aggression, and dissidents, such as Jan Urban and Gaspar Miklos Tamas, with easy media access in the West, have brilliantly but unrealistically interpreted their new irrelevance as a sign that they are being singled out for special obloquy and that a general hunt for guilty parties is under way.

11. *East European Constitutional Review* (Spring 1995), p. 11

12. Louisa Vinton, "Walesa and the Collaboration Issue," *RFE/RL Research Report*, no. 6 (February 5, 1993). Admittedly, a handful of embarrassing show trials have taken place in Tirana, but even there, where retribution is traditionally considered sweeter than honey, "strikingly, Albanians are not interested in taking revenge on those responsible for the previous era." See James Whettington, "Albania Clings to Some Repressive Levers of State," *Financial Times*, September 12, 1994, p. 3. Criminal law is apparently being used in Albania in a political struggle, to eliminate political rivals, not in a quest for historical justice, and thus not to find the guilty or to right perceived wrongs and thereby to absorb psychological anxieties.

13. "People didn't want to get even with the communists. Many of them were card-carrying members and all of them had relatives and friends among the rank and file." Vassily Aksyonov, "A Changing Russia Full of Familiar Communist Faces," *International Herald Tribune*, November 23, 1994, p. 9.

14. Special issue on the Politics of Intolerance, *RFE/RL Research Report* 3, no. 16 (April 22, 1994).

15. "Torgyan, Csurka, and Thurmer (in that order) have recently been coming in last when Hungarians are asked to rank 26 politicians in order of popularity." Edith Oltay, "Hungary," *RFE/RL Research Report* 3, no. 16 (April 22, 1994), p. 61. Since 1995, admittedly, Torgyan's popularity has grown.

16. Gale Stokes, *The Walls Came Tumbling Down* (New York: Oxford University Press, 1993), p. 6.

17. Marie Mendras, "La Russie dans les têtes," *Commentaire,* no. 71 (Autumn 1995), pp. 501–509.

18. Jon Elster, "Consenting Adults or the Sorcerer's Apprentice?," *East European Constitutional Review* 4, no. 1 (Winter 1995), pp. 36–41.

19. Anne Applebaum, "The Fall and Rise of the Communists: Guess Who's Running Central Europe?," *Foreign Affairs* 73, no. 6 (November/December 1994), p. 9; old Poles who collect old postcards of Vilnius and Lvov are not necessarily irredentists.

20. Erich Fromm, *Escape from Freedom* (New York: Avon Books, 1969).

21. George Schöpflin, *Politics in Eastern Europe* (Oxford: Blackwell, 1993), pp. 256–300.

22. See Ernest Gellner, *Nations and Nationalism* (Oxford: Blackwell, 1983); one basic insight here is that nationalism requires identification with people you will never see, and therefore differs fundamentally from tribalism.

23. In "recent national elections in Poland, Hungary, Slovakia, and Bulgaria," again, "anti-Romany extremists failed to gain much support." Zoltan Barany, "Grim Realities in Eastern Europe," *Transition* 1, no. 4 (March 29, 1995), p. 3.

24. More modestly, Serbia-contra-mundum narratives, based on a long historical memory of Serbia as a loser state and an unappreciated defender of the West against the Turks, even if they did not *motivate* aggression, may have *paralyzed* or *silenced* many potential opponents of a policy of Serbian expansion.

25. Karen Dawisha and Bruce Parrott, *Russia and the New States of Eurasia* (Cambridge, England: Cambridge University Press, 1994), p. 292.

26. Wendy Slater, "Russia," *RFE/RL Research Report* 3, no. 16 (April 22, 1994), p. 23.

27. Sharon Fisher, "Slovakia," *RFE/RL Research Report* 3, no. 16 (April 22, 1994), p. 70.

28. This is not to deny, for instance, that local narratives of "failed reform" have been successfully used by resurgent communist parties to oust their liberal-reformist rivals.

29. Remember that Archduke Franz Ferdinand was assassinated in retaliation for the Austro-Hungarian annexation of Bosnia.

30. Jonathan Steele, *Eternal Russia* (Cambridge, MA: Harvard University Press, 1994), p. xiv; "How could there be a return to Russian nationalism if no such feeling existed before?" (ibid.).

31. *The Economist*, April 22, 1995, p. 69.

32. Nicholas Eberstadt, "Demographic Disaster: The Soviet Legacy," *The National Interest*, no. 36 (Summer 1994), pp. 53–57.

33. Jirina Siklová, "Backlash," *Social Research* 60, no. 4 (Winter 1993), pp. 736–49.

34. *Open Media Research Institute Daily Digest* (OMRI), no. 81 (April 25, 1995).

35. Richard Rose, "Getting by without Government: Everyday Life in Russia," *Daedalus* 123, no. 3 (Summer 1994), p. 52; see also ———, "Russia as an Hour-Glass Society: A Constitution without Citizens," *East European Constitutional Review* 4, no. 3 (Summer 1995), pp. 34–42.

36. Rose, "Getting by Without Government," pp. 55–56.

37. Ibid., p. 58.

38. That is to say, by preserving cynical Marxism while discarding utopian Marxism, they have a ready-made intellectual framework that "makes sense" of their current predicament—explaining to all, in the simplest terms, how low-salary officials can build fancy dachas. In my view, this particular cultural legacy, which is cognitive, not attitudinal, eases public anxieties in the face of a novel situation and considerably reduces public demand for paranoid narratives of blame.

39. "In fact, what is truly extraordinary is that, cheated out of their wages by the government and by company managers who use the money to play the

markets, Russia's workers have not yet staged a truly general strike, or for that matter rioted." *The Moscow Times*, International Weekly Edition, April 16, 1995, p. 8.

40. Martin Seligman, *Helplessness* (New York: W. H. Freeman, 1992).

41. Elemér Hankiss, "European Paradigms: East and West, 1945–1994," *Daedalus* 123, no. 2 (Summer 1994), p. 117; summarizing this theory, J. F. Brown remarks: "the argument holds that the communist system turned most East Europeans into vegetables." *Hopes and Shadows*, p. 312.

42. Martin Malia, *Alexander Herzen and the Birth of Russian Socialism* (New York: Grosset and Dunlop, 1965), pp. 269–74.

43. Jacques Rupnik, "The Post-Totalitarian Blues," *Journal of Democracy* 6, no. 2 (April 1995), p. 68.

44. The freelancing officials involved in the sale were presumably more interested in their private overseas bank accounts than in the welfare of their country.

45. The Russian Federal Tax Service, as of May 23, 1995, estimated that tax arrears in the Russian Federation were 28 billion rubles or $5.7 billion. (*OMRI Daily Digest* Part I, May 23, 1995.)

46. *The New York Times*, October 7, 1994, p. A6.

47. Jacek Kochanowicz, "The Disappearing State: Poland's Three Years of Transition," *Social Research* 60, no. 4 (Winter 1993).

48. In Bulgaria, "18 people have died over the past year owing to 'carelessness' on the part of the police." *OMRI Daily Digest*, April 13, 1995.

49. By "insolvent" I mean not poor or resourceless states, but states unable to tax efficiently and to target extracted resources to the provision of public services.

50. Jiri Pehe, "A Leader in Political Stability and Economic Growth," *Transition* 1, no. 1 (Special Issue, January 30, 1995), p. 30.

51. In March 8, 1995, the Czech Constitutional Court upheld the 1945 Benes decrees, despite their references to *národnost* and insinuations of collective guilt. This was a political, not a moral or judicial, decision, based on realpolitik, not justice, blatantly violating the great market principle: give back what has been stolen!

52. Steve Kettle, "Of Money and Morality," *Transition* 1, no. 3 (March 15, 1995), pp. 38–39.

53. Klaus's scheme to raise campaign contributions for his own party from state enterprises that had been bailed out by his government brought the conflict-of-interest question into the public eye; it is not enough to point to the existence of similar scandals in western Europe and add that the Czech Republic is just "a normal country," for private holdings in western Europe have a much greater social legitimacy than those in any postcommunist society.

54. In any case, the mighty Russian anarchy will not bend easily to the fiat of the Kremlin, no matter who sits in the citadel of power. When Hitler took over Germany, a very effective bureaucracy and judicial system was still in place. Zhirinovsky's Russia would be much less amenable to centralized control. Khorzhakov is reportedly building a private security force of

40,000 men. Such troops may be useful for protecting Yeltsin and his friends, but would they allow the Kremlin to control Russia?

55. Juan J. Linz and Alfred Stepan, "Political Identities and Electoral Sequences: Spain, the Soviet Union, and Yugoslavia," *Daedalus* 121, no. 2 (Spring 1992), pp. 123–39.

CHAPTER TWO

The State and Economy: Reflections on the Transition from Communism to Capitalism in Russia

Robert Skidelsky

Interpretations of the collapse of communism have lacked a significant general dimension. In most commentaries, the communist state is treated as a unique kind of state, which generated unique pathologies that destroyed it. This perspective is a natural outgrowth of Sovietology and, more generally, Cold War thinking, which divided the world into two discrete systems, capitalism and communism, competitive but not interactive. The fall of communism was thus, at the same time, the victory and the vindication of capitalism: "We won."

This perspective is not wrong but incomplete. The Communist Party state was a unique twentieth-century form of life. It not only monopolized political power but, unlike the fascist states, owned and commanded the whole economy as well. So when the party lost its power to command the polity, the economic system stopped working, and had to be rebuilt on completely different lines. That is why the transition to postcommunism is much more traumatic than was the transition to postfascism after World War II, and no more so than in Russia, where capitalism came later and communism sooner than in Central Europe.

However, from the political economy standpoint—one that deals with the relationship between the state and economy—communism was not unique, but an extreme development of collectivism—of the doctrine that the state knows best, and the application of this doctrine to the shaping of economic and social life. Most capitalist societies shared collectivist features with communism, such as central planning, large public sectors with bureaucratic allocation of resources, manipulated trade and currency regimes. These were the common inheritance of the first half of this century. In the 1950s and 1960s it was fashionable on the center-left to suppose that the capitalist and communist worlds would converge on moderate collectivism. The main change in political economy since the 1970s has been the general retreat from collectivism. The death of a monstrous mutation (Soviet communism) is the most dramatic episode in the failure of a species (collectivism). To focus on the particular reasons for the fall of communism is a valid exercise. But it should not stop us from reflecting on the general reasons for the failure of state-led or state-controlled economies; or from realizing that the problems of the transition are, to some extent, worldwide, even though they vary enormously in scope and existential import from society to society.

The political economy standpoint gives us a point of entry into the debate between the pessimists and optimists. This debate largely reflects disciplinary divides. General history, sociology, and political science tend to be pessimistic disciplines because the stories they tell are so often ones of failure: failure to transcend the past, to overcome deep-seated cultural attitudes and racial and religious conflicts, to establish legitimate forms of political rule. On the optimistic side are the economists and economic historians, who usually know little general history, have a scant feel for the peculiarities of culture or the constraints of politics, but can point to the undoubted progress humankind has made in solving its economic problems. Economists are essentially problem-solvers. They drop out of the sky with a dispensary of portable science and "core institutions" to be met by a barrage of pessimistic analysis explaining why these medicines will not work in these particular circumstances or why the transplants will not take in these particular conditions. At root this disciplinary divide probably reflects the fact that we have been more successful at economics than at politics.

On balance the political economy approach is optimistic, because it believes that experience and theory both show that there are good and bad ways of arranging economic life, that transplants of modern institutions take quite readily even in very traditional soil (such as, the Meiji Restoration), and that "cultural resistances to change" often turn out to be state-created vested interests. All the great economists, from Adam Smith to Keynes and Hayek, have emphasized the heuristic value of ideas; the Austrian school of economics has pinpointed the role of the risk-taking entrepreneur in creating and exploiting favorable market opportunities, a standpoint that can be applied readily to political leadership. In other words, the postulate of inventiveness or voluntarism is needed to break the closed circle of pessimistic structuralist analysis, with its terraces of preconditions. The political economy approach offers a further ground for optimism by linking the collapse of communism not to the "tumult of ethnicity"[1] but to the global trend toward a capitalist and democratic future.[2] This is the most substantial ground for optimism today.

THE CRISIS OF THE STATE

In the notion of the breakdown of the overambitious state we have a single perspective for understanding the collapse of communism, the problems faced by postcommunist countries, and the process of "remarketizing" nominally capitalist economies that started in the late 1970s. There has been a restructuring of political economy that is global in scope, encompassing countries as varied as China, Britain, Mexico, Argentina, New Zealand, Sweden, India, and Russia. Domestically and internationally the state has retreated and the market has advanced. This movement has been driven by new ideas and new technology. But a common catalyst was the "fiscal crisis" of the state: its inability to raise the taxes required to pay for its expenditure. This led to widening budget deficits, inflation, and finally a process of divestment by the state of many of its responsibilities. This process of "structural adjustment" of the political economy has brought serious problems to all countries that have experienced it, though none so acute as to the postcommunist countries, where the state had to divest itself of ownership of the entire economy.

This perspective gives us a far more encompassing notion of the "transition." The remarketization of economies started in China in 1978, spread to Britain, the United States, and Latin America in the early 1980s, and reached the European communist world in 1989. This worldwide movement had many motives and causes, but a common thread was the attempt by governments to preserve or reconstitute state revenues by restoring economic profitability.

Communism collapsed because the Soviet state ran out of the will to enforce the command economy, the source of its profits. At the same time, the weakness of the postcommunist state explains many features of the actual transition process in the chief successor republic, Russia—notably hyperinflation and criminality. Under communism the state was connected to the economy in a particular manner. The state owned the economy; the central planning system set the production goals; ideology and terror provided the incentives. Once the incentives ceased to work, the planning system broke down, and with it the economy and the source of state revenues. There was no legal, political, or attitudinal basis for the more familiar Western pattern, whereby the state provides the public goods of a market economy characterized by the private ownership of firms.

At a minimum, a successful transition to a capitalist market economy thus requires the creation of a type of state capable of providing the public goods of a commercial society. The archaic and retrogressive character of the Soviet system has meant that, in Russia, where it took its deepest hold, many institutional features of the modern capitalist state have had to be invented from scratch—notably the legal system, the political system, the tax system, and social safety nets. Belatedly, the realization has now taken hold that progress in developing appropriate legal-political institutions for a capitalist market economy will have a far bigger effect on the outcome of the transformation process than the precise sequencing of particular economic policies—the main subject of debate in the earlier phase of the transition. In fact, no coherent sequencing is possible when the state structure itself is incoherent.

This is not to deny that economic policy and institution building interact. For example, persisting high rates of ruble inflation in Russia push economic activity into the informal and "dollarized" sectors. This reduces the central government's tax take and encourages monetization of the deficit, inflation, and continued dollarization. Although ending inflation is a necessary condition for restructuring the economy, the structure of Russia's economy encourages inflation. An act of political will is needed to break this vicious circle. Such acts are always very difficult for a weak government, though there are encouraging signs that the Russian government, with imported financial strength from the International Monetary Fund (IMF), has finally decided to take the plunge.

Russia will have to sort out its own problems in its own way. It is too big, too proud, too distinctive, and still too powerful a country to be told what to do. In the end, there probably will be a "Russian model of capitalism" to add to all the others. Russia's reentry into the community of nations also will influence the norms of international and domestic conduct in disturbing ways. Under communism, Russia was an enemy that had to be contained; but its self-imposed quarantine meant that it did not properly interact with the West. The more "normal" it becomes, the more it will become a giver as well as a receiver of values.

The West can hope to facilitate a relatively benign transition to postcommunism, but only if Western countries ponder seriously the conditions of their own political and economic stability. This also involves rethinking the relationship between the state and the economy. The current general problem—leaving all variations aside—is too little Keynes and too much welfare. This is a scenario for global instability. Too much welfare builds fiscal instability into the macroeconomy; macroeconomic instability encourages trade wars and protectionism; protectionism sours international relations and makes reintegrating the former communist countries into the global economy more difficult. Exclusion or humiliation will promote Russian xenophobia and

militarism. Few doubt that western Europe's unwelcoming economic and incoherent political reaction to the recovery of the
"lost lands" is heavily influenced by its own heavy unemployment, which now is its only weapon to keep inflation down.

Although this chapter focuses on the distempers of communism, communism was only an extreme expression of the collectivism that had gotten practically all economies into trouble
by the late 1970s and early 1980s. Welfarism was the democratic form of collectivism, militarism the autocratic form, but
in the end both systems ran up against resistance to the preten-
sions of the state. This chapter looks at the role of the state in a
commercial society. Communism is a distorting mirror of ourselves. By looking at it we can hope to understand what we must
do if we are to be any use to former communists.

In the following section I offer a stylized account of the
pathologies of the collectivist economy, of which the Soviet system was an extreme case. I then apply this to the reform efforts
of Gorbachev and Russia's postcommunist governments, before
concluding with what the West can do to bolster a benign transformation.

THE PATHOLOGIES OF THE REVENUE ECONOMY

In his *Theory of Economic History*, the economist John Hicks
distinguished between a "revenue" and a "market" economy. In
the traditional revenue economy, the goods and labor of subjects
are considered fit for rulers to command at will, for their greater
power, splendor, and prestige. In a market economy, goods and
labor are exchanged between free citizens, and the "wealth of
nations" increases through the effects of the division of labor and
accumulation of stock described by Adam Smith. In such an economy, the ruler's "take" is restricted by legally defined and enforceable property rights and by a constitution obliging him to
obtain consent for supply from private property owners. There
is no doubt that the market economy is a more dynamic and successful type of economic organization than the traditional revenue economy. Under conditions of revenue economy, the wealth

of nations failed to increase over thousands of years. Economic progress starts with the emergence of market economies in western Europe in the eighteenth century.

In the nineteenth century the revenue economy was in retreat. The ruler's take as a share of national income declined as the area of market exchange expanded, though his revenue grew in absolute terms as a result of the growth in aggregate wealth. The world economy started "growing" at the end of the eighteenth century, and its growth tended to accelerate as the century wore on. In the twentieth century, as Hicks noted, there has been a "massive swing-back toward the Revenue Economy."[3] This can be demonstrated easily. In 1880 the average of public spending as a share of gross national product (GNP) in six selected Organization for Economic Cooperation and Development (OECD) countries was ten percent; in the early 1960s it was about a third—roughly the share the Moguls are estimated to have taken from the farmer in seventeenth-century India; by 1985 it had reached 47 percent.[4] An interesting question arises. Is the twentieth-century revenue economy a more rational and successful form of economic organisation than the nineteenth-century market economy, or is it a return to the pre-market predatory state?

The crucial differences *seem* to be ones of knowledge and motive. The modern state (unlike its archaic predecessor) is held to have the knowledge to formulate and pursue coherent developmental and welfare objectives. Certainly the state's claim to revenue is now couched in these terms. The most extreme expression of this claim was in Soviet communism. Second, it is widely held that, outside the communist countries, the revenue economy has been brought back by popular demand—through the ballot box. This is said to guarantee that the revenue raised from taxes will be spent according to the preferences of the citizenry rather than those of the rulers and their servants. The modern revenue economy is thus seen to be distinguished from its traditional predecessor by welfare goals and popular control. The real question is whether the change in the purposes and conditions of revenue collection has succeeded in making the modern state an engine of growth and welfare rather than a predator.

The answer afforded by twentieth-century experience is: not as much as might have been expected. On the plus side is the undoubted fact that world economic growth, as conventionally measured, has been faster in the twentieth than in the nineteenth century (two percent a year in real per capita terms as against less than one percent) and, partly as a consequence, partly as a matter of design, the explicit "welfare" component of state spending is higher than in the traditional revenue economies. However, some acceleration of growth was always a likely consequence of the spread of market relations; and there seems to be no clear correlation between the proportion of output spent by the state and the growth of output. Since World War II, the countries with the fastest sustained rates of growth have been the East Asian capitalist economies, which have the smallest state sector, measured by expenditure. On the other hand, countries such as Germany and France, which had historically high rates of growth from the 1950s to the 1970s, had relatively large state sectors; and the United States, which had a relatively small state sector, also had a relatively slow rate of growth (see table 1).

However, it must be noted that in all these countries, the share of state spending in the economy rose markedly in the 1970s, a rise associated with a growth slowdown and the start of "fiscal crises."

Against the faster growth record of the twentieth century must be set the much larger share of gross domestic product (GDP) taken by military spending. From the welfare point of view, this is largely waste. Of the additional resources produced

TABLE 1—ANNUAL AVERAGE PERCENTAGE INCREASES IN GDP PER CAPITA, AND GOVERNMENT OUTLAYS AS A PERCENTAGE OF GDP, 1950–73

	Growth of GDP per capita	Government Outlays
Japan	7.6	18.0
Germany	6.0	35.5
France	5.0	36.1
United Kingdom	3.2	36.5
United States	2.4	28.6

Source: N. F. R. Crafts and Nicholas Woodward, *The British Economy Since 1945* (Oxford: Oxford University Press, 1991), pp. 8, 10.

in the twentieth century, about 20 percent have been wasted, on a conservative estimate. The twentieth-century revival of the revenue economy has been associated with a big increase in warlikeness, with two world wars, a number of very costly smaller wars, and a big increase in the incidence of civil wars and mass murder of civilians. On a commonsense reading, the connection has been reciprocal: the revenue economy was put back into business by the rising costs of "protection," but the revival of such economies, particularly though not exclusively in their fascist and Soviet form, increased the costs of protection all around.

The fundamental theoretical reason why the twentieth-century revenue economy cannot be judged to be unambiguously welfare-enhancing is that it is neither scientific nor democratic in the usual meaning of these terms. Contrary to much elite expectation, the modern state's claim to superior knowledge has proved invalid. It has proved impossible to centralize knowledge concerning the public good or the community's preferences or even how the economy works sufficiently to provide a "scientific" or "objective" basis for the pursuit of ambitious collective goals. These goals are therefore still inevitably determined by the private preferences and subjective beliefs of rulers and officials, who may or may not be benevolent in intention.

Further, the fact that public spending has risen in part at least as a by-product of the competition for power should alert us to the presence of traditional patronage and clientage motives in the spending decisions of the modern welfare state.

Thus "public choice" as practiced by self-interested politicians and bureaucrats in a setting of genuine ignorance, competition for votes, and pressure from vested interests has turned out to be a mechanism for diverting income flows to those groups and sections of the electorate on whom governments and political parties depend for support, irrespective of the general utility—which is not, after all, so different from the behavior of the traditional autocrat who shared out his "take" with those whose support he needed to stay in power. In fact, it has been argued that the "fiscal outcomes emerging from the democratic process can in general be expected to serve the interests of us, the citizens, [no] more than the exactions of the absolute monarchies of the past."[5]

If this is true, it follows that the twentieth-century revenue economy is not much better placed than its traditional predecessor to close the "preference gap": the gap between the government's choice of output and what the population at large would choose if it had free disposal of its resources. This is the insoluble contradiction of all revenue economies. It explains why they were all in the end subject to "fiscal crisis"—from democratic Sweden with its once-vaunted welfare state to militarized, autocratic Soviet Russia. Democratic legitimation only postpones the day of crisis for the revenue economy.

The crisis is signaled by the emergence of tax resistance. As taxes rise, the rewards from tax evasion or avoidance rise, while the rewards from taxed activity fall. There are many forms of tax resistance, but they all share one aim, which is to place some portion of wealth and income-generating activity beyond the reach of the tax collector. In India, the traditional method was to hoard precious metals—to the great detriment of the nation's economic development. Tax resistance can take the form of capital flight, fiscal separatism, growth of the informal economy, or inflation. All signify an unwillingness to buy the state's services at the prices the state charges for them.

It is impossible to identify a single tax/income ratio at which tax resistance develops, valid across all societies and at all times. Tax tolerance undoubtedly increased in the first half of this century, though not by as much as governments wanted to spend, probably as a result of the two world wars and the Great Depression.[6] Otherwise, the ratio depends on the efficiency of the tax-collecting system, the size and nature of the revenue base, the degree of respect for the law, the efficiency with which state services are provided, and other things. Tax resistance may develop at quite low levels of taxation, if the taxes are incompetently or inequitably levied, or if the goods and services they pay for are inefficiently provided.[7]

A crude indicator of tax resistance is the emergence of price inflation. John Maynard Keynes was the first to state clearly that inflation is a form of taxation:

> A government can live for a long time ... by printing paper money. That is to say, it can by this means secure the command over real resources, resources just as real as those obtained by taxation. The method is condemned, but its efficacy, up to a point, must be admitted. A government can live by this means when it can live by no other. It is the form of taxation which the public find hardest to evade and even the weakest government can enforce, when it can enforce nothing else.[8]

Like any form of taxation, inflation enables a government to shift resources to its clients and dependents as well as to its own staff, when the general public is unwilling to pay for these benefits through taxes openly levied.[9]

From the later 1960s most Western governments increased taxes to pay for increased social spending. Receipts of European OECD governments as a share of GDP rose from 32 percent during the years 1960–67 to 39 percent in 1974–79. However, current outlays went up from 33.1 percent to 43.2 percent in the same periods, with inflation rising from 3.8 percent per annum to 12.8 percent. Evidently, a sizable part of the increased spending was paid for by the inflation tax. One way in which tax resistance produces inflation is through the process of tax-shifting—transferring the initial impact of the tax to someone else. Employees retaliate against tax-imposed cuts in their take-home pay by demanding a compensating increase in gross pay, which transfers the tax to their employers. For a time employers are able to pass this on to the consumer in higher prices, which the state accommodates, so employees end up paying the tax as consumers. However, when they notice that the real value of their personal income has fallen, employees demand further increases in gross pay, setting off a wage-price spiral, as employers again attempt to shift the tax to the consumer. Who ends up paying the "inflation tax" depends on the relative bargaining power of different groups. In the 1970s the tax, broadly speaking, fell more on profits than on wages, so inflation turned into "stagflation" as employers laid off workers. However, the important point is that the process would never have got going had the additional output, which the governments were providing through higher taxes, corresponded to the preferences of their beneficiaries.[10]

The "new political economy" of the 1980s marks a (so far modest) swing back from the revenue to the market economy, driven by tax resistance. The seemingly inexorable long-term growth in the share of public spending in GDP has been slowed, arrested, and in a few countries even reversed. It is still early, and the tax resistance crunch has yet to come in most of western Europe.

The fall of Soviet communism may be seen as an extreme example of tax resistance generated by excessive exactions. Mancur Olson has provided a stylized account of communism's rise and fall by considering what would happen if a mafia chief took complete control of a region or country—that is, became a "stationary bandit." The rational stationary bandit, Olson argues, is a long-run revenue maximizer. He settles down, assumes the crown, and limits his take to what is needed to maintain (and even increase) the income of his territory, and thus his own future income; the rational autocrat chooses the revenue-maximizing tax rate.

Olson extends this model of rational autocratic behavior to cover the case of Stalin. He credits Stalin with having realized that by seizing the capital stock of the Soviet Union, using it for capital-intensive investment, and depressing private consumption through a colossal implicit tax on intramarginal work (while providing bonuses, prizes, and special perquisites for especially productive workers and managers—directly contrary to the Western system of progressive taxation), Stalin could obtain a "larger proportion of the national output for his own purposes than any other government in history has been able to extract." This went mainly for military and prestige spending, which was consequently a higher share of national income than even the most powerful traditional autocrat had achieved.

In Olson's stylized account, Soviet communism decayed and collapsed because of the growth of resistance to the very high level of implicit tax collections on managers' and workers' incomes. Competition between managers to offer more output for given inputs (in order to earn bonuses) gives way to collusion between managers to understate how much they can produce in order to keep the surplus. Workers collude to reduce the implicit tax burden by only pretending to work. As coercion weakens, the whole population bands together in collusive groups to deprive the dictatorial center of revenue. "Ultimately even the republics in which language and ethnic loyalties facilitate collective action can become conspiracies at the expense of the center," Olson writes. Since the Stalinist autocrat owned 100 percent of the property of his domain, only he had an incentive to guard it and preserve or increase its productivity. Everyone else had an incentive to steal it, restrained only by ideology and fear; and the conspiring coteries of "burglars" were too narrow to have any "encompassing" interest in the health of the whole. As communism weakened and devolved, it was bound to collapse. But the only successor were groups of robber barons formed to take back some of what the stationary bandit had stolen. This was the debris of communism out of which a "normal" capitalist society had to be constructed.[11]

FROM GORBACHEV TO YELTSIN

The collapse of Soviet communism and the transition to market economy can be understood as an ongoing episode in the "struggle for revenue." The proximate cause of the fall of the Soviet Union was state bankruptcy. The Soviet state went bankrupt because its investments were unprofitable. Its tax take declined precipitately and it had no collateral for borrowing. Paradoxically, the long-run financial viability of the state depends on its *not* owning the economy. This is because the system of incentives the state owner substitutes for private ownership and market exchange is guaranteed, terror apart, to make the economy unprofitable. The Soviet economy was like a single firm owned by the state. If this firm is unprofitable, the state runs out of money. Because the firm is the economy, it cannot simply be liquidated. It is the owner that is liquidated, and the residual assets are acquired by anyone who will take them. This is the meaning of privatization. Privatization is simply the recognition de jure of the inability of the state owner to make profits. The only way for the state to preserve sources of revenue is to hand over the economy to entrepreneurs who can. The analogous development in the capitalist world was the privatization of loss-making state industries. But since the revenues of the state never depended importantly on the profits of these industries, the fact that they incurred losses did not bring about the ruin of the state, although the losses contributed to the growth of the state's budget deficit.

Since Soviet prices and the budgetary accounts were fictitious, it is impossible to get an accurate idea of the share of the national output spent by the state. The whole output of the economy was produced by the state; the whole of it was allocated by the state; but of course not all of it was literally "consumed" by the state, even though the state maintained a vast bureaucratic, party, and military apparatus. According to the official budgetary figures, the Soviet state spent about 50 percent of the national income in 1981, not much higher than the share being spent by capitalist states at the same period. Thirty percent of this output was invested, the capital formation of the whole economy being financed out of the state budget. Because of the high implicit taxes levied on private consumption, Soviet economies were able to achieve a substantially higher rate of capital formation than capitalist economies (except Japan). In the reasoning of their leaders, the larger the share of investment in total spending, the faster the growth rate of output and the greater the output (revenues) available for the upkeep of the state. Since little attention was paid to the productivity of investment, the economy could generate a surplus of output over input only if the costs of the factors of production—land, capital, and labor—were kept artificially cheap. The rewards to these factors were thus systematically depressed (the reward to capital eliminated entirely) in order to yield the Soviet state the surplus of output to pay for its investment and own consumption.

The growing inability of the Soviet state to "pay its way" is revealed in the revenue side of its budget. Its two main sources of revenue were the turnover tax, a sales tax levied on consumption, and the profits tax, levied at a rate of 100 percent, on production. According to official statistics, the Soviet budget remained balanced until 1990. But according to the Soviet economist Konstantin Kagalovsky, the budget deficit in 1986 was already between eight and nine percent of GNP.[12] Government borrowing from the Central Bank concealed the shortfall in tax revenue. The deficit was caused by a decline in the profitability of Soviet enterprise (surplus of output over input), the concealment of profit, and the concurrent increase in subsidies to keep production going and consumer dissatisfaction at bay. Since the inflation was repressed by maintaining fixed prices, the actual cost of the inflation tax was borne by the state itself—it lost the resources that the firms gained. By 1990 the deficit was openly admitted, and in 1991, the last year of the Soviet Union, it reached 16 percent of GNP: the state was still spending over 50 percent of national income, but was appropriating only 35 percent. Table 2 shows the progressive reduction in in the state's "take" of the national income.

The fraction of official national income taken by the post-communist state (federal and regional) is now about two-thirds of a typical west European "welfare state." In fact it is even lower as a fraction of total income, since the informal (unmeasured and therefore untaxed) economy is estimated to be between 25 percent and 40 percent of the total. The revenue of the *central* government was only 13 percent of official national income in 1994 (as against expenditure of 23.2 percent), showing the extent to which fiscal federalism has proceeded. Essentially, the central government in Moscow lost most of its revenue to the newly in-

TABLE 2—CONSOLIDATED GOVERNMENT REVENUES AND EXPENDITURES
AS A PERCENTAGE OF GNP
SOVIET UNION, (1986–91), RUSSIA, (1992–94)

	Revenues	*Expenditure*
1986	52.5	52.2
1990	47.2	51.3
1991	35.1	50.8
1992	33.6	42.5
1993	25.8	35.3
1994 (% GDP)	27.3	37.3

Sources: J. Sachs, "Russia's Struggle with Stabilization: Conceptual Issues and Evidence," unpublished manuscript, *World Bank Conference on Development Economics* (April 1994), p. 54; *Russian Economic Trends* (Moscow: Government of the Russian Federation/London School of Economics, 1995), vol. 4.1, p. 28.

dependent republics, the 89 autonomous republics and provinces that make up the Russian federation, and the informal economy, while retaining responsibility for the upkeep of the military-agrarian sector—that part of the economy it still "owns." That is what is meant by the collapse of the Soviet Union.

How did it happen? The story of Mikhael Gorbachev's failure to maintain the state's revenue base is now well known. The basic problem diagnosed by Soviet economists in the 1980s was that the Soviet system had exhausted its possibilities for "extensive" growth and needed to shift to "intensive" growth. The high Soviet growth rates of the 1950s and 1960s were achieved mainly by mobilizing the factors of production, especially labor, capital, land, and minerals: the contribution made by the growth in factor productivity was much lower than in capitalist countries. The potential for extensive growth is finite. After all possible labor has been mobilized, the cost of using it (wages) rises; this reduces the amount of capital (investment) that can be squeezed out of the economy by *force majeure*. In a Stalinist economy, that means a fall in output (revenues) available to the state. By the late 1970s some investment was already being financed by inflation. So Gorbachev tried to "accelerate" growth by increasing capital and labor productivity. The only way the Soviet state knew of achieving these twin objectives was to order a huge investment in machine tools regardless of the means of paying for them and to reduce the quantity of vodka available in state shops. The attempt to restructure the productive system at madcap speed—a speed dictated by the need to keep up with the United States in the arms race—started the fall in output by disrupting all the productive chains. The attempt to restrict the consumption of vodka knocked a big hole in the state budget by cutting the proceeds of the turnover tax. This restricted the state investment fund and accelerated the growth of the informal economy, with illegal distilling making up for the shortfall in official sales.

Gorbachev's most radical move to "perfect the economic mechanism" was the 1987 Law on State Enterprises. This law aimed to improve incentives by limiting firms' obligations to supplying state orders and allowing them to retain the profits from "ordinary" trade, which would be conducted with competing firms at market prices. Although this law implied a narrowing of the state's revenue base, the hope was that improved company profitability would increase the state's revenue and reduce its subsidies. However, with private ownership still taboo, the incentive signals were confused. Crucially, Gorbachev's government shrank from price liberalization, which would have meant shifting the inflation tax from the state to the consumer. The Law on State Enterprises allowed workers to elect their managers. This gave them control over the wages fund. Nominal wages rose rapidly from 1989 onward while prices remained fixed. Rising input and fixed output prices was the royal road to firm, and therefore state, bankruptcy.

With *perestroika* faltering, Gorbachev tried to build a mass base for himself outside the party. The transition to democracy and federalism in 1989–90 led to an explosion of social expectations, with parties competing with each other in extravagant promises of social spending, and with the center competing with the republics for control of resources and resource flows. With central control weakened, open resistance to the government's exactions replaced covert resistance: stocks were hoarded, goods were diverted onto the black market, workers struck for higher wages, regions withheld payment from the center. The autocrat's exactions from his estate were replaced by economic lobbies in parliament exacting subsidies from the budget and subsidized credits from the central bank. With goods disappearing from state shops, rationing of most basic items had to be reintroduced. With cash balances piling up ("monetary overhang"), price liberalization became ever more difficult. An aborted currency reform in 1991 led to a panic flight from the ruble into dollars and physical commodities, increasing shortages still further. An alternative economy, based partly on dollars, partly on barter, and partly on the regions, grew up around the ruins of the official economy.

When the Soviet Union broke up at the end of 1991, Boris Yeltsin inherited a weak but hypertrophied state: its reach far exceeded its grasp. The problem of macroeconomic stabilization resolved itself into how to rebalance state obligations and resources at a much lower level of taxation. The Russian state—the chief successor state of the Soviet Union—could save itself only by shedding responsibilities it could no longer fulfill. In a series of dramatic and very brave moves starting in January 1992, Yeltsin's acting prime minister, Yegor Gaidar, slashed military orders by 70 percent, freed most prices, and started mass privatization through vouchers—in effect giving away most state firms to whoever wanted them. But Yeltsin also inherited a constitution that, in effect, gave control of the money supply to a producers' political cartel in the Duma, which coalesced in the summer of 1992 around the issue of enterprise arrears—nonpayments for production. This cartel has so far defeated three attempts to stabilize the macroeconomy and end inflation— Gaidar's first effort in 1992, Boris Fyodorov's more gradual attempt in 1993, and Victor Chernomyrdin's attempt in 1994. The new constitution, approved in December 1993, after Yeltsin had dispersed the old Duma by force, proved more workable than the old. It centralized economic power in the president's hands, removing the Duma's veto on monetary policy. The price Yeltsin had to pay for this new constitution was the relatively poor showing of the reformers in elections to the new Duma in the same month, the legitimization of extremism in the shape of Vladimir Zhirinovksy's misnamed Liberal Democrats, and the reinforcement of the "soft inflation" lobby. Since then Yeltsin has found it prudent to balance different factions in his government. That has meant a compromise between the pro- and anti-inflationists, with an emerging "centrist" consensus on gradual disinflation and liberalization.

The debate between the anti- and pro-inflationists is not without interest or substance. Russian economists and politicians are now replicating the debate between the monetary and structural causes of inflation that raged in Latin America in the 1960s and 1970s. The conversion of a command economy geared to military orders for market production inevitably takes time. The amount of time is even longer if no legal framework for commercial activity exists. The pro-inflationist argument is that without the crutch of subsidy, such an economy simply collapses. Any attempt to balance the budget on the basis of a collapsing economy is illusory: revenue will continue to drop faster than expenditure. So the priority must be to maintain production with the help of inflation and protectionism, enabling conversion to proceed gradually as circumstances allow.

The pro-inflationists point out that the big difference between conversion in (say) West Germany after the end of World War II and in Russia after the fall of communism is that in the former, the legal-institutional framework of a commercial society was in place and the state was, in effect, supplied initially by the victorious Allies. This is the *rational* argument for gradualism. The actual arguments of the military-industrial, agrobusiness cartel for protection and continued emissions from the Central Bank are much more straighforwardly self-interested, with a strong overlay of nostalgia and regret for the vanished certainties of communism.

More interestingly, Grigori Yavlinsky, head of the Yabloko faction in the Duma, argues that if monetary policy is overrigid, heavy unemployment will develop, reversing the political will to continue with reform. His argument is a good example of conversion pessimism. But he lacks a coherent alternative.[13]

The anti-inflationist position is characterized by conversion optimism. The anti-inflationists argue that the ending of inflation is a necessary and sufficient condition for economic restructuring and the recovery of output. Vladimir Mau has claimed that within a year of stopping inflation, the fall in production ceases, and six months later the economy starts to recover.[14] Inflation does not ease restructuring for market demand, it delays it and hence delays economic revival. Moreover, it perpetuates the political dominance of the pro-inflation cartel. The anti-inflationists say that, anyway, the fall in output is greatly exaggerated, as the informal economy is unmeasured. The anti-inflationist reformers argue that rather than squandering subsidies on the mastodonic remnants of the old economy, the state should focus its available resources on providing the genuine public goods of a commercial society: an appropriate legal system, an effective tax system, enforcement of contracts, social safety nets, education, research, and health care. A key element in the anti-inflationist program is military reform—replacing the conscript army with a much smaller professional army under civilian control. The anti-inflationists argue that this kind of refocusing of state activities, together with a commitment to end Central Bank emissions and open the economy to foreign competition, will induce an inflow of both private and official capital to kick-start the ailing economy and finance the budget deficit.

Russian experience provides no way of testing these two opposing propositions, because the Yeltsin governments have pursued neither pro-inflation nor anti-inflation policies consistently. They have oscillated between one and the other, with the recent tendency being to turn the tap off more often than on. On the other hand, there is now ample experience from other postcommunist societies that if inflation is brought below 40 percent per annum, production starts to recover.[15]

At the time of this writing (April 1995), the scene is set for the fourth big postcommunist effort to stabilize the macroeconomy and revive the microeconomy. One can be optimistic or pessimistic about the outcome. The monthly rate of inflation has fallen to 3 percent a month; output has stopped falling. The Duma has approved a budget that aims to cut the deficit to 5.5 percent in 1995. The Central Bank will no longer be allowed to finance the deficit by printing money. The tax base has been expanded to cover hitherto exempt or privileged energy, gas, and oil industries. In return for these commitments, and tied to progress in meeting them, the IMF has made available substantial resources to finance the budget deficit. At the same time, the president has finally come down in favor of trade liberalization. He has ended import and export quotas and licenses, reduced the list of fixed prices, and proposed new laws governing shareholders' rights and joint stock companies. The sale of many remaining state assets for cash has finally started. On paper, the anti-inflation reform agenda has triumphed.

The question of course is whether the political will exists to see it through. Elections to the Duma are scheduled for December 1995, to be followed by the presidential election in June 1996. This will be a time of political turbulence, and many observers anticipate heavy defeats not just for the first wave of reformers but for the more cautious groups that support the prime minister, Chernomyrdin. Yeltsin's future is also in doubt. On the other hand, with the privatization of the economy, there is now a much stronger pro-reform, anti-inflation base than existed in 1992 and 1993, centered on the banking sector.

I argued earlier that an act of political will is necessary to break the vicious circle whereby inflation precludes restructuring and the structure of the economy precludes ending inflation. Probably the most substantial ground for pessimism is the continued weakness of the Russian political system and in particular its inability to create an "encompassing" reform party. This places almost the sole responsibility for articulating and representing the general interest on the president—with the political factions left free to pursue narrow interests of their own.

The presidency is too slender a reed to carry the whole burden of the reforms. Even the strongest presidential systems—in France and the United States—are effective only when they have the support of an organized majority in the legislature. Had the reformers been united in December 1993, there would have been more consistent backing for the reform policy than has been available from the current Duma. One hears too often for Western liking that Russia is not "structurally" ready for democracy. But the more people believe that Russia's culture precludes democracy, the less likely it is that democracy will emerge.

WHAT THE WEST CAN DO

The West's contribution to the success of the Russian reforms is usually discussed in terms of aid, inward investment, and advice. This viewpoint has the advantage of diverting discussion from how Western economies might need to reform themselves to assimilate a raft of 27 postcommunist countries. It is no use to talk about opening up the postcommunist markets to Western penetration if these countries are at the same time stopped from exporting their goods to the West.

The best way the countries of the West can help former communist states move toward capitalism is to open up their markets to their goods and services. The biggest obstacle to such an opening is the present economic condition of developed capitalist countries, especially European ones. A combination of deflation and rapid technical change has left them with a legacy of long-term unemployment. Underemployment undoubtedly reinforces the tendency to protectionism. "In the 1990s," writes Paul Krugman, "the world is ripe for another outbreak of trade war."[16]

The prospects for economic liberalism are thus tied up with the fuller or better utilization of resources, including human resources, in both western Europe and the United States. Much of the current debate in the West concerns the nature of the supply-side measures needed to bring this about. Without caricaturing too much, we are offered the choice between an "American" solution, based on labor market flexibility, which has kept registered unemployment (and the quality of new job creation) fairly low, and the "European" solution, based on large public investments in education and training and advanced infrastructure.

The name missing from these arguments is Keynes. Supply-side policy, necessary though it is, does not guard against the danger of economic volatility—not the best environment for trade liberalization. Keynes argued that capitalist economies were inherently unstable. If an economy suffers a shock, it does not simply return to its previous position: extra unemployment or underemployment develops and persists. The experience of the 1980s and early 1990s vindicates this insight.

Keynes brought in the state to smooth the business cycle. Today this particular function of government is widely discredited. What financial markets want from governments is sound money. In a world of footloose capital, this discipline has become universal.

The financiers have a point. Keynesian full-employment policy came to be associated with accelerating inflation, seemingly uncontrollable public-sector growth, and growing public-sector deficits. As I have suggested, these phenomena were widely connected through the mechanism of tax switching, as tax resistance grew to the state's "welfare" function.

The logic of the argument is that if we are to resist protectionism, we must restore a financial regime that excludes inflation while allowing the state to stabilize the business cycle. Doing so requires both a financial rule curbing inflationary finance while guarding against recessionary shocks and an anticollectivist rule aimed at slashing the revenue economy—the chief source of inflationary finance.

There is no space here to develop a rigorous rationale for such a "Western" reform program, so I will simply restate its basic logic.

A level of government spending that exceeds the willingness of the public to make resources available to the government generates inflationary pressures that can be suppressed only by low levels of economic activity. These in turn generate a political demand for increased public spending. Governments are forced to use Keynesian policy to *destabilize* their economies, which makes nonsense of Keynes. As we have seen, there is no definite tax/income ratio at which tax resistance may be said to start, valid for all economies at all times. However, experience of the "golden age" of Western economies—from 1950 to 1968 before inflation took off—suggests that the feasible tax/income ratio—that consistent with stable prices and employment—is much nearer 30 percent than the 50 percent prevalent in western Europe today.

Getting down the share of public spending to anything approaching the "golden" ratio has so far defeated the liberal-conservative revolution that swept the world in the 1980s—except in the postcommunist countries, where state revenues simply collapsed. The problem is that deep cuts in public spending, allowing deep cuts in taxes, cannot be made without reducing the *social agenda* of the state. This agenda has been extended from the original welfare function, which was to provide a social safety net, into a system of universal entitlement to services that most of the population could now afford to buy for themselves if they were not so heavily taxed. A reduction of the state's social agenda would create a pattern of spending and saving that more closely approximates what most people want for themselves and their children.

Supporting the existing revenue economies in western Europe are all those who benefit from state cash payments and also from benefits in kind that they cannot imagine being provided in any other way. As in Russia, an act of political will is needed to break these structural conditions of alternating inflationary pressure and heavy unemployment. The age of the revenue economy will not be over until state spending has been drastically pruned. This pruning is the essential condition for restoring states as stabilizers of economies, which in turn is the best assurance of a liberal postcommunist world.

NOTES

1. As does Daniel Moynihan in *Pandaemonium: Ethnicity in International Relations* (Oxford: Oxford University Press, 1993), p. 15.
2. See Francis Fukuyama, *The End of History and the Last Man* (London: Hamis, Hamilton, 1992). Fukuyama is too optimistic, but with necessary qualifications, his thesis remains the most plausible medium-term (ten to 20 years) extrapolation of current trends.
3. John R. Hicks, *A Theory of Economic History* (Oxford: Oxford University Press, 1969), p. 24.
4. Percival Spear, *A History of India*, vol. 2. (London: Penguin Books, 1991), p. 43.
5. Deepak Lal, *Fighting Fiscal Privilege* (London: Social Market Foundation, 1990), p. 10.
6. For a classic discussion, see Alan T. Peacock and Jack Wiseman, *The Growth of Public Expenditure in the United Kingdom* (Princeton, NJ: Princeton University Press, 1961).
7. David Calleo, *The Bankrupting of America* (New York: William Morrow and Company, 1992), pp. 88 f.
8. John Maynard Keynes, *A Tract on Monetary Reform*, vol. 4, 1923, in *The Collected Writings of John Maynard Keynes* (London: Macmillan, 1971), p. 37.
9. The mechanism is as follows. When the government spends the money it prints, prices rise: the government and its clients get more of a given supply of resources, the general public less.
10. For good accounts of the mechanism of "tax inflation," see Robert Bacon and Walter Eltis, *Britain's Economic Problem: Too Few Producers* (London: Mamillan, 1976), pp. 96–99; Ronald Burgess, *Public Revenue without Taxation* (London: Shepheard-Walwyn, 1993), pp. 41–42. The locus classicus of this kind of analysis is Colin Clark, "Public Finance and the Value of Money," *Economic Journal* (December 1945).
11. Mancur Olson, "The Devolution of Power and the Societies in Transition: Therapies for Corruption, Fragmentation and Economic Retardation," in Robert Skidelsky, ed., *Russia's Stormy Path to Reform*, (London: Social Market Foundation, 1995).
12. Janos Kornai, *The Socialist System* (Oxford: Clarendon Press, 1992), p. 538 n.
13. Yavlinsky's view is taken from his speech to a conference in Moscow, organized by *IRIS*, University of Maryland, attended by the author in April 1995.
14. Vladimir Mau, *Russia's Choice: Background to the Chechnya Crisis* (London: Social Market Foundation, 1995).

15. European Bank for Reconstruction and Development, *Transition Report: Economic Transition in Eastern Europe and the Former Soviet Union* (London: EBRD, update, 1995), tables on pp. 24, 25.
16. Paul Krugman, *Peddling Prosperity* (New York and London: W.W. Norton and Company, 1994), p. 28.

CHAPTER THREE

Democracy, Capitalism, and the End of Transition

John Mueller

A couple of Polish writers were discussing conditions in their country on a street corner in Warsaw fairly recently. At one point, one reflected, "I think we all must now believe that this is it."

It is the central contention of this chapter that most of the postcommunist countries of central and eastern Europe have essentially completed their transition to democracy and capitalism: what they now have is, pretty much, it. They are already full-fledged democracies if we use as models real Western countries (as opposed to some sort of vaporous ideal), and by most realistic standards they have already substantially achieved the kind of capitalism found in the West, where governments still control and regulate much of the economy.

There will, of course, be continued political and economic change in these countries, and some of this will be quite important. Politicians will come and go; parties will fall in voter favor and others will rise (with luck perhaps the beer-lovers party will once again capture seats in the Polish parliament); constitutional and legal structures will undergo development; controversial issues will emerge and decline; new businesses will rise and others will go bankrupt; economic structures will be reshaped and refined; trade patterns will change; governmental subsidies will be increased and decreased; tax laws will be altered.

But, barring some sort of extraordinary, and probably violent, upheaval, the time of fundamental change is substantially over: further developments will take place in environments that are essentially democratic and capitalistic. The societies may become more or less efficient, humane, responsive, productive, corrupt, civil, or effective, but these changes probably will have to come about within (or despite) the present political and economic framework, not through further fundamental institutional transformation. In consequence, it may be sensible now to decrease the talk of "transition" and to put a quiet, dignified end to the new field of transitology.

Actually, there is some danger in continuing to refer to the process that is going on as "transitional" because the word suggests that the postcommunist countries are still moving toward future institutional patterns that will somehow be crucially different from the ones that prevail today. This can inspire or reinforce a short-term perspective, something that is undesirable from either a political or an economic standpoint, as Stephen Holmes also notes in chapter 1 of this book.

The experiments in political and economic change that are taking place in the postcommunist countries of central and eastern Europe have been quite remarkable not only for themselves but also for the way they force us to reexamine the concepts of democracy and capitalism.[1] In particular, the experience suggests that preexisting negative attitudes—cultural legacies, in Holmes's expression—need not necessarily be a notable hindrance to the establishment of democracy or capitalism. In the 1970s even Russians who yearned for democracy anticipated that it would "take generations to evolve."[2] A Czech entrepreneur voiced a common concern when he argued, "We are fighting a deformation of the human mind. During 40 years of the totalitarian regime people have formed the opinion that all private businessmen are thieves trying to get money without doing any work." And in 1992 Sovietologist Stephen Cohen gloomily concluded that "Any hope for real markets and real democracy in Russia is a matter of a generation."[3] These concerns, it seems, have been substantially exaggerated: the results suggest that minds were not permanently deformed by the communist experience, that whatever deformation took place is rather readily overcome, or that any such deformation is essentially irrelevant.

More broadly, the transitional experience in many of the postcommunist countries and elsewhere suggests that democracy as a form of government and capitalism as an economic form are really quite simple, even natural, and, unless obstructed by thugs with guns, they can emerge quite easily and quickly without any special development, prerequisites, or preparation. It seems to me that democracy is fundamentally about leaving people free to complain and that capitalism is fundamentally about leaving people free to be greedy. Neither emotional quality, it seems, can be stifled easily, and neither is terribly difficult to inspire.

At the same time, there is something of an image problem: in practice, democracy seems to be quite a bit worse than its popular image, while capitalism is quite a bit better. And these disconnections between image and reality have the potential to cause problems.

This chapter is divided into three parts. The first assesses democracy and compares the European postcommunist states with real, functioning, long-established democracies—not with an abstract, theoretical democratic image that does not exist, has never existed, and will, in all probability, never exist. By that comparison, it seems, most of these states have already become democratic, and their experience suggests that, contrary to the gloomy prognoses of generations of observers and theorists, democracy can be managed quite easily.

The second part assesses capitalism. It argues that capitalism, like democracy, is already substantially in place in most of these countries. Further, it compares capitalism to its image and develops the argument that, although it is often held primarily to require and inspire deceit, dishonesty, and discourtesy, in fact capitalism systematically rewards honesty, fairness, civility, compassion, and heroism. Moreover, where people cling too strongly to the popular negative image of capitalism, the result often is inefficiency and a lack of economic growth. With this as background, the prospects for further economic development in the postcommunist countries of Europe are assessed. On the whole, they seem rather good because of the ready possibility of imitating successful Western business practices and because of a fundamentally sound preexisting value system concerning private behavior.

The third part offers some conclusions and further reflections. It begins by comparing democracy and capitalism, concluding that the postcommunist experience suggests there is little or no necessary connection between them: they can coexist, or either can exist without the other. Some speculations about the prospects for international influence on domestic developments in the area are proffered, and it is proposed that NATO be expanded to include Russia in part for this purpose, since alliances historically have often (sometimes chiefly) been used to control allies. I then argue that, as democracy was sold partly under the misguided assumption that it necessarily leads to capitalist wealth, there is now a danger, perhaps, that both democracy and capitalism will, equally erroneously, become detrimentally associated with crime. I also assess concerns about the development of effective legal systems to improve the functioning of democracy and capitalism; generally, it seems, while valuable, they are less important than often considered. In addition, I reflect on the role intellectuals play, and I suggest they could prove to be a danger to the actual carrying out of democracy and capitalism because they often are revered and because many of them have disproportionately become attached to a romantic notion of what democracy is all about and an embittered one of what capitalism is all about. However (and finally), on what might be taken to be the brighter side, historical experience suggests that democracy and capitalism often can work quite well even if people do not understand them very well.

DEMOCRACY

A famous Norman Rockwell painting purports to show democracy in action. It depicts a New England town meeting in which a working man has risen in a contentious situation to present his point of view. His rustic common sense, it appears, has cut through the bickering to provide a consensual solution to the problem at hand, and others in the picture are looking up to him admiringly.

As it happens, that misty-eyed, idealized snapshot has almost nothing to do with democracy in actual practice. Democracy is not a process in which one shining idea conquers all as erstwhile aspirants fall into blissful consensus. Rather, it is an extremely disorderly muddle in which contending ideas and forces do unkempt, if peaceful, battle and in which ideas often are reduced to slogans, data to distorted fragments, evidence to gestures, and arguments to poses. Speculation is rampant, caricature is routine, and posturing is de rigueur. If one idea wins out, it is likely to be severely compromised in the process, and no one goes away entirely reconciled or happy. It is a mess and as unromantic, in Charlotte Brontë's phrase, as Monday morning. The only saving grace is that other methods for reaching decisions are even worse.

This disconnection between image and reality and the consequences that flow from it are the central issues of the following considerations.

Assessing Democracy in the Postcommunist Countries

The word "democratization" often is applied to the process that is going on in the postcommunist countries of central and eastern Europe, and the phrases "transition to democracy" and "democratic consolidation" are equally common. The implication of such characterizations, of course, is that these countries have not yet achieved full democracy.

Asked, "How's your wife?" comedian Henny Youngman responds, "Compared to what?" When those European postcommunist countries not in the midst of civil wars are compared with such mature democracies as the United States, Canada, Britain, and Japan (as opposed to some evanescent, ungraspable, Rockwellian democratic ideal), it seems difficult to discover a sense in which they are not already democratic.[4]

Freedom of Press, Speech, Assembly, Petition, Organization, Elections. It is central to democracy that the press must be free to publish and that people must be free peacefully to complain, petition, and organize. In my view, democracy emerges when a simple (but nontrivial) deal is effectively consummated: the people agree not to overthrow the government by force, and the government leaves them free to try to overthrow it by any other means. With that, the point of democracy is likely to be achieved: to have a form of government in which political officeholders are routinely and necessarily responsive to the citizenry. This comes about in a democracy because people have the right to work nonviolently to influence the officeholders and to organize to throw them out if sufficiently riled.

The exact formal and informal institutional mechanisms used to facilitate this core relationship seem secondary to me, and they vary from democracy to democracy—though this does not mean that all institutions are equally fair or efficient. Virtually all conceptions of democracy also require a specific device for changing and evaluating governments: elections that are free and fairly contested. However, the experience in Mexico and Hong Kong suggests that government that is routinely and necessarily responsive can be achieved even without this device, and the experience of nineteenth-century feminists suggests that people can be politically effective even when they do not have the vote.[5]

There may be worries in some postcommunist countries, but by and large, the press is free and thoroughly disputatious (although not always ideally objective—unless the standard is the London tabloids). Moreover, elections, if one accepts them as essential to democracy, are fairly contested, and parties are almost too vibrant. (At first campaigns in these countries were not commonly decorated with funny hats, noisemakers, and cascades of balloons as they often are in older democracies, but it seems that campaigners in these new democracies are already beginning to catch on to such essentials.) And, most important, people appear to be only too willing to complain, organize, and petition. Darina Malová shows that in a very brief time, there has been a proliferation of political interest groups in her country: before 1989 there were only 306 officially permitted associations in Czechoslovakia; by the end of 1992 there were over 5,000 in Slovakia alone. Moreover, this counts only national associations; there are thousands more at the local level.[6]

Concern about press bias and democratic inadequacy in the postcommunist countries is most commonly focused on television, and this appears to be a reasonable complaint in many instances. The experience in such Western countries as France, however, suggests that government control of television can lead to similar problems even in established democracies. The best guarantee seems to be for there to be a proliferation of channels, something that is advancing rapidly: by the spring of 1994 some 50 percent of Hungarian households were already hooked up to cable and satellite TV; a year later Hungary had twice as many cable connections as telephones.[7] Beyond that, the vibrancy of the print media (in France as well as in the postcommunist countries) goes a long way toward providing the outlets for the free expression of opinion that is important for a democracy.

Political Participation. Some people hold that wide political participation is necessary for democracy to flourish.[8] However, in mature democracies many citizens routinely decline to participate. Nearly half of Americans fail to vote even in high-visibility elections, and only a few percent ever actively participate in politics.[9] The winner of a recent election for the mayor of Rochester, New York, received only about six percent of the vote of the total electorate. (However, he was a very popular choice: if everybody had voted, he almost certainly would have achieved the same victory.)

Actually, if broad political participation is an important standard, most postcommunists countries are *more* democratic than the United States. For example, the 1994 parliamentary elections in Ukraine showed participation levels that should make the mouth of a political participationist water. Some 5,833 candidates registered, for an average of 13 candidates competing for office in each of the country's 450 electoral districts. Of these, only 11 percent were proposed by political parties, while 27 percent were put forth by "workers' collectives" and the remaining 62 percent by "simple groups of voters." And turnout "reached a surprisingly high average of about 75 percent."[10] (Of course, one could deftly reverse the argument and contend that these numbers show Ukrainians to be democratically naive, and that it will take time for them to sink to participation levels found in mature democracies such as the United States.)

Romanticism about political participation has led to the rather bizarre and even potentially disruptive legal requirement in some postcommunist countries that at least 25 or 50 percent of the electorate must vote for an election to be valid. This stipulation seems to arise from a misty caricature of democratic reality, one that has been thoroughly discredited in practice. If this were the law in the United States, huge numbers of elected offices would be vacant.

Social Organization. Some analysts, such as Robert Putnam, argue that the key to making democracy work is the presence of "dense networks of social exchange." Actually, he seems to be arguing that such networks may be more helpful for effective government than for democracy itself when he concludes that "*good government* in Italy is a by-product of singing groups and soccer clubs."[11] However, as Malová's analysis cited earlier suggests, those sorts of networking groups seem to be proliferating quite nicely in many postcommunist societies.[12] And nowhere does there seem to be a notable dearth of political groups and parties.[13]

Effective Courts. An effective court system is desirable for many reasons, but, as will be discussed somewhat more fully in the third part of this chapter, it is not clear how necessary it is for democracy (or for capitalism). Certainly there have been many court failings in established democracies.

For a functioning democracy, it is important—vital—that people's civil liberties be preserved, that individuals maintain the freedom and right peacefully to speak, protest, petition, and organize. Since people in most postcommunist countries seem to be substantially unfettered in this, the central democratic goal that the courts would enforce seems largely to have been achieved. Nor do people seem unwilling to try to use the courts to advance policy agendas—though they may find it no easier there than it is in the United States.

Separation of Powers. The separation of powers is a common quality in democracies, sometimes slavishly imitated from the U.S. Constitution. Moreover, as the new democracies of central and eastern Europe establish their day-by-day working rules, they are thrashing out, sometimes quite acrimoniously, the political patterns and traditions that will govern them in the future. However, it seems unwise to require that a democracy be characterized by this particular device, since it is not a formal part of the British system.[14] A government with an overwhelmingly strong executive or legislature is not undemocratic because of that.

Political Instability, Democratic Fragility, Reversibility. Democracy has not been entrenched very long in the European postcommunist countries, and already there have been a rather large number of shifts of government. Some people see this as a sign of political instability. But these changes have been legal and quite orderly, and if substantial shifts of governments are a sign of "instability," then Italy and Japan would also have to be so labeled. And no postcommunist country has suffered a parliamentary gyration as radical as that venerable democracy, Canada, where voters in the last elections dropped the majority party to two seats and tossed in two new parties to fill the gap.

Those who worry about "democratic consolidation" often focus on Latin America and southern Europe, where the military, once a central political force, could rise to overthrow young democracies (as occurred in Haiti in 1991).[15] With the possible (and important) exception of Russia, this sort of worry seems less arresting in the postcommunist countries of Europe. The militaries there are often small, and they do not have the tradition and experience of political meddling.

Analysts sometimes argue that for democracy to be "consolidated," a country must hold a "consolidating election" in which an orderly change of government takes place. How that actually "consolidates" democracy is not terribly clear, since a successful election presumably means democracy was already consolidated and stable when the country first turned democratic. It is like testing negative for a disease: the test means you do not have (and never had) the disease; it does not cause the diseaselessness. At any rate, most of the new democracies in central and eastern Europe have already passed this questionable test with considerable success, even élan.

In some quarters alarm has been expressed because countries such as Poland, Hungary, Lithuania, and Bulgaria have elected former communists to office. Although the new officeholders may have the same faces and DNA as many of the old ones, their policies rather closely resemble those of the centrist parties they replaced—they promise economic and social reform, but pledge to be more humane and competent in carrying it out. In particular, the new/old communists do not seem to be bent on retreating from, much less dismantling, democracy.[16]

Corruption. There have been many charges that some of the postcommunist countries are quite corrupt. But corruption is extensive in such accepted democracies as Italy and Japan, and it has been widespread in other democracies in the past, certainly including the United States. Corruption may be undesirable and debilitating, but it is neither surprising nor completely incompatible with democracy.

The Desire for a Strong Leader. It is often said that people in the postcommunist countries, particularly in Russia, are not ready for democracy because they still yearn for a strong leader.[17] The implication, apparently, is that real democrats prefer weak ones. Yet, oddly enough, people campaigning for office in democracies never seem to parade their weakness. Instead, they characteristically promise to be firm and decisive and to "get things done" as they try to explain as forcefully as possible their miraculous plan to rid the nation of all its ills with little or no pain.

Democratic Values. This is a rather murky area. Over the course of its long democratic history, the United States has experienced a considerable amount of political bigotry at various times. There is a substantial literature showing that the American public often has been willing to give lip service to principles about free speech while at the same time standing ready to restrict them for people whose views seem threatening.[18] Using similar measures and comparing the results with what has often been found in the United States, it does not appear that people in the postcommunist countries subscribe to notably undemocratic beliefs.[19]

Political Awareness and Knowledge. Robert Bellah and his colleagues argue that "one way of defining democracy would be to call it a political system in which people actively attend to what is significant."[20] But if democracy requires such political awareness and knowledge, the one in the United States is in big trouble. Few Americans, it appears, spend much time trying to figure out what is going on. Recent surveys find that around half do not have the foggiest idea which party controls the Senate or what the first ten amendments of the Constitution are called or what the Fifth Amendment does or who their congressional representative or senators are. Moreover, this lack of knowledge has generally increased (particularly when education is controlled for) since the 1940s.[21]

A month after the 1994 election that, Republicans said, was all about their highly touted "Contract with America" and that propelled one of their most vocal and energetic leaders, Newt Gingrich, into the media stratosphere, a national poll found that 72 percent of the public claimed never to have heard or read anything about the legendary "Contract," while 50 percent had not heard enough about Gingrich even to have an opinion about him.[22] Four months later, after endless publicity over the varying fortunes of Gingrich and the "Contract," neither number had changed.[23]

By contrast, a poll conducted in Slovakia in October 1993, when the country was only ten months old, asked its respondents about a list of 31 politicians, many of them quite obscure, and found the public's ignorance level reaching that of the Americans' about Gingrich only for eight of them.[24] It appears that, after only a few months of trying, Slovakia surpassed the United States on this dimension.

It is not clear, however, why one should expect people—in Slovakia or anywhere else—to spend a lot of time worrying about politics when democratic capitalism not only leaves them free to choose other ways to get their kicks but in its seemingly infinite quest for variety is constantly developing seductive distractions. Democratic theorists and idealists may be intensely interested in government and its processes, but the suggestion that other people are somehow inadequate or derelict unless they share the same curious passion verges on the arrogant.

Extreme Nationalism. As has been shown in Yugoslavia, ultranationalism can be a major danger to democracy, not to mention peace and tranquillity. However, it seems possible that extreme nationalism in central and eastern Europe may not be an increasing problem as the "ancient blood feuds" literature would have it. Rather, it may have had its day and may now be in some degree of remission in many areas. Hypernationalists (and even some that are not so hyper) who were once threateningly formidable often seem to have been reduced in elections to the point of near extinguishment, particularly in Lithuania, Poland, Slovakia, Bulgaria, and Hungary. To a degree, this is true even in Serbia, where a proposed policy in 1995 of essentially cutting off the Bosnian Serbs found few public opponents.[25] Hypernationalism was dangerous only if it had some real demagogic appeal. It did for a while, but—perhaps—no longer.

This is not to deny that nationalism itself is quite robust in Europe. I have found in Norway that it is remarkably easy to get Norwegians to say some really quite nasty things about the Swedes, for example. And the legendarily tolerant Dutch seem to be fully capable of publicly delivering racial slurs against Germans ("They're fat, ugly, and eat too much," "They're just so full of themselves").[26] But that is not the sort of nationalism that threatens to lead to armed conflict. It is not that people have suddenly fallen in love with each other, but simply that they are being motivated far more by economic and other issues. It seems rather like the "family values" balloon the Republicans tried to launch in the United States in 1992: many people agreed with their perspective on this issue, but they wanted to hear about jobs and the recession. Under the right (or wrong) circumstances things could reverse, of course, but for now militant nationalism does not seem to be gaining in appeal.

If this notion is correct, Yugoslavia is doubly tragic. If the Serbs could have held their cool in the face of regimes in Croatia and Bosnia that they had (some) reason to feel would persecute them, the threatening regimes might now have been quite adequately mellowed by the trends of the time.[27] (Of course, one reason the militants have often done so badly at the polls in other countries of late is exactly the disastrous Yugoslav example, which shows what their policy can lead to.) Of less concern, this notion also suggests that the split of Czechoslovakia might never have happened if the issue had been debated longer.[28]

Cynicism about the Democratic Process. Bismarck once observed that "If you like laws and sausages, you should never watch either one being made." A fundamental property—and perhaps defect—of democracy is that it allows citizens to watch laws being made. And when they do so—in the East or West—they often come to view the process with righteous disdain, even outrage, opaquely dismissing it as bickering and correctly, but uncomprehendingly, labeling it "politics as usual." Effectively, however, politics as usual is often the same as democracy in action.

Rather than accepting democracy for what centuries of experience have shown it to be, many democrats—both in old democracies like the United States and in new ones in the postcommunist countries of Europe—still yearn for the ungraspable Rockwellian ideal and get very angry and cynical when they watch the process in all its chaotic, unkempt finery.

In the United States in October 1990, President George Bush and the Democrats went at each other over the budget: there was a difficult deficit to confront, and this required such painful remedies as spending cuts or increased taxes or (as it turned out) both. In due course they worked out a sensible compromise, but people, incensed over the furor, started screaming—as the cover of the October 22, 1990, issue of *U.S. News & World Report* headlined—to "throw the bums out." The popularity of both Congress and the president reached conspicuous lows.[29]

More recently, it could be argued that the health care debate in the United States in 1993 and 1994 showed democracy at its finest. A problem the voters had sensibly determined to be important was addressed and debated. President Bill Clinton had a solution, others in Congress had theirs, affected interested groups appropriately weighed in with theirs, and there were months of thoughtful and nuanced (if sometimes confusing and boring) discussion of this difficult topic. Admittedly, a solution (apparent or real) to this complicated concern was not smoothly worked out in two years of effort, but the problem does not have to be solved immediately, and there is plenty of time in the next years to devise judicious remedies with this groundwork laid. Yet voters, few of whom paid much attention to the substance of the often tedious debate, dismissed it as "bickering," cried "gridlock," and often became angry and cynical.[30]

Predictably, the popularity both of the president and of Congress plummeted. Exacting revenge in 1994 for the unpleasant untidiness, the voters threw many of the leading bums—the ones who had started the contentiousness in response to the voters' earlier concerns—out. Thus, an analysis of exit polls in the election finds "no unifying theme among voters who supported Republican candidates" except for "an overall distaste for government." It suggests that Clinton got the election's message, such as it was, when he concluded that the voters were saying "Look, we just don't like what we see when we watch Washington. And you haven't done much about that. It's too partisan, too interest-group oriented, things don't get done. There's too many people up there playing politics. Democrats are in charge—we are holding you accountable."[31] Emerging from this was a swelling demand for term limits and perhaps for a third party under the highly questionable assumption that the people elected under such conditions will behave notably differently from the ones elected under the present ones.

Thus, Congress tends to slump in popularity whenever it is caught in the act of trying to solve or resolve a contentious problem, and cynicism rises when politicians wrestle with difficult issues such as the deficit and health care (problems that, as it happens, largely stem from the rather pleasant facts that people are living so long and that health care has gotten so good). It is accordingly reasonable to find, as Charles Gati does in chapter 4 of this book, that cynicism has flourished in the new democracies of eastern and central Europe where politicians deal daily with issues that are far more difficult. American politicians agonize for months over raising the gasoline tax a few cents; politicians in the postcommunist countries regularly have to consider changes that, however potentially beneficial in the long run, will necessarily cause enormous social disruption and pain. Indeed, a much-underdiscussed aspect of the transition period has been the lowering of life expectancies in the postcommunist countries, something substantially caused, it appears, by increases in psychological stress.[32]

Nonetheless, one analyst is shocked at a poll showing that 79 percent of the Romanian population feel politicians were "ready to promise anything to get votes," while 65 percent say politicians are more interested in strengthening their own parties than in solving the country's problems.[33] Another commentator asserts that Russian voters have "lost their faith in all politicians."[34]

The implication, apparently, is that this condition is notably different in real democracies, such as the United States or Great Britain—something strongly disputed by political developments there. Only six percent of Russians in a poll conducted in 1994 say they trust political parties.[35] But a 1994 poll in the United States discovered only ten percent willing to rate the "honesty and ethical standards" of congressmen as "very high" or "high," tidily placing them twenty-fifth on a list of 26, just ahead of car salesmen.[36] And a poll in Britain found that 73 percent of Britons think the ruling Conservative Party is "very sleazy and disreputable."[37] In 1994, after a tumultuous political year, only 12 percent of Russians said they trusted their parliament.[38] But in 1992, after decades of comparative political placidity, only 17 percent of Americans approved the job their Congress was doing,[39] while a mere 14 percent said they were satisfied with the way things were going in the country and over 80 percent opined that "things have gotten pretty seriously off on the wrong track."[40]

Seymour Martin Lipset twice quotes with alarm a Hungarian analyst:

> All the surveys and polling data show that public opinion in our region rejects dictatorship, but would like to see a strong man at the helm; favors popular government, but hates parliament, parties, and

the press; likes social welfare legislation and equality, but not trade unions; wants to topple the present government, but disapproves of the idea of a regular opposition; supports the notion of the market (which is a code word for Western-style living standards), but wishes to punish and expropriate the rich and condemns banking for preying on simple working people; favors a guaranteed minimum income, but sees unemployment as an immoral state and wants to punish or possibly deport the unemployed.[41]

And Richard Rose argues, "An election produces a representative government if those elected are trusted representatives of those who voted for them. The current Russian government is democratically elected but distrusted."[42] But much the same could be said for the United States at many points in its history. Indeed, in the postcommunist context a healthy distrust of all politicians has probably helped, as Stephen Holmes suggests, to keep extremists from gaining much political ground.

The Simplicity and Ease of Attaining Democracy

We seem to be learning from the experience of many countries, including the postcommunist ones in Europe, therefore, that democracy is not terribly difficult to institute. No elaborate prerequisites or cultural developments are necessary for it to emerge, and an agonizing process of "democratization" is not required. It seems likely that democracy can come about rather naturally, almost by default, unless devices and gimmicks are fabricated to suppress it.

John F. Kennedy once proclaimed, "Democracy is a difficult kind of government. It requires the highest qualities of self-discipline, restraint, a willingness to make commitments and sacrifices for the general interest, and it also requires knowledge."[43] From time immemorial statements like this have raised derisive hoots from antidemocrats, and as noted above, modern polling data quantitatively confirm their argument: when it comes to either the grand or the narrow issues of politics, the average American voter hardly displays such qualities. If Kennedy was right, democracy would be impossible.

By contrast, the recent experience in the postcommunist countries and elsewhere suggests that democracy is at base a fairly simple thing—even a rather natural one. If people feel something is wrong, they will complain about it; and some of the complainers will be led to organize and to try to convert others to their point of view. People do not need to be encouraged or coaxed; nor do they first need to be imbued with the democratic spirit or achieve broad literacy or a high degree of development. They will just *do* it. This is suggested by the way the Bill of Rights is worded in the U.S. Constitution. Nowhere does it admonish citizens to complain or to lobby: rather, it restrains the government from restricting their ability to do so. The framers seem to have been well aware that complaint and pressure would emerge without any encouragement from the government.

Unless this natural tendency is artificially stifled by thugs with guns, and unless the complainers resort to violence to get their point of view across, democracy will take effect. What seems unnatural is to try to *stop* people from complaining. This requires a lot of work: thought police and informers and dossiers and organized social pressure.

As it happens, therefore, democracy is really quite easy, and it can function remarkably well even when people exhibit little in the way of self-discipline, restraint, commitment, knowledge, or, certainly, sacrifice for the general interest: a system built on perpetual self-sacrifice, in fact, is doomed to eventual failure. Democracy's genius in practice is that it can work even if people rarely, if ever, rise above the selfishness and ignorance with which they have been so richly endowed by their creator. People do not need to be good or noble, nor do they need to be deeply imbued with the democratic spirit, whatever that may be. They need merely to calculate their own best interests and, if so moved, to express them.

A most spectacular case of a new, instant democracy is Paraguay, a country that had never known any kind of government except Jesuit theocracy or rigid military dictatorship. In 1989 Paraguay's guiding autocrat, entrenched since 1954, was overthrown by a man who had been one of his chief henchmen and who had become fabulously wealthy in the process. The new leader was sensitive to the fact that democracy is what everyone is wearing nowadays—that "despots have gone out of style," as a reporter from *The Economist* put it.[44] Accordingly he held fair elections and promised that, if elected president, he would guide the country to full democracy in four years. Paraguayans, in the first free election in their grim history, took him at his word. Then in 1993, on schedule, another election was held and another man became president.[45] Albania might form a somewhat comparable extreme example in Europe.

Samuel Huntington argues, "Political leaders cannot through will and skill create democracy where preconditions are absent. In the late 1980s, the obstacles to democracy in Haiti were such as to confound even the most skilled and committed democratic leader."[46] But a few years earlier, some might have said the same thing about poor, isolated countries such as Paraguay and Albania. The obstacle to democracy in Haiti seems to have been a group of thugs with guns, not the absence of "preconditions," and it will be interesting to see if the current experiments there take long-term effect as they apparently have in Paraguay.[47] Or, putting the argument another way, it is likely that the *only* thing keeping isolated, backward, impoverished, prerequisite-free Burma from being democratic is a group of thugs with guns.

The notion that democracy is difficult to institute and that all sorts of attitudinal, cultural, economic, and atmospheric developments are necessary before it can function has led in the past to considerable pessimism about the prospects for democracy. In a classic article, Dankwart Rustow envisioned the establishment of democracy as a gradual process in which national unity leads to prolonged and inconclusive struggle, which leads in turn to a conscious decision to adopt democratic rules followed by habituation to these rules.[48] Writing early in 1989, Robert Dahl concluded that "it would be surprising" if the proportion of the countries in the world that are democratic "were to change greatly over the next twenty years."[49] In 1975 Daniel Patrick Moynihan concluded gloomily that "liberal democracy on the American model increasingly tends to the condition of monarchy in the nineteenth century: a holdover form of government . . . which has simply no relevance to the future."[50] In 1984 Huntington concluded that:

> [W]ith a few exceptions, the prospects for the extension of democracy to other societies are not great. These prospects would improve significantly only if there were major discontinuities in current trends—such

as if, for instance, the economic development of the Third World were to proceed at a much faster rate and to have a far more positive impact on democratic development than it has had so far, or if the United States reestablished a hegemonic position in the world comparable to that which it had in the 1940s and 1950s. In the absence of developments such as these, a significant increase in the number of democratic regimes in the world is unlikely.[51]

By contrast, recent experiences in the postcommunist countries and elsewhere suggest that such pessimism is very substantially overdrawn, that democracy is really quite easy to institute, that it can come about very quickly, and that it need not come accompanied with, or preceded by, the social, economic, and cultural clutter that some have declared to be necessary. The experience also severely tests Huntington's previously unexceptionable observation that "democratic regimes that last have seldom, if ever, been instituted by mass popular action."[52]

Some of this might have been anticipated. After all, in 1956 Hungary declared it planned instantly to become a multiparty democracy. This scheme, of course, was destroyed by Soviet tanks, but the 1989 experience suggests that only the tanks were necessarily hampering the plan's consummation. Relatedly, the 1989 experiences suggest that Brezhnev was right in 1968 when he sent tanks forcefully to stifle liberalization in Czechoslovakia on the grounds that, although its leaders protested much to the contrary, the country was on the slippery slope out of the Soviet bloc and into Western democracy.

Thus it seems that democracy is essentially a state of mind, not a logical or empirical consequence of other factors. As Dahl points out, the role of beliefs is "pivotal" for the rise of democracy: it is difficult to see, he notes, how democracy could exist if political elites "believed strongly that a hegemonic regime was more desirable."[53] By the same token, a country can quite easily become democratic—fully democratic—without any special historical preparation and whatever the state of its social or economic development if elites generally come to believe that democracy is the way things ought to be done and if they aren't physically intimidated or held in check by authoritarian thugs.[54]

The rise of democracy over the last two centuries—of which the developments in postcommunist Europe have been a highlight—does not seem to be best explained as a predetermined consequence of broader social or economic processes. There clearly is a correlation between economic development and democracy, for example, but the experience of Paraguay, Albania, and many other countries suggests there is no necessary causal connection: democracy, after all, is also correlated with the rise of the string quartet. Rather, the rise of democracy appears to be the result of successful efforts by idea entrepreneurs who have sought actively to promote—or market—the concept to political elites around the world. Democracy, it seems, is an intellectual construct that has an intrinsic appeal and has proved in market tests to be notably better (or less bad) than the competition. Despite some occasional overeager and inflated claims, it has been rather well promoted by its advocates who, through luck, fashion leadership (or demonstration effects), agile undermining of the competition, and patient, persistent salesmanship, are now cashing in. In general, economically advanced countries have tended to buy this idea (as well as many other related ones) comparatively early, but the exertions of idea entrepreneurs have been more determining of the pace of democratization than the correlated wealth of their customers.[55]

CAPITALISM

Capitalism can be defined as an economic arrangement in which the government substantially leaves people free to pursue their own economic interests as long as they do so without physical violence (including physical theft). That is, capitalism emerges when it is legal and possible to make a profit nonviolently.

Assessing Capitalism in the Postcommunist Countries

By that perhaps rather minimalistic standard, most of the countries of central and eastern Europe have basically become capitalistic: people are essentially free to plot their economic destinies for themselves. There seems to be a great deal of economic scrabbling going on as people, with varying degrees of

eagerness, pain, and success, seek to cope and to find or fabri-
cate economic security under the new system.

Economist Anders Åslund uses rather more stringent standards to define capitalism, but he finds that Russia, in only a few
years, has substantially fulfilled them: the economy has been
emancipated from politics; ownership, credit, and pricing have
been depoliticized; centralized state allocation has been ended;
and the market has been monetized with currency that is reasonably convertible and with a floating exchange rate that is market determined.[56] And generally, it seems, Åslund's conclusions
also could be applied to most of the postcommunist countries to
Russia's west. As with democracy, this basic transition seems to
have been rather easy to accomplish and did not require decades
of agonizing attitude change.

This is not to deny, of course, that improvements can be
made in the effectiveness, efficiency, and fairness of the capitalist system in these areas. (There are those who irreverently suggest that improvement is possible even in the American system.)
In Russia, Åslund is particularly concerned about improving the
judicial system, expanding private ownership, policing crime, reducing corruption, and getting inflation under firmer control.
But, as he stresses, these are all modifications within capitalism,
not visceral alterations of it.[57] Using realistic standards, then,
capitalism fundamentally has been achieved in Russia, where six
out of seven nonfarm workers are now employed by private
business, and in most of the other postcommunist countries of
central and eastern Europe.[58]

Capitalist Values: Capitalism and the Milk of Human Kindness

While many of the postcommunist states in Europe may have
become essentially capitalist already, however, one important
hindrance to economic effectiveness and growth can be capitalism's image. This could be a special problem in these countries
where the system has been systematically discredited for decades.

Although capitalism generally is given credit, even by its
many detractors, for generating wealth and for stimulating economic growth, it commonly is maligned for the dishonesty,

inhumanity, and cruelty that are widely taken to be the normal consequences of its apparent celebration of greed. This negative image of capitalism has been propagated for centuries not only by communists and socialists, but by the church, popular culture (including capitalist Hollywood), intellectuals, aristocrats, and often capitalists themselves.

Swindlers and moral monsters sometimes do become rich (in both capitalist and noncapitalist systems), but capitalism, contrary to its popular image, by its nature inspires, enforces, and rewards many important values that are highly regarded. Capitalism generally rewards business behavior that is industrious, prescient, diligent, and prudent, of course; but it also tends, all other things being equal, to reward honesty, fairness, civility, compassion, and heroism. Capitalists do not pursue these virtues, it should be emphasized, to the point of stupidity—the virtues do not require one to cut an unfavorable deal or to keep open an unproductive factory. But many capitalists have found that virtue is, on balance, essentially smart business.

In addition, I will argue in the next section that these capitalist virtues appear to be necessary, or at least extremely helpful, for economic growth. And in the section after that I apply this observation to conditions in the new capitalist countries of postcommunist Europe.

The capitalist I have in mind in all this is the same one envisioned by capitalism's caricaturists: one who has no higher motivation than greed—to make as much money as possible—and who, while eschewing violence, is generally left free to lie, cheat, swindle, misrepresent, and engage in fraud. The word "greed," as used here, generally implies a long-term acquisitiveness. ("Short-term greed" seems almost oxymoronic to me.) Some individual capitalists may actually be impelled as well by other motivations—ones generally more esteemed. But the point to be developed here is that under capitalism, greed alone encourages certain kinds—though not necessarily *all* kinds—of behavior that are generally held to be moral, virtuous, and admirable.

Capitalists often spend a great deal of money on advertising, but as any advertiser will readily agree, the most generally effective advertisement is word of mouth. Thus the best way to get ahead (that is, to become rich) in the long term is to establish a good word-of-mouth reputation. Conversely, a wealth-seeking capitalist can be severely punished, often at little cost to the aggrieved, if the word of mouth becomes unfavorable. According to a business slogan, "A customer who goes away happy will tell three friends; a customer who goes away unhappy will tell ten." This phenomenon gives individual customers and fellow deal-makers a considerable enforcement mechanism. They can punish behavior they find unsuitable by refusing to deal with someone they have had a bad experience with or have heard unfavorable things about. Thus, if the community generally values honesty, fairness, civility, and compassion, the sensible capitalist will, because of greed, seek to furnish them—or at least seem to furnish them—in full, unambiguous measure.

Honesty. It is impossible to create a perfect written contract, and it would be wildly inefficient to require even an imperfect one for every transaction. It would be even more inefficient to have contracts regularly adjudicated in court. That is, while a fair and reliable judicial system facilitates capitalism by providing a mechanism for enforcing contracts and for protecting against fraud, it is a clumsy and costly expedient. Moreover, a huge portion of transactions do not involve enough money to make a civil suit a sensible recourse.[59]

Thus, in its general day-to-day dealings, capitalist business necessarily requires, relies upon, and inspires integrity, honesty, trust, and reliability to achieve its vaunted efficiency and growth.[60] And, most important, this quality is generally enforced by the market—and probably much more efficiently and effectively than it could ever be enforced by the courts. As the Better Business Bureau puts it, "Honesty is the best policy. It's also the most profitable." That is, although it is certainly possible to make a quick profit by cheating and lying, the best prospects for secure, long-term wealth derive from honest business practices.[61]

An interesting case in point derives from the experience of the Quakers, a religious group that requires absolute honesty from its members. Because of this quality (and hard work), the Quakers soon found that they enjoyed a competitive advantage.

All other things being equal, customers preferred a business run by a Quaker because they knew they could trust the Quaker to be honest. Accordingly, Quakers became prosperous.[62] But because the image of capitalism holds that one can become wealthy only by cheating, Quakers have regularly been accused of being hypocrites.[63]

The experience of the legendary P. T. Barnum forms another arresting example. He is best known for supposedly having coined the phrase "There's a sucker born every minute." Not only did Barnum never make this statement, but it would have been out of character.[64] Although a few of his famous "humbugs" early in his career did have a degree of (rather good-natured) fraud about them, he became wealthy in the circus not by bilking "suckers," but by providing a good, honest show that people appreciated and were quite happy to spend money on. Before Barnum, circuses were very often run by fly-by-night cheats: ticket takers would regularly shortchange customers; pickpockets, working on a commission, would roam the fairways; "Monday men" would steal clothes on lines or burglarize homes when the citizenry was at the performance or watching the circus parade; shows would be frauds; games would be fixed. Quick profits were made this way, but soon the entire industry was on the verge of extinction because its customers, through experience, no longer were foolish enough to go. Barnum was one of those circus innovators who changed all that. He used honest ticket takers, hired private detectives to police pickpockets, and spent a lot of money and energy creating what he (with characteristic understatement) called "The Greatest Show on Earth." Whether customers always fully agreed with that characterization, they did find the show, and the whole experience of attending the circus, enjoyable, and they were happy to come back year after year. Accordingly, Barnum and like-minded circus managers, such as the Ringling Brothers, soon became far richer with their "Sunday School" approach than the cheats who had preceded them.[65]

In his spirited pamphlet and popular lecture "The Art of Money Getting," Barnum stressed that integrity "is more precious than diamonds or rubies" and argued that "the most difficult thing in life is to make money dishonestly," since "no man can be dishonest without soon being found out" and "when his lack of principle is discovered, nearly every avenue to success is closed against him forever." Thus, even "as a mere matter of self-ishness," he concluded, "honesty is the best policy."[66]

This conclusion holds also for businesses that generally do not service the same customer repeatedly. For example, since a taxi driver is unlikely ever to see the rider again, it is to the driver's short-term advantage to cheat the rider. However, where this is common, the taxicab system as a whole gets the reputation for fraud, and people take cabs only when they have no other choice. Thus the industry as a whole makes much less money than it would if it had a reputation for honesty and integrity. Consequently, taxi companies often have found it very much in their interest to establish industry regulations that keep their drivers from cheating.[67]

The principle can be writ larger. In general, as the organizers of the Better Business Bureau strongly suggest, it is harmful for swindlers to be able to flourish, since they taint all business, reducing sales in the aggregate. Honest business is good for business as a whole and, as will be suggested more fully later, for economic growth.

Fairness. The issue of fairness is closely related to the one of honesty. A vendor or deal-maker who is perceived to be unfair—even though essentially honest—will do less well in the long run than one who appears to be fair.

This can be seen quite clearly in the phenomenon of price stickiness. There seems to be a nearly universal aversion to what is called price gouging, and even when demand clearly comes to outstrip supply, a smart business will be careful about suddenly boosting prices. Thus ski resort owners know that "if you gouge them at Christmastime, they won't come back in March."[68]

A similar phenomenon happens in consummating a business deal. Unless one can make so much money from the deal that one is set for life, it is to the capitalist's long-term economic advantage that the other party walk away from the deal feeling fairly treated, even though this might mean cutting a deal that is somewhat less favorable or immediately profitable. Or, to put it the other way, nothing riles people more—causes more fury and long-term resentment—than the feeling that they have been "taken," or been taken advantage of. (It can also lead to the feeling that one has been cheated, in which case the deal-maker will get the undesirable reputation not only for unfairness, but for dishonesty.) As Barnum put it succinctly, "Men who drive sharp bargains with their customers, acting as if they never expected to see them again, will not be mistaken."[69]

Civility. Although rudeness is hardly unknown among capitalists, the system itself rewards civil behavior: in Barnum's words, "politeness and civility are the best capital ever invested in business."[70] James Q. Wilson argues that capitalism fosters "a reasonable concern for the opinions of others";[75] or, as a Scottish historian put it in 1769, commerce "softens and polishes the manners of men."[72] The philosophy "the customer is always right" is self-effacing, even cravenly self-abnegating, but it brings maximum profits. That is, in general, nice guys finish first.

It seems reasonable to speculate that McDonald's does not insist that its employees treat its customers with courtesy because Mr. McDonald (or whoever runs the company) is an especially nice person, but because the company knows that when salespeople are pleasant and polite to their customers, the customers return to buy more and might even bring their friends. As Barnum observed, "Large stores, gilt signs, flaming advertisements, will all prove unavailing if you or your employees treat your patrons abruptly."[73]

Similarly, employers who are considerate and courteous to their employees will tend to find them working harder for less money or doing more work for the same money—and being more impervious to the potentially problematic attractions of union organizers.[74] A form of this phenomenon is found even in the extreme case of slave systems in which masters were mostly unable to use economic incentives to encourage more output (and hardly had unions to worry about). If one looks not at theoretical discussions of the system but rather at how slave owners actually carried out their business, one finds them commonly and routinely discovering that "humaneness and self-interest were inseparably intertwined."[75]

And capitalists who are pleasant to work with tend to find other deal-makers willing to cut special, favorable agreements.

Rudeness was routine—notorious—in communist enterprises, and, more generally, it is commonly found in government shops and agencies and in places like the University of California, where demand outstrips supply and where the seller is unable to raise the price. Under these conditions customers become supplicants, and there is no economic disincentive to incivility, surliness, and arrogance.[76] Since one cannot ration by price, one is inclined to ration by rudeness, by creating inconvenience or, where possible, by corruption—demanding side payments to obtain the product.[77]

The point here, of course, is not to argue that incivility never shows up in a capitalist system, but rather that the system encourages and rewards civility. Sometimes capitalists may decide that there are things more important than economic gain: for example, individual executives may take pleasure in lording it over underlings. But such behavior is a distortion of sensible greedy behavior, and people indulging themselves will pay an economic price.

Compassion. Logically, appropriately greedy capitalists should be essentially indifferent to any human suffering or inadequacy that does not affect their own enterprises: neither supportive nor opposed. In strict economic principle, capitalism does not oppress the unfortunate so much as it simply neglects them.

In practice, however, it is to the capitalist's advantage—that is to say, it is good for business—to show a sense of compassion, of community responsibility, of charity, and of altruism. People who do have money to spend and deals to make like doing business with people like that, and a reputation—image—for decency and community concern, consequently, is good for profits. Barnum, none too surprisingly, had something to say on this issue: "Of course men should be charitable, because it is a duty and a pleasure. But even as a matter of policy, if you possess no higher incentive, you will find that the liberal man will command patronage, while the sordid, uncharitable miser will be avoided."[78]

The belief that their firm is run by caring, compassionate, socially responsible people also can make employees (even slaves) happy and proud and hence willing to work harder for less money.

Of necessity, however, capitalism requires acts that can be viewed as lacking compassion: the firing or laying off of employees for cause or when business slackens, for example. Even in this case, however, the wise capitalist will seek to be as compassionate as possible—striving to ease the blow—since a reputation for casual heartlessness can harm employee morale, foster hostile union relations, and pose difficulties in times of labor shortage.

Heroism. Most popular caricatures present capitalists as effortlessly (and unfairly) rich. In developing this perspective, they conveniently leave out, or assume away, the crucial element of risk, something that is particularly notable in the traditional vilification of speculators.

However, to be successful a capitalist must continually run risks. Indeed, as it is often put, "the greatest rewards are usually not far from the greatest risks." Often, in fact, entrepreneurs risk their financial future on a venture, and a large proportion of them fail, often with consequent harm to their long-term (and in some cases short-term) health.

In war, risk-taking behavior is considered heroic. However, creative, risk-taking capitalists, whether they experience success or failure, are never given anything like the same credit.[79]

The Essential Insincerity of Capitalist Morality. It should be acknowledged that the honesty, fairness, civility, compassion, and heroism that characterize successful capitalism are essentially insincere—or even cynical and hypocritical. That is, capitalism encourages capitalists to be honest, fair, civil, compassionate, and heroic not because those qualities are valued for themselves, but because of greed, the desire to become rich.[80] Accordingly, if one walks into an automobile showroom and says, "I want to buy that car over there, but I demand that I be treated dishonestly and with consummate discourtesy," one can reasonably expect the dealer to evince few moral qualms in complying. A true saint, by contrast, would likely undergo a certain angst when trying to service that improbable request.

But essential insincerity often is found in other moral systems as well. For example, the soldier may be heroic not because he values heroism for itself but because it leads to medals and admiration. And the common moral injunction "Do unto others as you would have them do unto you" rather implies that the moralizer is chiefly inspired not so much by conscience as by a cagy calculation of ultimate, if collegial, self-interest.

Moreover, most people find it difficult to counterfeit morality. Sam Goldwyn is alleged to have said, "The most important thing about acting is sincerity: once you've learned to fake that, you've got it made." This may well be true for acting, but it is not so for real life: most people cannot consistently and routinely fake sincerity. And people using not much more than common sense can, at least on substantial exposure, generally spot pretenders.[81]

Thus the best way to *seem* honest and fair and civil and compassionate is to *be* honest and fair and civil and compassionate. Barnum's observation bears repeating: "The most difficult thing in life is to make money dishonestly! . . . [N]o man can be dishonest without soon being found out and when his lack of principle is discovered, nearly every avenue to success is closed against him forever."[82] A clerk or manager who actually hates people is unlikely to be successful because the customers and employees eventually will see through the act.[83] And most salespeople find that it is much easier to sell a product if they truly believe in it: the common injunction is "If you can't feel it, you can't sell it."

Thus capitalists who seek to become successful (that is, rich) either will be naturally honest and fair and civil and compassionate, or will tend to become so by their experience in business. If not, either they will make less money than they would otherwise, or they will fail completely and be selected out of the system.

Capitalism, the Milk of Human Kindness, and Economic Development

If honesty, fairness, civility, compassion, and business heroism help to make one rich, it follows that, all other things being equal, places where those qualities are common, valued, and habitually encouraged will be more prosperous than places where they are not. Policies such as price controls or high taxes that can cramp free economic activity will hamper economic growth, as economists point out all the time. But so will cultural attitudes of distrust, mendacity, incivility, and hostility to entrepreneurship. Accordingly, for the postcommunist states to prosper, it is important that they develop the appropriate business norms.

The Role of Norms in Economic Development. I was once struck by a passage in a guidebook to Italy. Travel guides tend to be very upbeat, but when the author got to Naples he became unhinged: a beautiful spot, he pointed out, but avoid dealing with Neapolitan merchants because they are unrelievedly vicious. This sort of reputation, one suspects, was none too good for the local tourist industry or for the area's economic development more generally.

Society in that area, it is said, subscribes to such cheerless folk maxims as these: "He who behaves honestly comes to a miserable end"; "Damned is he who trusts another"; "Don't make loans, don't give gifts, don't do good, for it will turn out bad for you"; "Everyone thinks of his own good and cheats his companion"; "When you see the house of your neighbor on fire, carry water to your own."[84]

Edward Banfield tells of the labor situation in a southern Italian town. "An employer who can get away with it is almost sure to cheat his employees," and relations with employees are accordingly poisoned by "anxiety, suspicion, and hate." The result is not only that the employees work less hard and less reliably for the employers, thus reducing profits to the enterprise, but that the economic development of the whole system suffers: "Rather than work a larger unit on shares, an arrangement which would be more profitable but which would necessitate getting along with a landlord, the peasant prefers to go it alone on his uneconomic holding." Banfield also notes that in some towns the upper class, out of tradition, "has always been brutal toward the peasants," a phenomenon that would similarly hamper economic development.[85]

It has been argued earlier that, although capitalists can be uncivil or dishonest or unfair or lacking in compassion or incapable of taking risks, capitalism systematically rewards—though not evenly—those who appear civil and honest and fair and compassionate and who take judicious risks. In some places, such as southern Italy, however, a social norm toward dishonesty or rudeness or even brutality may prevail—that is, social norms get in the way of natural, mellowing greed. An area like that, while fully capitalist, will be less economically developed than an area where a sense of honesty, fairness, civility, and compassion prevails.[86]

Norms are important to economic development because people who generally expect to be treated dishonestly, unfairly, or discourteously in business will avoid making transactions as much as possible, and hence there will be less wealth because there will be less economic activity. Where this sort of distrust or lack of confidence is extremely high and where the business is not necessary for survival, the economy will simply collapse, as has happened, for example, in the case of the traveling door-to-door salesman.

Norm-based Models of Economic Development. In attempting to account for economic development, Douglass North stresses the role of formal institutions that regulate, police, and enforce contracts and agreements. He uses, as a prime example, markets in the Middle East and North Africa, where exchange skills are "the primary determinant of who prospers in the bazaar and who does not," and where "haggling over terms with respect to any aspect or condition of exchange is pervasive, strenuous, and unremitting." "The key," he observes, "is men seeking gains at the expense of others. In essence, the name of the game is to raise the costs of transacting to the other party to exchange."[87]

But the high transaction costs in this system are not so much the "name of the game" as the unintended, detrimental result. And, most important, given the sheer difficulty of dealing, and the considerable danger of being treated dishonestly or unfairly, people—particularly insecure and underinformed bargainers—will tend to avoid engaging in economic exchange when they can. Thus just about everyone will be poorer.

North argues that it is difficult to "understand why these inefficient forms of bargaining" persist. One would expect, he suggests, that "voluntary organizations would evolve to ensure against the hazards and uncertainties of such information asymmetries." But that has not happened because "the fundamental underpinnings of legal institutions and judicial enforcement that would make such voluntary organizations viable and profitable" are missing. "In their absence," he concludes, "there is no incentive to alter the system."[88]

But this reasoning seems to have gotten the causal flow backward. As North himself stresses, the mechanical imposition of appropriate legal and judicial mechanisms is not adequate. Third World countries often remain poor even though they have adopted the laws and institutions of developed countries.[89] Moreover, any superimposed regulatory mechanisms will be swamped quickly if undesirable economic behavior is common: policing will be effective only when such behavior is fairly rare. In addition, government policy does not seem to be hampering the development of sensible voluntary organizations in the markets North is assessing: the economy, perhaps mostly by default, is essentially free.[90]

What seems to be missing is not so much formal institutions of control or incentives to change the system as the realization that honest, fair, civil, and compassionate dealing furnishes a competitive advantage. What the bazaar needs, then, are not institutions, but people with the enlightened greedy business mentality of a Barnum. Neither he nor the Quakers needed "the fundamental underpinnings of legal institutions and judicial enforcement" to discover that honest, fair, civil, and compassionate dealing was a smart, profitable way to do business.

The mechanism of economic development, then, would run something like the following. Someone comes to the simple, but apparently nonobvious, realization that honest, fair, civil, and compassionate dealing will lead to greater profits. Shattering tradition, that person puts together a business with those qualities. The business enjoys a competitive advantage and accordingly prospers. Other businesses, noticing the success of the innovator, follow suit. Since the sheer pain (or transaction cost) of doing business has been substantially reduced, people more and more overcome their traditional, well-founded aversion, and cheerfully do business with such enterprises. Economic activity therefore increases overall, and the general economy grows.

Next, the greedy, honest, fair, civil, compassionate businesses that now dominate the industry become concerned that the whole industry is given a bad name by the relatively few members who still engage in (economically foolish) dishonest, unfair, uncivil, and uncompassionate business practices. Accordingly, the dominating greedy, honest, fair, civil, compassionate businesses form associations, and they work, informally or with the government, to force the dishonest, unfair, uncivil, and uncompassionate businesses to shape up or to leave the industry. Since undesirable economic activity is quite rare, the institutions of regulation are capable of policing the situation. People become more and more pleased with the ease and pleasure of doing business, and confidence soars. Growth happens. It seems likely, then, that effective institutions are more the result of virtuous norms than the cause of them.

The economic development process I suggest can be illustrated by the experience of American retailing entrepreneur John Wanamaker. Judging from his recollections, American business practices in the 1860s were quite similar to those discussed by North for the Middle East and North Africa:

> The law of trading was then the law of the jungle, take care of number one. The rules of the game were: don't pay the first price asked; look out for yourself in bargaining; haggle and beat the seller as hard as you can.... And when a thing was once sold—no returns.... Schools in stores for training employees were unknown.

Shattering this ill-tempered tradition with its high transaction costs, Wanamaker consciously set out to provide "a service exactly opposite to the ancient custom that 'the customer must look out for himself.'" He applied set prices and, importantly, combined this with a money-back offer that essentially guaranteed a low price. Moreover, he instructed his employees as follows: "place yourself in the customer's place and give such service as you would like to have given to you were you buying instead of selling"; "give information and show new goods just arriving without allowing an unspoken grumble to appear on your face"; and, when customers come back with goods to return, "be, if possible, more agreeable than if they had come to make other purchases."[91]

The approach proved, in the words of business historian Joseph Appel, "sound not only in morals, but in economics as well."[92] Wanamaker became rich, his success was imitated by his competitors, a retailing revolution took place, and the economy prospered.[93]

North notes that "we are not yet able to explain precisely the forces that shape cultural evolution," but he stresses the importance of "path dependence," the notion that current developments are the result of forces set in motion long ago in the society.[94] By contrast, the explanation for economic development here stresses only greed and the grasping of the very simple, but nonobvious, idea that honesty, fairness, civility, and compassion give one a competitive advantage.[95] Economies prosper when that visceral emotion is given free play and when that simple idea is grasped. Indeed, the emotion seems built in, and the idea appears to be easy to grasp and imitate once it is effectively demonstrated. Accordingly, whatever their historical path, economies can turn around quickly, as has happened, despite North's rather gloomy implication, in Spain and in a number of Latin American countries.[96]

It is curious, however, that greedy capitalists seem to have taken so long to see the economic benefits of honesty, fairness, civility, and compassion. The Quakers were early, but they were virtuous for religious reasons, and their wealth was therefore in considerable part accidental or incidental. As early as 1748 Benjamin Franklin stressed the economic value of honesty in enhancing one's ability to obtain loans,[97] and there have long been informal reputational mechanisms such as guilds for policing honesty among businesspeople.[98] But as an elaborated, self-conscious principle, the notion that honesty, fair dealing, civility, and compassion bring wealth seems to have been generally discovered only in the last century or two—though undoubtedly many capitalists saw the virtue of virtue earlier and either did not articulate the practice as an explicit business principle or were intimidated about doing so because it somehow seemed unseemly to appear to glorify greed. The setting of prices for retail goods, and the sense of fairness the practice induces, began only in the nineteenth century. Concentrated efforts by businesses to establish agencies to police profit-harming fraud and misrepresentation began only around the turn of the century: the Better Business Bureau, for example, was not founded until 1912.[99]

And when experiments at the Hawthorne Works of Western Electric in the 1920s pointedly concluded that higher employee morale led to greater and more efficient production, it seems to have come as quite a revelation.[100] Rather curiously, then, capitalism per se does not seem necessarily to generate a long-term perspective: that is, however natural greed may be, it has apparently often taken an effort for people to come to grasp the concept of enlightened, long-term self-interest. Indeed, it is conceivable that one of the reasons for capitalism's negative image is that for millennia capitalists often were dishonest, unfair, and uncivil (at least at the retail level) because they were foolishly unaware of their own greedy long-range interests. But eventually, it seems, they discovered that under capitalism, virtue is considerably more than its own reward.

Relevance to the Postcommunist Experience

The traditional caricature of capitalism could hinder its advancement in the new capitalist democracies of central and eastern Europe, where it often seems that any successful businessman is automatically assumed to be dishonest and "mafia." Moreover, the communist system tended to discourage initiative and the kind of risk-taking heroism characteristic of entrepreneurial capitalism. There are reasons for some degree of optimism, however.

The Public and the Private Spheres. As the Polish sociologists Mira Marody and Piotr Sztompka have observed, under communism there was actually a curious duality between the public and the private (or, perhaps better, personal) spheres for most people.[101] The public sphere was characterized by mendacity, deception, laziness, cynicism, rudeness, social helplessness, mediocrity, and a devaluation of work. By contrast, the private sphere—which, unlike southern Italy, extended far beyond the immediate family—was characterized by risk-taking, resourcefulness, initiative, civility, self-fulfillment, considerateness, and appreciation of work. Stealing from the state was accepted; stealing from a private individual was not. Cheating on a university exam was accepted, even lauded; cheating in a personal relationship was not. Thus honesty, fairness, civility, compassion, and initiative were not stamped out but simply relegated to the private sphere. Contrary to Robert Putnam's concern, then, the social atmosphere in former communist countries does not appear really to resemble that of economically backward areas like southern Italy.[102]

What may happen now in the postcommunist states is that the private attitudes will freely find application in the rapidly expanding business sphere (neither exactly public nor exactly private) because the private values will be rewarded there. Old habits may still dominate relations between the individual and the state—as, to a lesser extent, they also do in the West.[103] But as the capitalist sphere expands in central and eastern Europe, relations between the individual and the state become a decreasingly important element of life.

Thus it is not necessary for old habits to be unlearned. Rather, one preexisting set of habits and perspectives may gradually (or perhaps suddenly) become eclipsed by the other preexisting set.[104] All this could make economic development comparatively easy. It would hardly require decades of pain, trauma, uncertainty, and effort.

Barnum's observations that "no man can be dishonest without soon being found out" and that "when his lack of principle is discovered, nearly every avenue to success is closed against him forever" can already sometimes be seen at work in the new capitalist countries of Europe. For a while, economist Michael Hobbs observes, Czech security dealers, following the popular sleazy image of capitalism, frequently would conclude a deal, then find a better one and renege on the first. Very soon, however, such dealers obtained a reputation for unreliability, and they are now going bankrupt because no one will deal with them.[105]

Opportunities for honest business abound in these areas. Going back to communist days, it has been common for automobile mechanics to cheat their customers: an automobile brought in for repairs would be fixed, but at the same time the mechanic would remove good parts from the car, replacing them with inferior (thought still functional) ones. The result, however, is not that mechanics become rich. Rather, the customers do everything to repair their cars themselves. Thus an honest repair business—which, precisely because of its honesty, can charge higher prices—can prosper. I was recently talking to a resident of Warsaw who complained about the difficulty of getting repairs done competently and honestly there. When I suggested there must be some competent and honest repair businesses, she observed, "Yes. But they have so much business, you have to wait for months."

Some of the more entrepreneurial people were systematically discouraged under communism and thus dropped out, submerging themselves into the private/personal, leaving the running of things to others. But some entrepreneurial people probably decided to work the system—to seek, perhaps rather cynically, to advance in it. Thus in an age in which individual entrepreneurs are systematically rewarded, we would expect many who were excluded from the old communist system to rise, but also many to come from within it. Thus it is not surprising to find that in Poland "every second top manager in the private sector used to be the director of a socialist enterprise."[106] Although the perception is that the old communists are still running the system and thus that nothing has really changed, in fact everything has.

Imitation of the West. Imitation and competition are likely to help in all this. For the most part, the postcommunist countries want to achieve the wealth of the West, and many seem quite willing to imitate Western business practices to do so. Moreover, they have local role models in the newly established branches of successful Western businesses that routinely and prominently apply established and tested procedures of honesty, fairness (including set prices accompanied by a return policy), civility, and compassion to their business practices.

Thus the invasion of institutions like McDonald's and K-mart can have a very beneficial impact on the business climate.[107] A vivid case in point are the new Russkoye Bistros opening in Moscow that provide "fresh ingredients and fast and pleasant service in a clean environment." Says the marketing director of the Moscow McDonald's, "I really see it not so much as competition as the acceptance of our way of doing business. They have seen what we can do and I hope they will learn from it."[108] Indeed, local businesses that fail to follow suit, by, for example, continuing to treat their customers with incivility, are likely quickly to find themselves in financial trouble.

Special Problems in Postcommunist Societies. There could be special problems because the people in the postcommunist countries lived so long under regimes that tirelessly, if hypocritically, stressed the moral virtues of economic equality. Although these regimes have been substantially discredited in the eyes of most, this intuitively appealing central dogma may linger on.

Moreover, in the old days there was an "us versus them" mentality.[109] Members of the elite *nomenklatura* were obviously better off, but those less well-off could console themselves with the knowledge that their comparatively humble position in society derived not from any inherent lack of worth, but because they (nobly) refused to subordinate themselves to the party nonsense. Under capitalism and democracy, however, this excuse will no longer be available: now economic inequalities will rise among the "us" as some do better in business, creating new jealousies.

And there may be special resentments as people see that the (presumably more capable) members of the *nomenklatura* remain in place or even prosper and, increasingly it seems, win elections.[110] In addition, resentment is likely in the postcommunist countries when certain people advance more by luck than by skill, as is inevitable from time to time in capitalism.

It is important to note, however, that these are not new problems for capitalism and that a negative, resentful image of capitalism is found as well in the capitalist West: ask the Quakers, or check out almost any Hollywood movie that purports to portray business in action.[111]

Finally, as noted at the outset, the notion that one is still in transition toward a fundamentally different economic system can be dangerous because it inspires a short-term perspective: transitology encourages transitory thinking. As argued earlier at length, capitalism requires greedy long-term thinking for its virtues—and for the growth the virtues induce—to emerge effectively. Consequently, the more people in the postcommunist countries are persuaded that "this is it," the better.

DEMOCRACY AND CAPITALISM

In general, the recent experience in the postcommunist countries of central and eastern Europe suggests that, using realistic (as opposed to idealistic) standards, democracy and capitalism are essentially in full operation in most places there; that, despite decades of concentrated efforts to turn minds against them, neither democracy nor capitalism is particularly difficult to institute when people are freed to give in to natural impulses to complain and to be greedy; and that such fundamental changes can take place with a speed and thoroughness that might have seemed miraculous only a very few years ago.

Some final comments are in order on several issues: on the connection, if any, between democracy and capitalism, on the effects of international pressures, on the potentially damaging connection democracy and capitalism may popularly develop with crime, on the importance of an effective judicial system, on the role of intellectuals in the new capitalist democracies of Europe, and on the connections, if any, between the images and the realities of democracy and capitalism.

Connections between Democracy and Capitalism

Although there is a notable correlation between democracy and capitalism, the postcommunist experience in Europe suggests there is little necessary relation between them.

It is no news to observe that capitalism can exist without democracy, but the postcommunist experience seems to do considerable damage to the commonly accepted and previously unassailable notion of Charles Lindblom and many others that to become a democracy, a country must have a market-oriented economy.[112] The postcommunist countries in eastern and central Europe quickly became democracies even while the vast majority of the people there still continued to work for the government, even while the economy continued to be centrally planned, and even while most property was still state-owned. They have worked (and continue to work) to change that, of course, but only because the old economic system has become discredited, not because the process of democracy mandates it.

Some analysts have held to the related notion that a sizable middle class is necessary for democracy: as Barrington Moore put it, "No bourgeois, no democracy."[113] The cases of India and quite a few other places call that generalization into question, and the recent experience in central and eastern Europe seems to shatter it.

In practice, democracy does give to property owners a certain confidence that they can protect themselves from arbitrary seizure of their property—or at any rate that they will have recourse if such seizure does take place. Insofar as that confidence is necessary to encourage capitalism and its effects, such as economic growth and efficiency, democracy will have an economic leg up on authoritarian regimes—or at least on those of the more absolutist sort.[114] But while capitalists have generally been able to use democracy to keep confiscation of their property to a bearable level, there does not seem to be a necessary link between capitalism and democracy as institutions.[115]

The Role of Outside Countries and of NATO

It is important to keep in mind that all the postcommunist countries—and almost all political factions within them—want most of all to join Europe and the West. Accordingly, the West is in an excellent position to discipline democratic and capitalistic backsliders by denying them something they value highly. In the extreme this can be carried out through explicit economic sanctions of the sort that have devastated the economies of Serbia and Iraq at remarkably little cost to the sanctioners. But much of this effect can come about even without such formal measures because severe backsliding is likely to cause quick and substantial economic distress through capital flight and withdrawn investment.

The role of outside countries, both eastern and western, also may be important for ethnic conflicts. In some cases, as with the

Serbs in Yugoslavia, outsiders have sought to inflame nationalist tensions in a nearby country with disastrous consequences.[116] But this may not be the wave of the future. A study by Ellen Gordon and Luan Troxel notes that Turkey, concerned about the condition of Turks within Bulgaria, opened its borders to Bulgarian Turks in 1989—but then soon closed them again when the new immigrants caused so many problems. Thus they find, "Turkey, while being supportive of the Turkish minority in Bulgaria, has little interest in inflaming internal ethnic relations in Bulgaria." Poland, they also note, has come to a similar conclusion with respect to the Polish minority in Lithuania.[117] Similarly, Russia, as Stephen Holmes notes, has done remarkably little about Russians living in other countries. And in the 1994 election in Hungary, politicians found that calls to help Hungarians in other countries were ineffective with a troubled electorate, which responded, "What about the Hungarians *within* Hungary?"[118]

An important international medium of management in all this could be NATO. Of late, commentators often have routinely complained, sometimes in the same breath, that NATO no longer has a purpose, and we cannot let Russia into NATO because that would ruin its purpose. In fact, this shows an incomplete understanding of alliances. As Paul Schroeder has demonstrated, alliances in Europe have characteristically been designed in part to control an ally—often, in fact, that has been the *main* purpose of the alliance.[119] Indeed, although not often mentioned, one notable role of NATO itself has been to control Germany: as it has been irreverently put, NATO was designed to keep the Soviets out, the Americans in, and the Germans down.

Variously uncontrollable remnants of disintegrating armies have been important in all the warfare that has taken place recently in Europe (and in the Caucasus). By integrating the militaries of central and east European countries, including Russia, into NATO, the organization would gain important leverage over one of the chief potential instruments of trouble in the area. It would have lines to major players, and by treating them as valued members of the community rather than as inscrutable second-class citizens, it would keep them tied to, and in direct, systematic contact with, the peaceful, advanced West.

In the past NATO played a useful role—for example, in undermining the 1981 coup attempt by the military in Spain and in keeping the contest between member states Greece and Turkey from getting worse. If Yugoslavia had been a member—it was moving in that direction in the 1950s—NATO would have had direct lines to leaders of the Yugoslav army; accordingly, it would have been in a far better position to understand, and to deal with, problems as they emerged in that area rather than treating the army essentially as an incomprehensible marauding force made up of a bunch of guys with *c*'s at the end of their names. According to Susan Woodward, in fact, the Yugoslav army was trying at one crucial point early in the war to become a peaceful buffer between warring Croats and Serbs, a role that never came to fruition in part because the West uncomprehendingly labeled it an occupation force and refused to talk to its leaders.[120]

This scheme is no panacea, but an expansion—including Russia—would put NATO in a far better position to deal with future problems of the kind that have ravaged much of the former Yugoslavia.

Crime

A potential danger to democracy and capitalism in the postcommunist countries comes from crime, something that, polls suggest, is at least as big a concern as economic problems such as inflation and unemployment.

Democracy and capitalism were bought by many people on the questionable grounds that they guaranteed, or at any rate implied, prosperity. (Everyone looked at Germany and the United States, no one at India or the Philippines.) However, although democracy and capitalism do not, by definition, allow for violence, they may now come to be causally (and casually) linked to crime: people look particularly at the United States, where colorful stories of criminal mayhem abound, never at capitalist democracies such as Canada, Japan, or Switzerland, where crime is quite low.

Two responses to this concern are unlikely to be very helpful. One is to observe (correctly) that crime in the postcommunist countries is, for the most part, still actually quite low, especially compared with that enjoyed in the exemplary United States.

The other is to suggest that one must grin and bear it, since Western standards of justice require that, essentially, it is better to let a lot of criminals roam free than to imprison a few innocent people. This response merely reinforces the connection with crime, and the understandable rejoinder is to suggest that the choice actually then is between locking up a few innocent people and locking up all of them as, out of fear, they place themselves essentially into house arrest. What good, some may well ask, is "freedom" if one no longer feels free to walk the streets? People are now far freer to speak their minds, of course, but not that many people ever say things that anyone, even the most paranoid of dictators, would want to suppress, whereas everybody uses the sidewalks.

Concern about crime is, of course, also very high in the United States, and, as in the 1994 elections, it can be a hot topic with voters. An important difference, perhaps, is that concern about crime does not translate in the United States into demands to get rid of democracy and capitalism; in the postcommunist countries it conceivably could. Alarmist Hitler analogies should be avoided, but it was the demand for order (in that case from street fighting by political gangs) as much as economic instability that helped him into office.

Obviously, efforts to improve police work in central and eastern Europe could help with this concern. But, as in the United States, the fear of crime is often essentially psychological.[121] Moreover, with a free capitalist press, crime, which sells papers everywhere, is more likely to be reported and dwelled upon—often in gruesome detail—and it is likely to be handled in the usual incompetent, anecdotal manner so common in America.[122]

The Relevance of an Effective Legal System

An effective legal and criminal justice system is probably significant for maintaining democracy and capitalism in the indirect—essentially political or public relations—sense just suggested. In addition, it is important that courts enforce civil liberties in a democracy, since the freedom to speak, protest, petition, and organize is what democracy, is all about. However, as noted earlier, civil liberties are generally in rather good shape in most of the postcommunist countries of Europe, so the establishment of a good court system seems more nearly to be a hedge against a potential danger than a requirement to service a pressing one.

As Åslund and many others stress, an improved judicial system is important for the further development of capitalism as well, particularly as the ultimate arbiter of contracts and property rights and as final recourse against fraud. However, if the experience in the capitalist West is any guide, an effective court system may be somewhat less vital than it might first appear.

As Stewart Macaulay shows, people in American business rely on trust and reputation, and they studiously avoid the courts or even threats of legal action. That is, if there is even a small chance the courts will be required to make a deal work, the deal probably will not be consummated in the first place. Macaulay is able to find remarkably few reasons that written contracts exist at all, and many of these are essentially extralegal. He points out that contracts sometimes serve as a useful communication and clarification device, particularly when the issue at hand is complex and likely to take place over a long period of time, and often contracts are put together mainly because they are required by the federal government or by a lender of money or for the convenience of outside lawyers who, obsessed with avoiding "any possible legal difficulty," demand a formal contract because it makes their job easier in the (highly unlikely) event that a future dispute will have to be settled in court or by legal pressure.[123]

Capitalism is more likely to work well if property rights are clearly and unambiguously understood, and the legal system can be important as the ultimate referee in this regard. But the actual private ownership of real property—land and buildings—is not necessarily required. If the state owns all real property, lease agreements can be worked out if profit-making is legal. Traditionally, Jews were not permitted to own real property in many places in Europe; yet they clearly were able to prosper and to contribute enormously to the economy.

In chapter 1, Stephen Holmes stresses the importance of enforceable antifraud legislation. This is surely desirable, but it is worth noting that even in the United States, with a highly developed and substantially incorruptible court system, the buyer still must be wary of fraud. A consumer who has been cheated can report the fraud to the authorities, and the cheater perhaps may eventually be put in jail. But as a practical matter, the swindled have very little chance of ever getting their money back, particularly since the courts are already jammed with criminal (especially drug) cases.

What is mainly needed, as argued earlier, is the development of a norm of honesty, integrity, fairness, reliability. At that point, the relatively few miscreants will stand out and can perhaps be dealt with by the courts; without the norm, the courts would be utterly overwhelmed. And because those adhering to the norm have a competitive advantage in the long run, it should emerge naturally out of normal competition when competitors are aware of the advantage. On these grounds, as suggested earlier, the postcommunist countries of Europe are generally in good shape.

The Intellectuals

It is conceivable that there may be special problems with intellectuals in the postcommunist areas. Obviously, many intellectuals have been extremely valuable to the successful transition process, and their actions and advice have proved knowledgeable, realistic, and politically adept. But many others, including many former dissidents, are traditionally drawn toward an oppositional pose that has often been quite romantic.[124] Moreover, intellectuals there tend to pay a larger political role than their Western counterparts and to form themselves into a sometimes-perceptible class—the "intelligentsia," a category not duplicated in most Western countries.[125]

It has been argued here that, in practice, democracy is enormously messy, a severe contrast with the romantic image that often envisions democracy as some sort of gracious ideal of genteel discourse. It also has been argued that the democratic ideal—or myth—could be dangerous since it causes people to expect much more than they are realistically likely to get. This problem could be most severe with those intellectuals whose concept of democracy has often been "homogenizing, idealized, and despite their profession to the contrary, utopian."[126] They dream of Elysian Fields of consensus and are quick—even eager—to succumb to cynicism when reality intrudes. Many of them have been yearning for democracy for decades and are appalled to find it an unseemly and often corrupt mess. Thus Aleksandr Solzhenitsyn holds that there is no democracy in postcommunist Russia at all, rather opaquely arguing that "today we have an oligarchy since power belongs to a limited number of people." And he romantically calls for the revival of *zemstvo*—grassroots self-government bodies that existed in precommunist Russia.[127]

Intellectuals seem to be regrettably quick to use the epithet "antidemocratic" to characterize people or policies they do not like.[128] But the success of politicians such as Vladimir Zhirinovsky in Russia and Vladimir Mečiar in Slovakia does not stem so much from antidemocratic actions (at least so far) as from a willingness and ability to get their hands dirty in the drudge work of political campaigning—such unpleasant tasks as raising (or begging) for money; learning how to use the media slickly and skillfully; establishing and nurturing local organizations; fabricating appealing, if simplistic, slogans; finding out what the voters want and then promising to deliver it.

Well-bred intellectuals who snobbishly turn their noses up at such work, and who continually squabble divisively from the pristine shelter of tiny, unelectable parties that exist only in major cities, show their naïveté about the realities of democracy.[129] If they insist on wallowing in the romantic image, they will lose out in the competitive reality.

The problem could be even greater for capitalism, since intellectuals have classically had a notable antipathy toward the economic form.

The negative image of capitalism sees to have come from a considerable variety of sources. To begin with, greed has never been an easy sell, and promoters of capitalism often try to maintain, utterly unconvincingly, that greed is somehow not central to its functioning, stressing capitalism's efficiency and economic productivity and leaving those who argue that capitalism is characterized by deceit, dishonesty, and cruelty uncountered.[130]

Some critics, such as socialists and communists, champion an alterative economic system, and over the last couple of centuries many of these have proved to be extremely adept propagandists—well organized and colorful. Another traditional enemy of capitalism and an effective source of anticapitalist propaganda has been the church. Capitalists can profit only if they are able to come up with a product or service people genuinely value and (therefore) are willing to pay for. Accordingly, they routinely pander to the capricious whimsy, frivolous self-indulgence, crass materialism, all-consuming selfishness, and flighty narcissism of their customers. The church, on the other hand, is selling spiritual commodities, and it perhaps has an incentive to reduce demand for the things it does not supply.[131] The hostility of those who exalt the aristocratic and martial virtues—chivalry, honor, nobility, glory, valor, martial heroism—also has been a problem for capitalism.[132] Indeed, appropriately greedy capitalists will routinely grovel: they will have no sense of honor or self-respect or dignity as they seek to satisfy the whims of the consumer, who, they feign to believe, is "always right," even when patently wrong. From such behavior, Adam Smith concluded that commerce "sinks the courage of mankind," with the result that "the heroic spirit is almost utterly extinguished," and the "bulk of the people" grow "effeminate and dastardly" by "having their minds constantly employed on the arts of luxury."[133]

Along with all of this there seems to be a natural antipathy toward capitalism among intellectuals, something that, Donald McCloskey argues, has escalated to a "sustained sneer" during the last century and a half.[134] For example, storytellers, quite apart from any leftist leanings, generally have found irrational capitalism to be more dramatic and interesting than its actual, boring rational self. Thus gambling mobsters always seem inexplicably to rub out their debtors rather than cutting deals that might at least give them partial recompense. Employers who foolishly create dissension by brutalizing their charges are more engrossing than ones who maximize profits by cleverly maintaining a contented workforce. Landlords who mindlessly harass their tenants supply more dramatic grist than ones who realize they can charge higher rents if the tenants find the building to be especially desirable. Overseers who sadistically whip their slaves make for better drama than ones who treat them well in order to maximize production and who realize that scars from beatings reduce a slave's market value. Labor negotiations that break down and lead to pitched battles between strikers and company goons are far more colorful than ones that lead to mutually satisfactory agreement. Swindling adds grist to a tale even if it requires positing an improbable gullibility to the swindled. Wall Street entrepreneurs who cheat are found to be much more fascinating than typical ones who profit from integrity. And capitalist risk-taking has been found to be difficult to portray, perhaps because no one gets shot or involved in a car chase and because the costs of failure, the occasional suicide aside, show up in such unphotogenic and comparatively mild conditions as ulcers, insomnia, quiet despair, and reduced life expectancy.[135]

Moreover, intellectuals, almost by definition, tend to prize flights of fancy, grand generalizing, and cosmic conceptualizing, whereas people who are successful in business must be comparatively practical, mundane, materialistic, banal, unreflective, methodical, pedestrian, unideological, routine, unromantic, tidy, and, ultimately, boring.[136] Adam Smith, an intellectual himself, argued that the "commercial spirit . . . confines the views of men," with the result that the "minds of men are contracted, and rendered incapable of elevation."[137] Some intellectuals who quest to change people's tastes also may be distressed at the drive of capitalists uncritically to service whatever tastes the consumer might happen to have at the moment.[138] In addition, the overly gregarious, glad-handing, hail-fellow-well-met demeanor characteristic of many people in business can seem offensive and phony to many garret-loving, library-haunting, muse-awaiting intellectuals.

Intellectuals also may be understandably turned off by the ingenuous prose of business books, most of which have all the wryness and subtlety of cheerleading as they exuberantly assemble lists of business principles that often seem banal, flip, corny, and perhaps hypocritical, and as they rail on and on about loving the customer and assembling a "winning team." And businesspeople often have been prone to high-minded rhetoric that could appear disingenuous at best and hypocritical at worst to skeptical intellectuals.[139]

From the perspective of the intellectual, then, people in business may appear small-minded, crass, and even stupid—though typically they will understand their business in greater depth and finer nuance than the average intellectual will ever understand anything. Thus the fact that the successful businessman (intellectuals routinely ignore the many unsuccessful ones) makes far more money than the average intellectual—a process well under way in postcommunist Europe—often inspires a special resentment among intellectuals.

Images and Realities

It has been a recurring theme of this chapter that there is a considerable disconnection between the images of democracy and capitalism and their realities.

Both in mature democracies and in new ones, many still cling to a fuzzy, romantic, Rockwellian image that, centuries of experience suggest, is quite fantastic. In the United States there is, for example, the noisy, perennial clamor against "special interests." But in a democracy the free, competitive play of "special interests" is fundamental—indeed, that is democracy's whole *point*. To reform this out of existence would be uncomprehending and profoundly antidemocratic.[140] Relatedly, there is endless talk about "negative campaigning," which, studies show, increases cynicism about politics.[141] As William Riker has observed, there is nothing wrong or indecent about negative campaigning if it helps to differentiate candidates and issues—as it almost always does—and it is a commonplace in democratic campaigns, never more so than in the intensely contentious and politically manipulative ratification campaign for the since-sanctified U.S. Constitution.[142] But democracy, it has been argued here, is not about active mass participation, heartwarming consensus, or dewy-eyed tolerance.

Similarly, even capitalists—when they trouble to generalize about it—often have a remarkably cynical view of the economic form. And the general view of capitalism suggests that it is somehow vicious and reprehensible or at least devoid of virtue. This image holds even though the daily business experience of people in advanced capitalist countries—where they are treated overwhelmingly (though not unfailingly) with honesty, fairness, civility, and even compassion by greedy proprietors—constantly belies the negative image. Indeed, studies comparing attitudes toward capitalism in the East and the West find remarkably little difference on many issues. For example, most New Yorkers agree with most Muscovites that it is "unfair" for an entrepreneur to raise prices merely because demand increases, and New Yorkers are, if anything, *less* tolerant of economic inequality, *more* distrustful of "speculators," and *less* appreciative of the importance of material incentives.[143]

But these faulty popular images—that democracy ought somehow to be much better than experience has shown it to be, and that capitalism deep down is somehow really much worse than experience routinely shows it to be—do not seem to have notably hampered the workings of either institution. In operation democracy is far from ideal, but it seems to be the best (or least bad) form of government. And in operation capitalism, for all its real and imagined flaws, seems the best way to run an economy for the greatest benefit of the greatest number.

Hence, although each can exist without the other, capitalism and democracy are a great deal like each other in a very important sense. Although there probably ought to be *some* guiding minds at work for democracy and capitalism to be properly instituted and maintained, it does not appear necessary for people in general fully to understand them, or even to believe in them, for them to work. For the posttransitional postcommunist countries of Europe, that somewhat perverse message could be the most hopeful of all.

ACKNOWLEDGMENTS

For comments and suggestions, I would like to thank Michael Mandelbaum and members of the Council on Foreign Relations symposium, as well as Ted Bird, Randall Calvert, Henry Carey, Ian Fried, James Johnson, Henry Manne, Mira Marody, Normand Perreault, Ralph Raimi, William Riker, Richard Rosecrance, Andrew Rutten, Edward Schleh, Kenneth Shepsle, Randall Stone, Eric Uslaner, David Weimer, and especially Stanley Engerman. For support for a semester in Slovakia, I thank the Civic Education Project.

NOTES

1. Although many of the observations may apply to them, this discussion mostly excludes the postcommunist states of Asia, including the trans-Caucasian ones.
2. Hedrick Smith, *The Russians* (New York: Quadrangle, 1976), p. 507.
3. "MacNeil/Lehrer NewsHour," March 12, 1992.
4. However, although democracy has been under substantial assault in war-racked Croatia, Bosnia-Herzegovina, and Serbia, it is remarkable how much of it survives and persists. Of course, the episode in Moscow in 1993 in which parliament was shelled by troops loyal to the president will not be held out here to be a shining example of democracy in action. The Russian invasion of Chechnya in December 1994 often is taken to be a failure of democracy, but that is not clearly true. George Bush said both before and after the event that his decision to invade Iraq in January 1991 was not dependent on congressional approval, and I suspect that if the Chechnya adventure had proved as militarily successful as the Gulf one, antipathy to the move in Russia would have dissipated quickly. Although there was great opposition to the invasion in the Russian parliament, the fact that those so disposed were not able to muster the votes to undermine the military move is no more surprising than the fact that doves in the American Congress were unable to force the United States from Vietnam. On the other hand, the fiasco in Chechnya apparently reduced Boris Yeltsin's reelection prospects substantially—which, after all, is what is supposed to happen in a democracy. And if the Gulf War had proved unacceptably costly, Bush and the Republicans would have been in devastating political trouble. See John Mueller, *Policy and Opinion in the Gulf War* (Chicago: University of Chicago Press, 1994), pp. 58–60, 128–29. Democracy is no guarantee against foolish policies. It does, however, hold fools (and geniuses) finally responsible for their policies, and it provides a method for removing them should people so decide after assessing their record and the alternatives.
5. On these issues, see John Mueller, "Democracy and Ralph's Pretty Good Grocery: Elections, Inequality, and the Minimal Human Being," *American Journal of Political Science* 36, no. 4 (November 1992), pp. 983–1003; John Mueller, *Quiet Cataclysm: Reflections on the Recent*

Transformation of World Politics (New York: HarperCollins, 1995), pp. 156–59. On the requirements for a democracy, see also Robert A. Dahl, *Polyarchy* (New Haven: Yale University Press, 1971), p. 3; Philippe Schmitter and Terry Lynn Karl, "What Democracy Is . . . and Is Not," *Journal of Democracy* 2, no. 3 (Summer 1991), p. 81. For disagreement with Dahl's emphasis on political equality, see John Mueller, "Minorities and the Democratic Image," *East European Politics and Societies* 9, no. 3 (Fall 1995), pp. 513–22.

6. Darina Malová, "The Relationship Between the State, Political Parties and Civil Society in Postcommunist Czecho-Slovakia," Bratislava, Slovakia, Department of Politology, Comenius University, 1994.

7. *RFE/RL Daily Report*, April 5, 1994; "Voice of America," March 1, 1995. Expanded television choice also could form a partial palliative for some of the pains of transition. See also John Mueller, "New, Improved Opiates for the Masses!," *The Wall Street Journal*, May 23, 1989, p. A18. The bulk of what keeps masses of Westerners contentedly in their living rooms, despite a wealth of nontelevision alternatives, has been substantially missing in the postcommunist countries—a variety of breezy and engaging shows devoted to comedy, adventure, mystery, romance, and so forth. That is, Western television already has proved itself to be a highly successful opiate for the masses. (And lively sports channels might do a great deal to reduce alcoholism, or at least public drunkenness, where that is a problem.) That television entertainment importantly affects the perceived living standard is clear from the East German experience. During a period of approved emigration in 1984, the government found that the residents of the Dresden area—known as the "valley of the blind" because it was too distant to receive West German television—were some five times as likely to seek to leave as were people from other areas. They left, they told Western officials, because life under the communist regime was intolerable without daily exposure to the offerings of West German television. The government found that getting even ardent communist cadres to relocate to Dresden was difficult because of the city's television deprivation. Accordingly, it began to pipe in the foreign signals by cable. See William Drozdiak, "2 Germanys Slacken Ties after Allies Voice Unease," *The Washington Post*, June 1, 1984, p. A23; George Quester, "Transboundary Television," *Problems of Communism* (September–October 1984), p. 78. The Western experience guarantees that the importation of large quantities of Western television will generate a chorus of complaints from the elite about how cultural and intellectual standards are being debased. For a sample, see Václav Havel's comments in note 138, below. It is also completely predictable that television soon will be blamed for every social malady—something that ought to appeal to beleaguered politicians.

8. See, for example, Michael Lienesch, "Wo(e)begon(e) Democracy," *American Journal of Political Science* 36, no. 4 (November 1992), p. 1011.

9. See M. Margaret Conway, *Political Participation in the United States* (Washington, D.C.: CQ Press, 1991), ch. 1.

10. *RFE/RL Daily Report*, March 1, 1994; March 29, 1994.

11. Robert D. Putnam, *Making Democracy Work: Civic Traditions in Modern Italy* (Princeton: Princeton University Press, 1993), pp. 172, 196, emphasis added.

12. Malová, "The Relationship Between the State, Political Parties and Civil Society." See also Peter Rutland, "Has Democracy Failed Russia?," *National Interest* (Winter 1994/95), pp. 8–9.

13. For a critique of the rather murky "civil society," or "civic culture," concept, concluding that the "norms of a civic culture are better thought of as a *product* and not as a producer of democracy," see Schmitter and Karl, "What Democracy Is," p. 83.

14. Ibid., p. 84.

15. See, for example, Scott Mainwaring, Guillermo O'Donnell, and J. Samuel Valenzuela, eds., *Issues in Democratic Consolidation: The New South American Democracies in Comparative Perspective* (Notre Dame: University of Notre Dame Press, 1992).

16. See Marcin Król, "A Communist Comeback: Poland's Longing for Paternalism," *Journal of Democracy* 5, no. 1 (January 1994), pp. 85–95.

17. See Smith, *The Russians*, ch. 10; Rutland, "Has Democracy Failed Russia?," p. 8. See also Richard Rose, "Getting By Without Government: Everyday Life in Russia," *Daedalus* (Summer 1994), p. 57.

18. See, for example, Samuel A. Stouffer, *Communism, Conformity, and Civil Liberties* (Garden City, NY: Doubleday, 1955); James W. Prothro and Charles W. Grigg, "Fundamental Principles of Democracy: Bases of Agreement and Disagreement," *Journal of Politics* 22 (1960), pp. 276–94; John Mueller, "Trends in Political Tolerance," *Public Opinion Quarterly* 52, no. 1 (Spring 1988), pp. 1–25.

19. See James L. Gibson, Raymond M. Duch, and Kent L. Tedin, "Democratic Values and the Transformation of the Soviet Union," *Journal of Politics* 54, no. 2 (May 1992), pp. 329–71.

20. Robert N. Bellah et al., *The Good Society* (New York: Knopf, 1991), p. 273.

21. Michael X. Delli Carpini and Scott Keeter, "Stability and Change in the U.S. Public's Knowledge of Politics," *Public Opinion Quarterly* 55, no. 4 (Winter 1991), pp. 583–612.

22. CBS News/*New York Times* poll release, December 14, 1994.

23. Robin Toner, "G.O.P. Gets Mixed Reviews from Public Wary on Taxes," *The New York Times*, April 6, 1995, p. A1.

24. FOCUS, *Current Problems of Slovakia After the Split of the CSFR (October 1993)* (Bratislava, Slovak Republic: Center for Social and Market Analysis, 1993), pp. 10–11.

25. Christine Spolar, "U.S. Envoy Aborts Belgrade Mission," *The Washington Post*, May 24, 1995, p. A29.

26. Stephen Kinzer, "For Dutch It's O.K. to Despise Germans," *The New York Times*, February 8, 1995, p. A13.

27. Another problem in Yugoslavia may have been an acceptance of the popular image that democracy is centrally associated with political equality, majority rule, and active political participation by the mass of people. Taking these notions at face value, a national or other minority—particularly one that knows it inspires considerable hostility in the majority—is likely to conclude that it faces the potential of persecution in a democratic system because it will obviously be outnumbered. Democracy has generally had a good, if imperfect, record of dealing with minority issues, particularly when compared with other forms of government; but this is neither because democratic majorities have been notably tolerant of minority concerns, nor because majorities have shown a great deal of affection toward minorities. Rather, it derives from the fact that democracy leaves minorities free to increase their effective political weight—to become more equal, more important than their arithmetic size would imply—on minority issues. Moreover, the fact that most people most of the time pay little attention to politics—the phenomenon of political apathy—also helps to allow interested minorities to protect their rights and to assert their interests. For a development of this argument, see Mueller, "Minorities and the Democratic Image."

28. More broadly, although conflicts in Yugoslavia and elsewhere are commonly attributed to the nearly spontaneous burgeoning of ancient blood feuds, it may rather be that the conflicts have mostly been the result of the opportunistic work of local political entrepreneurs and, often, of unpoliced thugs. See Noel Malcolm, "Seeing Ghosts," *National Interest* (Summer 1993), pp. 83–88; Cheryl Benard, "Bosnia: Was It Inevitable?," in Z. M. Khalilzad, ed., *Lessons from Bosnia* (Santa Monica, CA.: RAND, 1993); V. P. Gagnon, Jr., "Serbia's Road to War," *Journal of Democracy* 5, no. 2 (April 1994), pp. 117–31; ———, "Ethnic Nationalism and International Conflict: The Case of Serbia," *International Security* 19, no. 3 (Winter 1994/95), pp. 130–66; Susan L. Woodward, *Balkan Tragedy: Chaos and Dissolution after the Cold War* (Washington, D.C.: Brookings Institution, 1995), pp. 236–46.

29. See Kelly D. Patterson and David B. Magleby, "Trends: Public Support for Congress," *Public Opinion Quarterly* 56, no. 4 (Winter 1992), p. 544; Mueller, *Policy and Opinion*, p. 180.

30. See Robin Toner, "Pollsters See a Silent Storm That Swept Away Democrats," *The New York Times*, November 16, 1994, p. A14.

31. Richard L. Berke, "Victories Were Captured by G.O.P. Candidates, Not the Party's Platform," *The New York Times*, November 10, 1994, p. B1.

32. For data, see Nicholas Eberstadt, "Demographic Disaster: The Soviet Legacy," *National Interest* (Summer 1994), pp. 53–57. Comparisons might be made with people who suddenly go from a situation of extreme security to one of great insecurity—who become utterly unanchored. Thus it may be that people who are released from prison after a long stay also have the same sorts of adjustment problems found in the postcommunist countries—or people who suddenly lose jobs they had previously

considered secure. Or there is another possible parallel: the demographics of newly freed slaves. It appears that the life expectancy of Southern blacks declined greatly when they were freed from slavery—and, most startlingly, that it did not recover to 1860 levels until the twentieth century. See Edward Meeker, "Mortality Trends of Southern Blacks, 1850–1910: Some Preliminary Findings," *Explorations in Economic History* 13 (1976), p. 14. The parallel is not precise and is probably extreme (I hope), but it is certainly suggestive. On the other hand, it might also be taken to suggest that substantial demographic shocks need not be particularly disruptive of social stability, as Eberstadt fears (p. 54). See also Judith Shapiro, "The Russian Mortality Crisis and Its Causes," in Anders Åslund, ed., *Russian Reform at Risk* (London: Pinter, 1995), pp. 149–78.

33. Michael Shafir, "Growing Political Extremism in Romania," *RFE/RL Research Report* (April 1993), p. 18.
34. Rutland, "Has Democracy Failed Russia?," p. 6.
35. Rose, "Getting By Without Government," p. 53.
36. Leslie McAneny and David W. Moore, "Annual Honesty & Ethics Poll," *Gallup Poll Monthly* (October 1994), pp. 2–4.
37. *Harper's*, February 1995, p. 11.
38. Rose, "Getting By Without Government," p. 53.
39. Patterson and Magleby, "Trends," p. 544.
40. Mueller, *Policy and Opinion*, pp. 281, 286. On various related U.S. trends (mainly downward), see Robert D. Putnam, "Bowling Alone: America's Declining Social Capital," *Journal of Democracy* 6, no. 1 (January 1995), pp. 65–78; Eric M. Uslaner, *The Decline of Comity in Congress* (Ann Arbor, MI: University of Michigan Press, 1993). Rose argues that "the communist regime has left a legacy of distrust" ("Getting By Without Government," p. 53), but Putnam and Uslaner suggest the United States has managed to pick up the legacy without that experience.
41. Seymour Martin Lipset, "Reflections on Capitalism, Socialism & Democracy," *Journal of Democracy* 4, no. 2 (April 1993), p. 51; ——— "The Social Requisites of Democracy Revisited," *American Sociological Review* 59 (February 1994), pp. 13–14.
42. Rose, "Getting By Without Government," p. 53.
43. *Public Papers of the Presidents of the United States: John F. Kennedy, 1963* (Washington, D.C.: United States Government Printing Office, 1964), p. 539.
44. *The Economist*, May 16, 1991, p. 48.
45. James Brooke, "Governing Party's Candidate Wins Paraguay's Presidential Election," *The New York Times*, May 11, 1993, p. A10.
46. Samuel P. Huntington, *The Third Wave: Democratization in the Late Twentieth Century* (Norman, OK: University of Oklahoma Press, 1991), p. 108.
47. Some examples of countries, besides Paraguay and Albania, that have gone democratic despite a notable lack of political or economic development or of painful transition to develop democratic attitudes: all the

new Caribbean countries (except Grenada for a while), Papua New Guinea, Botswana, Malawi, Namibia, Mozambique, Ghana, Portugal, Benin, Kenya, Zimbabwe, Gambia, and Senegal, as well as Nicaragua and many other Latin American states. Some of these may collapse, of course—but that is what they said about Portugal in the late 1970s.

48. Dankwart A. Rustow, "Transitions to Democracy: Toward a Dynamic Model," *Comparative Politics* 2, no. 3 (April 1970), p. 361.

49. Robert A. Dahl, *Democracy and Its Critics* (New Haven: Yale University Press, 1989), p. 26. Earlier, he had concluded that "in the future as in the past," democracy is "more likely to result from rather slow evolutionary processes than from the revolutionary overthrow of existing hegemonies," and "the transformation of hegemonic regimes" into democracies "is likely to remain a slow process, measured in generations" (*Polyarchy*, pp. 45, 47).

50. Daniel P. Moynihan, "The American Experiment," *The Public Interest* (Fall 1975), p. 6.

51. Samuel P. Huntington, "Will More Countries Become Democratic?," *Political Science Quarterly* 99, no. 2 (Summer 1984), p. 218. In 1993 economist Robert Barro confidently predicted that, because of "the country's level and distribution of income, the ethnic divisions, and the political and economic experiences of most of the counties of Sub-Saharan Africa," the establishment of democracy in South Africa was, quite simply, "not going to happen." See, "Pushing Democracy Is No Key to Prosperity," *The Wall Street Journal*, December 14, 1993, p. A16. When that analytically inconvenient result came about within a few months, he predicted with equal élan that the country had "probably already overshot the mark, and a substantial decline of political freedom is likely." See, "Democracy: A Recipe for Growth?," *The Wall Street Journal*, December 1, 1994, p. A18.

52. Huntington, "Will More Countries Become Democratic?," p. 212.

53. Dahl, *Democracy and Its Critics*, p. 260. See also Dahl, *Polyarchy*, p. 126.

54. On elite transformations, see John Higley and Richard Gunther, eds., *Elites and Democratic Consolidation in Latin America and Southern Europe* (Cambridge: Cambridge University Press, 1992).

55. For a fuller discussion of this process, see Mueller, *Quiet Cataclysm*, ch. 10. Huntington, although he has pointed out that countries "transit to democracy at widely varying levels of development" ("Will More Countries Become Democratic?," p. 200), continues to maintain that economic development is the most "pervasive force" for democratization in recent decades, and holds that "economic development makes democracy possible" (*Third Wave*, pp. 85, 316). This seems to suggest that despite the cases of India, Paraguay, Papua New Guinea, much of the Caribbean, Botswana, and eighteenth-century America, democracy is impossible without economic development. For another conclusion that social and economic requisites are necessary for democracy, see Seymour Martin Lipset, "A Comparative Analysis of the Social Requisites of Democracy," *International Social Science Journal* (May

1993), pp. 155–75. In his important study, *The Third Wave*, Huntington acknowledges "the beliefs and actions of political elites" as "probably the most immediate and significant explanatory variable" in the current wave of democratization. He concludes, however, that, while this may be "a powerful explanatory variable, it is not a satisfying one. Democracy can be created even if people do not want it. So it is not perhaps tautological to say that democracy will be created if people want democracy, but it is close to that. An explanation, someone has observed, is the place at which the mind comes to rest. Why do the relevant political elites want democracy? Inevitably, the mind wants to move further along the causal chain" (p. 36). As Huntington moves further along, he clings to the concept of economic preconditions, but his other explanations for the recent democracy wave stress persuasional and promotional elements: democracy's stylishness and the influence of fashion leaders, changes of doctrine in the Catholic church, the role of key converts such as Gorbachev, the failures of the competition, and patterns of imitation (pp. 45–46).

56. Anders Åslund, *How Russia Became a Market Economy* (Washington, D.C.: Brookings Institution, 1995), pp. 3–4. See also ———, "Ruble Awakening: Why the Economic News from Russia Is—Surprise!—Good," *Washington Post*, April 23, 1995, p. C4. On the various strategies that have been adopted—rather successfully, it seems—by Russians to cope with the changes, see Rose, "Getting By without Government."

57. Åslund, *How Russia Became a Market Economy*, pp. 5, 314.

58. Peter Passell, "Economic Scene: Russian Obstacles," *The New York Times*, April 20, 1995, p. D2.

59. Stewart Macaulay found in a classic study of actual business practices that only 5 of the 12 purchasing agents and only 2 of the 10 sales managers he interviewed "had ever been involved in even a negotiation concerning a contract dispute where both sides were represented by lawyers," and *none* had ever "been involved in a case that went to trial." Instead, he found that "disputes are frequently settled without reference to the contract or potential or actual legal sanctions." Indeed, "there is a hesitancy to speak of legal rights or even to threaten to sue." As one respondent put it, "You don't read legalistic contract clauses at each other if you ever want to do business again. One doesn't run to lawyers if he wants to stay in business because one must behave decently." "Non-Contractual Relations in Business: A Preliminary Study," *American Sociological Review* 28, no. 1 (Fall 1963), p. 61.

60. See also Donald McCloskey, "Bourgeois Virtue," *American Scholar* (Spring 1994), p. 183.

61. Specifically, Macaulay finds that the strong norm that "one does not welsh on a deal" is enforced because "both business units involved in the exchange desire to continue successfully in business and will avoid conduct which might interfere with attaining this goal." Thus each is "concerned with both the reaction of the other party" and "his own general

business reputation." "Non-Contractual Relations in Business," pp. 63, 66. On reputational effects, see also David M. Kreps, "Corporate Culture and Economic Theory," in J. M. Alt and K. A. Shepsle, eds., *Perspectives on Positive Political Economy* (New York: Cambridge University Press, 1990), pp. 90–143.

62. People discovered "that if they sent a child to their shops for anything, they were as well used as if they had come themselves," and the shopper's inquiry became "Where is there a draper or shopkeeper or tailor or shoemaker or any other tradesman that is a Quaker?": Paul H. Emden, *Quakers in Commerce: A Record of Business Achievement* (London: Sampson Low, Marston, 1939), p. 17. For a discussion, see Balwant Nevaskar, *Capitalists without Capitalism: The Jains of India and the Quakers of the West* (Westport, CT: Greenwood, 1971), especially pp. 219–22. As Nevaskar notes, the same phenomenon characterizes another pacifist group, the Jains of India.

63. As Nevaskar observes in *Capitalists without Capitalism*, "although they established a reputation as reliable merchants, the Quakers were often suspected of being shrewd, conniving, sly, and dishonest," p. 130.

64. See A. H. Saxon, *P. T. Barnum: The Legend and the Man* (New York: Columbia University Press, 1989), pp. 334–37.

65. Journalist George Ade observes that the Ringlings "found the business in the hands of vagabonds and put it into the hands of gentlemen." Thus they "became circus kings of the world by adopting and observing the simple rule that it is better to be straight than crooked." Quoted in David C. Weeks, *Ringling: The Florida Years, 1911–1936* (Gainesville, FL: University Press of Florida, 1993), p. 13. See also Gene Plowden, *Those Amazing Ringlings and Their Circus* (Caldwell, ID: Caxton Printers, 1967), pp. 66–68.

66. Phineas T. Barnum, *Struggles and Triumphs: Or, Forty Years' Recollections of P. T. Barnum, Written by Himself* (New York: American News Company, 1871), pp. 498–99. Of course, such conclusions hold only when government policies make it possible to profit honestly.

67. In Mexico City government-certified taxicabs cost *more* than other ones and do an excellent business with visitors who are willing to pay extra for assured honesty.

68. Daniel Kahneman, Jack L. Knetsch, and Richard Thaler, "Fairness as a Constraint on Profit Seeking: Entitlements in the Market," *American Economic Review* 76, no. 4 (September 1986), p. 738. See also Robert H. Frank, *Passions within Reason: The Strategic Role of the Emotions* (New York: Norton, 1988), p. 176.

69. Barnum, *Struggles and Triumphs*, p. 496. It is most interesting in this regard that in advanced capitalist areas, bargaining over prices has been abandoned almost entirely in ordinary retail commerce, a phenomenon that will be discussed more fully later. This practice was substantially begun, it seems, by the Quakers (Emden, *Quakers in Commerce*, p. 17),

and it has come about even though it has presumably been to the short-term disadvantage of retailers, who, since they bargain all the time, have an advantage, on average, over the casual ordinary customer. That is, businesses have found they tend to do better if they handicap themselves by setting (attractive) prices for a commodity, thereby reducing the customers' transaction costs by relieving them of the often unpleasant and emotionally unsettling task of haggling over a price and of the fear of being unfairly taken.

70. Barnum, *Struggles and Triumphs*, pp. 496–97.

71. James Q. Wilson, *On Character* (Washington, DC: AEI Press, 1991), p. 148.

72. Albert O. Hirschman, *The Passions and the Interests: Political Arguments for Capitalism before Its Triumph* (Princeton: Princeton University Press, 1977), p. 61.

73. Barnum, *Struggles and Triumphs*, p. 496. Such sentiments are commonly found in writings by businesspeople. An exuberant best-seller published more than a century after Barnum, stresses similar lessons. Excellent (and successful) businesses "love the customers," and "*really are* close to their customers" by learning their customers' preferences and catering to them. They even have an "*obsession*," which characteristically occurs "as a seemingly unjustifiable overcommitment to some form of quality, reliability, or service." Thomas Peters and Robert Waterman, *In Search of Excellence: Lessons from America's Best-Run Companies* (New York: Warner Books, 1982), pp. i, 29, 156, 157.

74. Peters and Waterman admonish: "Treat people as adults. Treat them as partners; treat them with dignity; treat them with respect. Threat *them*— not capital spending and automation—as the primary source of productivity gains. . . . In other words, if you want productivity and the financial reward that goes with it, you must treat your workers as your most important asset. . . . There was hardly a more pervasive theme in the excellent companies than *respect for the individual*." *In Search of Excellence*, pp. i, 238.

75. James Breeden, *Advice among Masters: The Ideal in Slave Management in the Old South* (Westport, CT: Greenwood, 1980), p. 30; see also Robert William Fogel and Stanley L. Engerman, *Time on the Cross: The Economics of American Negro Slavery* (Boston: Little, Brown, 1974), p. 73. This perspective was utterly unappreciated by Adam Smith, who held that "work done by slaves . . . is in the end the dearest of any" because "a person who can acquire no property, can have no other interest but to eat as much and to labour as little as possible. Whatever work he does beyond what is sufficient to purchase his own maintenance, can be squeezed out of him by violence only, and not by any interest of his own." *An Inquiry into the Nature and Causes of the Wealth of Nations* (Oxford: Oxford University Press, 1976), pp. 387–88.

76. One Soviet citizen tells of being kept waiting by a butcher who was chatting with a friend. When she asked for meat, he turned grumpily to her and said, "Next, I suppose you'll want me to cram it in your mouth for

you." Another observed, "They think, 'I am one and you are many, so why should I hurry? You have to wait for me anyway.' And they are right of course. Where else can you go if they have what you want?" Smith, *The Russians*, p. 67.

77. There are remedies against mistreatment by government agencies in a democracy, but they are awkward and indirect: an ill-treated customer can pressure an elected representative, who in turn can lean on the agency to treat its customer/supplicants with more civility.

78. Barnum, *Struggles and Triumphs*, p. 497.

79. See George Gilder, *The Spirit of Enterprise* (New York: Simon and Schuster, 1984). For the classic, if clearly erroneous, conclusion that heroic entrepreneurship must necessarily become obsolete as capitalism develops and as businesses grow and become bureaucratized, see Joseph A. Schumpeter, *Capitalism, Socialism and Democracy*, third ed. (New York: Harper & Row, 1950), pp. 131–34, 417. For a critique, see Neil McInnes, "Wrong for Superior Reasons," *National Interest* (Spring 1995), pp. 94–97.

80. Thus they do not seem to pass Wilson's test for a "moral man": "one whose sense of duty is shaped by conscience, that is, by the impartial spectator within our breast who evaluates our own action as others would evaluate it." *On Character*, p. 147.

81. As Wilson observes, "A person can be fooled by a chance encounter, but during a continuing relationship he will usually form an accurate assessment of another person's character." *The Moral Sense* (New York: Free Press, 1993), p. 102.

82. Barnum, *Struggles and Triumphs*, p. 489.

83. I have an acquaintance who became a doctor only to discover that he was ill-suited to the work because he had great difficulty dealing with people. Accordingly, he went back to school and became a pathologist and is now quite happy because the only patients he has to deal with come in the form of disembodied fluids and chunks of flesh. This seems to have been an especially wise career decision: a study has shown that doctors who are rude and inconsiderate with their patients are more likely to be sued for malpractice. *The New York Times*, November 25, 1994, p. B14.

84. Quoted in Putnam, *Making Democracy Work*, pp. 143–44. Related is the story of the peasant who was visited by a genie who promises to give him anything he wants with the proviso that his neighbor will be given twice as much. After some thought the peasant's request is "Kill one of my cows."

85. Edward Banfield, *The Moral Basis of a Backward Society* (Glencoe, IL: Free Press, 1958), pp. 93–94, 64, 79.

86. See also Francis Fukuyama, *Trust: The Social Virtues and the Creation of Prosperity* (New York: Free Press, 1995). Max Weber observes: "The universal reign of absolute unscrupulousness in the pursuit of selfish interests by the making of money has been a specific characteristic of precisely those countries whose bourgeois-capitalistic development, measured according to Occidental standards, has remained backward."

The Protestant Ethic and the Spirit of Capitalism (New York: Scribner's, 1958), p. 57.

87. Douglass North, *Institutions, Institutional Change and Economic Performance* (Cambridge: Cambridge University Press, 1990), pp. 123–24.

88. Ibid., p. 124.

89. Ibid., p. 101.

90. "Governmental controls over marketplace activity are marginal, decentralized, and mostly rhetorical." Ibid., p. 123.

91. Joseph H. Appel, *The Business Biography of John Wanamaker, Founder and Builder: America's Merchant Pioneer from 1861 to 1922* (New York: Macmillan, 1930), pp. 50–52, 370–73.

92. Ibid., p. 54.

93. Another illustration of the development process may come from a recent innovation in the automobile industry, which is just about the only American retail business after the Wanamaker revolution that still haggles with consumers. Venerable traditions, however, are now being challenged by the Saturn automobile, which charges set prices. Not only are Saturn sales brisk, but according to *Consumer Reports* (April 1995, pp. 270–71), questionnaires returned by 120,000 new car buyers indicated that Saturn placed solidly first in satisfaction with the car-buying experience, to which "the no-haggle policy . . . contributes greatly." There are signs other automobile dealers are beginning to follow Saturn's successful one-price policy. If so, it could mean the industry will enjoy greater overall sales because more people will buy more cars more often, essentially because the transaction costs have been substantially reduced. But the value of this approach, which may come to seem obvious, has clearly not been so until now. It will have taken an effort by one company to show its value, after which other greedy retailers follow suit.

94. North, *Institutions*, p. 87.

95. Many ideas seem simple and obvious in retrospect, but clearly are neither, since it took centuries—indeed millennia—for them to become accepted. These include Arabic numerals and the idea of zero, the wheel, the alphabet, the cotton gin, and home delivery of pizza.

96. North, *Institutions*, pp. 112–17.

97. *The Works of Benjamin Franklin* (Boston: Whittlemore, Niles, and Hall, 1856), vol. 2, p. 88.

98. For an example of such informal institutions in action, see Avner Greif, "Contract Enforceability and Economic Institutions in Early Trade: The Maghribi Traders' Coalition," *American Economic Review* 83, no. 3 (June 1993), pp. 525–48.

99. For a history of these early efforts, see H. J. Kenner, *The Fight for the Truth in Advertising: A Story of What Business Has Done and Is Doing to Establish and Maintain Accuracy and Fair Play in Advertising and Selling for the Public's Protection* (New York: Round Table Press, 1936).

100. See Elton Mayo, *The Human Problems of an Industrial Civilization* (New York: Macmillan, 1933).

101. Mira Marody, "Antinomies of Collective Subconsciousness," *Social Research* 55, no. 1–2 (Spring/Summer 1988), pp. 97–110; ———, "In Search of Collective Sense," *Polish Sociological Review*, 1994, pp. 17–22; Piotr Sztompka, "The Intangibles and Imponderables of the Transition to Democracy," *Studies in Comparative Communism* 24, no. 3 (September 1991), pp. 295–311.

102. Putnam, *Making Democracy Work*, p. 183.

103. It seems to be remarkably easy for different moral standards to prevail in dealings with the government. Honesty may be central to ordinary business transactions where both parties gain and where each has a long-term reputation to maintain, but the greedy have a strong incentive to minimize the confiscation of their wealth (for example, taxes) by any means feasible. Generally, even in societies where honesty is rampant, tax evasion may often be kept in check primarily by the effective threat of detection and coercion. It seems to be entirely possible for a society to exist in which tax cheats are lauded for their cleverness while they still are trusted fully in business or private life.

104. A student who visited Russia a few years ago came back with all the usual tales about the rampant discourtesy so characteristic of government stores. When asked about the private markets, she observed that the sellers there were, by contrast, wonderfully warm and friendly—they were, she said, "just like Americans." Actually, they were just like capitalists, though many of them would doubtless bridle at the comparison.

105. Michael Hobbs, "The Virtues of the Czech Republic's Invisible Exchange," unpublished manuscript, Brno, Czech Republic, 1994.

106. *The Economist*, April 16, 1994, p. 6. See also Tina Rosenberg, "Meet the New Boss, Same as the Old Boss," *Harper's*, May 1993, pp. 47–53.

107. This process may resemble the adjustments to traditional arrangements that occurred when Japan, China, and Korea were confronted with Western capitalism. See Fukuyama, *Trust*, pp. 349–50.

108. Michael Specter, "Borscht and Blini to Go: From Russian Capitalists, an Answer to McDonald's," *The New York Times*, August 9, 1995, p. D1.

109. See, for example, Teresa Toranska, *"Them": Stalin's Polish Puppets* (New York: Harper & Row, 1987).

110. See Jacek Wasilewski, "Communist Nomenklatura in the Post-Communist Eastern Europe: Winners or Losers of Transformation?," paper delivered at the Biennial Conference on Central and Eastern Europe (University of South Florida, Sarasota, FL, March 1995). Something like this also came about in the early days of democracy: once democracy was tried out, people tended to vote aristocrats (the very people democracy was supposedly directed against) into office. See Edmund S. Morgan, *Inventing the People: The Rise of Popular Sovereignty in England and America* (New York: Norton, 1988), pp. 147–48.

111. In *The Anticapitalistic Mentality* (Grove City, PA: Libertarian Press, 1972), Ludwig von Mises quotes the observations of an eighteenth-century German writer, Justus Möser: "Life in a society in which success would

exclusively depend on personal merit would, says Möser, simply be un-
bearable. As human nature is, everybody is prone to overrate his own worth
and deserts. If a man's station in life is conditioned by factors other than
his inherent excellence, those who remain at the bottom of the ladder can
acquiesce in this outcome and, knowing their own worth, still preserve
their dignity and self-respect. But it is different if merit alone decides. Then
the unsuccessful feel themselves insulted and humiliated. Hate and enmity
against all those who superseded them must result" (pp.10–11). Möser
therefore advocated promotion by blood lines—though, as the experiences
of the revolutions which began at the end of the eighteenth century were
to attest, his method of promotion actually did inspire quite a bit of
resentment.

112. Charles E. Lindblom, *Politics and Markets: The World's Political-Economic Systems* (New York: Basic Books, 1977), pp. 116, 161–69; Milton Friedman, *Capitalism and Freedom* (Chicago: University of Chicago Press, 1962); Huntington, "Will More Countries Become Democratic?," pp. 204–5, 214; William H. Riker, *Liberalism against Populism* (San Francisco: Freeman, 1982), p. 7. For a useful overview of this issue, see Gabriel Almond, "Capitalism and Democracy," *PS: Political Science & Politics* 24, no. 3 (September 1991), pp. 467–74.

113. Barrington Moore, *Social Origins of Dictatorship and Democracy* (New York: Basic Books, 1966), p. 418.

114. Mueller, "Democracy and Ralph's Pretty Good Grocery," p. 990; Mancur Olson, "Dictatorship, Democracy, and Development," *American Political Science Review* 87, no. 3 (September 1993), pp. 567–76.

115. See Mueller, "Minorities and the Democratic Image," pp. 516–17.

116. See Gagnon, "Serbia's Road to War."

117. Ellen Gordon and Luan Troxel, "Minority Mobilization without War," paper delivered at the conference on Postcommunism and Ethnic Mobilization (Cornell University, April 21–22, 1995).

118. In this regard, there has also been quite a bit of talk (mostly coming from Serbs and Greeks) about potential dangers arising from a desire in Tirana for a "greater Albania" (an oxymoronic concept if there ever was one). But the Albanian government, while concerned about Albanians elsewhere, is hardly hurting for additional problems, and it likes to point out that its citizens rather *resent* the uppity and socially distant Albanians of Kosovo and Macedonia and have little desire to combine countries with (and, potentially to be dominated by) them. See *The Economist*, May 21, 1994, pp. 56–57.

119. Paul Schroeder, "Alliances, 1815–1945: Weapons of Power and Tools of Management," in Klaus Knorr, ed., *Historical Dimensions of National Security Problems* (Lawrence, KS: University Press of Kansas, 1976), pp. 227–62. See also John Mueller, "Policy Principles for Unthreatened Wealth-Seekers," *Foreign Policy* (Spring, 1996).

120. Woodward, *Balkan Tragedy*, p. 257.

121. For example, although the crime rate had been declining for more than a decade, the issue suddenly became a prime one in the 1994 election in

the United States. See Mark Warr, "Trends: Public Opinion on Crime and Punishment," *Public Opinion Quarterly* 59, no. 2 (Summer 1995), pp. 296–310.

122. For example, buried in a sensational story in *USA Today* about the horrors of "driveway robberies" in Dallas was the observation that violent crime had dropped 32 percent in that city in the previous two years. See Mark Potok, "Fear Grips Dallas after Driveway Attacks," *USA Today*, March 22, 1994, p. 8A.

123. Macaulay, "Non-Contractual Relations in Business," pp. 65–67.

124. See Václav Havel, "The Responsibility of Intellectuals," *New York Review of Books*, June 22, 1995, pp. 36–37. As Holmes points out, rather paradoxically, dissidents have been "one of the groups that lost the most from the collapse of the old regime."

125. For a discussion of the influential role played by Yugoslav intellectuals in that country's descent into disaster, see Cvijeto Job, "Yugoslavia's Ethnic Furies," *Foreign Policy* (Fall 1993), pp. 52–74; Woodward, *Balkan Tragedy*, pp. 240, 484.

126. George Schöpflin, "Postcommunism: The Problems of Democratic Construction," *Daedalus* (Summer 1994), p. 130.

127. *RFE/RL Daily Report*, October 31, 1994.

128. For example, Igor Moloshenko, chairman of NTV in Russia, seems to suggest that the country is not democratic because it sometimes does things he does not approve of: "Yes, there is a public revulsion against this war in Chechnya.... However, we should keep in mind that Russia is not a democratic nation. And there is no democratic system of checks and balances and there is no political mechanism how public opinion can be implemented, so to say, how public opinion can be translated into political outcomes. That's why Russian politicians can disregard, in many instances, public opinion." "MacNeil/Lehrer NewsHour," March 6, 1995. Similarly, Democratic Russia Party co-chairman Lev Ponomarev supports efforts to reduce the number of deputies elected on party lists because he believes—patronizingly and apparently under the mistaken belief that things are different in real democracies—that "voters are not mature enough to sort out party programs and instead vote for personalities." *OMRI Daily Digest*, March 3, 1995. On this issue, see also n. 4 above.

129. On the Polish case, see Aleksander Smolar, "A Communist Comeback? The Dissolution of Solidarity," *Journal of Democracy* 5, no. 1 (January 1994), pp. 75–77.

130. For example, Milton and Rose Friedman's book, *Free to Choose* (New York: Harcourt Brace Jovanovich, 1980), a spirited defense of capitalism, tirelessly stresses the economic importance and value of freedom, but nowhere suggests that capitalism inspires, encourages, or rewards honesty, integrity, compassion, or civility—indeed, those words do not even appear in the index.

131. Thus, a papal encyclical rails against "consumerism" in which "people are ensnared in a web of false and superficial gratifications rather than being helped to experience their personhood in an authentic and concrete way."

The New York Times, May 3, 1991, p. A10. The church often seems to display what might be called a contempt for the consumer. For example, in such places as Germany and Austria, joining forces with like-minded socialists and with competition-fearing small businesses, it has successfully pushed for laws restricting shop hours in order to inconvenience trade and the general enjoyment of the mere material things in life.

132. Hirschman, *The Passions and the Interests*. Max Weber, after quoting Benjamin Franklin on the economic value of hard work, honesty, punctuality, and frugality, notes that such sentiments "would both in ancient times and in the Middle Ages have been proscribed as the lowest sort of avarice and as an attitude entirely lacking in self-respect." *Protestant Ethic*, p. 56.

133. Adam Smith, *Lectures on Justice, Police, Revenue and Arms* (Oxford: Clarendon, 1896), pp. 257–59. On this issue more generally, see John Mueller, *Retreat from Doomsday: The Obsolescence of Major War* (New York: Basic Books, 1989), ch. 2.

134. McCloskey, "Bourgeois Virtue," p. 188. See also Schumpeter, *Capitalism, Socialism, and Democracy*, pp. 145–55; von Mises, *Anticapitalistic Mentality*, pp. 12–14; Stephen Holmes, *The Anatomy of Antiliberalism* (Cambridge, MA: Harvard University Press, 1993), ch. 13.

135. Contrary to myth, in fact, capitalism is not treated sympathetically or realistically even in the Horatio Alger stories, where the typical boy hero is rewarded for integrity, propriety, and hard work not by success in business, but because he stumbles upon an inheritance or inspires the charity of a wealthy patron: "'Money is the root of all evil,' my young friend. It is an old proverb, and, unfortunately, a true one," one of these patrons philosophizes in typically stilted manner in Alger's "Shifting for Himself" of 1876. See Gary Scharnhorst, *Horatio Alger, Jr.* (Boston: Twayne, 1980), pp. 41–43, 142–44; Gary Scharnhorst with Jack Bales, *The Lost Life of Horatio Alger, Jr.* (Bloomington, IN: Indiana University Press, 1985), pp. 149–50. Much of the uninformed association of capitalism with the novels of Horatio Alger may stem from the propagandistic satisfaction of being able to ally business with works of fiction that are simplistic, banal, manipulative, and formulaic.

136. To Havel, "an intellectual is a person who has devoted his or her life to thinking in general terms about the affairs of this world and the broader context of things." "Responsibility of Intellectuals," p. 36.

137. Smith, *Lectures*, pp. 257, 259.

138. Bernard de Jouvenel, "The Treatment of Capitalism by Continental Intellectuals," in F.A. Hayek, ed., *Capitalism and the Historians*, (Chicago: University of Chicago Press, 1954), pp. 118–21. Thus, Havel exalts those intellectuals who care "whether a global dictatorship of advertisement, consumerism, and blood-and-thunder stories on TV will ultimately lead the human race to a state of complete idiocy." "The Responsibility of the Intellectuals," p. 37.

139. Thus, a book on the rise of the Better Business Bureau is subtitled, rather too nobly, "A Story of What Business Has Done and Is Doing to Establish and Maintain Accuracy and Fair Play in Advertising and Selling for the Public's Protection" (Kenner, *Fight for Truth in Advertising*). And in the book's introduction (pp. xiii–xiv), Joseph H. Appel intones with off-putting self-righteousness: "When advertising . . . becomes . . . untruthful, insincere, fraudulent, and thus misleading and unfair to the consumer, it merely reflects the evils that exist in our social, political, and economic circumstances, all of which are inherent in the nature of man himself. The basic cause of these evils is *selfishness*. Commercial selfishness arises from human selfishness. And human selfishness is the root of all our problems."

140. See also Kay Lehman Schlozman and John T. Tierney, *Organized Interests and American Democracy* (New York: Harper & Row, 1986), ch. 15.

141. Stephen Ansolabehere, Shanto Iyengar, Adam Simon, and Nicholas Valentino, "Does Attack Advertising Demobilize the Electorate?," *American Political Science Review* 88, no. 4 (December 1994), pp. 829–38.

142. William Riker, *The Strategy of Rhetoric* (New Haven: Yale University Press, forthcoming). Like other democratic values and practices, this seems to be something new democracies pick up with gratifying ease. A report from Paraguay after a mere two years of experience with the political form observed that "newspaper, television, and radio reports are filled with mud-slinging worthy of the most mature democracy." *The Economist,* May 16, 1991, p. 48.

143. Robert J. Shiller, Maxim Boychko, and Vladimir Korobov, "Popular Attitudes toward Free Markets: The Soviet Union and the United States Compared," *American Economic Review* 81, no. 3 (June 1991), pp. 385–400; ———, "Hunting for *Homo Sovieticus*: Situational versus Attitudinal Factors in Economic Behavior," *Brookings Papers on Economic Activity* (1992), pp. 127–81, 193–94.

CHAPTER FOUR

If Not Democracy, What?
Leaders, Laggards, and Losers
in the Postcommunist World

Charles Gati

I recall testifying before a House subcommittee in the mid-1980s. In response to a question by the chairman, I said rather cautiously that the future of communism in what was called Eastern Europe then was "uncertain." When asked to be more specific, I replied that, while it was hard to generalize, the region's Finlandization—domestic freedom combined with regular if indifferent support for Soviet foreign policy—was no longer unthinkable. "And when will that happen, professor?" the chairman wanted to know. "In my lifetime," I responded. As the silence that followed implied the chairman's reluctance to ask my age, I continued: "In your lifetime too, Mr. Chairman."

Intimidated by my desire to remain within the mainstream, I was still too cautious while drafting an essay in late 1988 for the January 1989 issue of Foreign Affairs. *I recall worrying for several days about the question mark after the title I chose, "Eastern Europe on Its Own." I kept adding it, removing it, adding it. . . . In the end I submitted it without a question mark, and the editors—Bill Hyland and Peter Grose—were good enough to leave it that way. But, sorry to say, the essay was full of qualifications; it was neither as forthright nor as prescient as the title suggests. My excuse: all the evidence was not yet in.*

Years later, it is even more difficult to generalize about the postcommunist world of 27 states in central and eastern Europe and the former Soviet Union. Conditions vary from country to country and from region to region, especially from central Europe to central Asia. And, once again, all the evidence is not in; the proverbial fat lady has yet to sing her last aria.

Still, in mid-1995, when this chapter was written, a trend can be discerned. Despite vast changes since 1989 in central and eastern Europe and not insignificant changes since 1991 in the former Soviet Union, the public mood in most postcommunist countries points to unsuccessful transitions to democracy. That it is seldom recognized to be so is because it does not fit into widely held Western notions of politics and economics. Many Americans, in particular, tend to assume that the road to democracy and the free market may be paved with bumps and detours, but at the end of the day there is no other road to be traveled. They take it for granted that the new, postcommunist states, having experienced tyranny for so long, have no choice but to proceed toward and eventually adopt something more or less similar to Western-style political and economic institutions and processes.[1]

The central argument of this chapter is that at least 20 of these states are facing the prospect of neither democracy nor totalitarianism. While the transition has neither completely failed nor completely succeeded anywhere—though democracy *is* taking root in central Europe and perhaps in the Baltics—the dominant trend of the mid-1990s is partial retrenchment. Most people in the postcommunist world have already made a choice between order and freedom, and their choice is order. Though approving a role for market forces, large majorities are nonetheless so nostalgic for the benefits of the communist welfare state, however meager, that they are prepared to do away with what they see as the cumbersome, dissonant, and chaotic features of democratic politics.

With rule by the few the familiar alternative, what they reject is not merely a leader or a party—as disillusioned Western publics would—but the very system and values of Western-style democracy. Thus, the transition is producing a group of semi-authoritarian (and therefore semidemocratic), nationalist, populist regimes that may permit free enterprise (so long as it is properly regulated), allow free parliamentary debates (so long as they are inconsequential), and even tolerate something resembling a free press (so long as it questions specific policies rather than the semiauthoritarian political order itself).[2] Only in central Europe (the Czech Republic, Poland, Hungary, and Slovenia) and to a lesser extent in the Baltic states of Estonia, Latvia, and Lithuania are the democratic prospects promising.

Persistent denial of the meaning of new realities in the face of growing evidence of retrenchment sustained and even prompted by public opinion suggests that the West suffers from a case of cognitive dissonance. Unpleasant facts, when noticed, are seldom characterized as part of a secular trend; they are called instead a "temporary setback." Election results revealing the appeal of reformed or even unreformed ex-communists and demagogic nationalist parties are explained away as a "protest vote," preference for "familiar faces," or simply the return of "experienced specialists." As election after election and poll after poll show immense and still increasing dissatisfaction with the region's democratic parties, the significance of such attitudes is minimized as "understandable reactions" to initial dislocations that accompany the introduction of democracy. The disparity between the few who are rich and the many who are poor—a major source of social strife—is seen as an "inherent" problem of "early capitalism." The power of, and atrocities by, criminals is compared to the situation in Chicago in the 1920s and thus excused.

Worse yet, those who look at the facts as they are rather than as they should be are mocked as "historical determinists" for assuming, it is charged, that only a few countries with "proper democratic genes" can have a democratic future.[3] Just the opposite is true. It is the superoptimists who seem to derive their assessments less from *contemporary* evidence than from the success of *American* history. Taking into account neither the legacy of the communism nor signs of retrenchment in the postcommunist world, they offer illusory forecasts based on hope, not on experience. Alas, American history as a guide to the evolution of the former Soviet Union and central and eastern Europe is about as helpful as an old Michelin guidebook is to present-day Yugoslavia.

To repeat, the argument advanced here is not that full restoration is taking place or is likely to take place. Most people in the postcommunist world are freer than they were ten years ago and will almost certainly remain so for years to come. Entirely unreformed communist politics has no significant following in central and eastern Europe, and only some in parts of the former Soviet Union. Even in Russia, where a bitter sense of humiliation obtains, only an extraordinary combination of economic and political developments—comparable to those that destroyed Weimar Germany in the 1930s—could mobilize sufficient forces to turn the clock back and reinstall old-fashioned communist controls. Humpty-Dumpty cannot be put together again; the return of ex-communists does not necessarily signify the return of the communist system.

The point that is being made here, then, is that the transition to democracy has lost its early popular appeal and therefore its early momentum. The glass is no longer half full. On the defensive, the demoralized champions of Western ways in Russia and elsewhere too have already begun to reposition themselves on the political spectrum. As pluralism is being blamed for living standards that are lower for most than they were even under communist rule, the eventual product of today's trend is the adoption of semiauthoritarian patterns combined with the pursuit of largely nationalist and populist policies.

THE GOALS OF TRANSITION

Most Western governments and observers view the changes that have taken place since the fall of communism in central and eastern Europe in 1989 and in the former Soviet Union in 1991 as far-reaching and encouraging. Although the overwhelming majority of the people of the postcommunist world certainly no longer like what they experience, it would be misleading to deny that the three basic goals of transition—independence, political pluralism, and free market economics—have been pursued vigorously and successfully in some countries.

The first goal was sovereign existence, which is to say independence from Russia, liberation from decades of foreign domination. Given the collapse of the Warsaw Pact together with the withdrawal of Soviet forces from central and eastern Europe and of Russian forces from most parts of the Soviet Union, this goal in fact has been achieved. In central and eastern Europe, except in Serbia and Bulgaria, not only Russian military power but Russian influence also has disappeared.

Alas, independence has brought with it two new disappointments and a potential threat. One disappointment is the rise of nationalist fervor—wars in the North Caucasus and in ex-Yugoslavia, tension elsewhere over the treatment of minorities, especially of Russians, Hungarians, and Turks who live in inhospitable neighboring countries. The other new disappointment is the inability of the postcommunist states to make use of their independence by joining the West through formal ties to NATO and the European Union. In the past it was Moscow that stood in the way; now it is the West that keeps stalling about the conditions of and the timetable for admission to these institutions. Finally, the threat to newly gained independence stems from Russia's lost status as a great power. The question its worried neighbors now ask is not whether but when Russia will be strong enough to revive its imperial ambitions.

Despite such disappointments and the fear of Russian intentions, independence has yielded results that are largely but not exclusively positive. While it has produced expressions of nationalist assertiveness rather than integration with the Western democracies, and it also has sparked new fears about Russia's future designs, it has brought to the surface long-suppressed national aspirations and strengthened national identities.

THE GOAL OF POLITICAL PLURALISM

The second goal of transition was political pluralism in an environment of open societies that observe human rights and follow democratic processes and procedures. As the yearly ratings by Freedom House's authoritative surveys indicate (see table 1), there have been far-reaching changes in the realm of political rights and civil liberties throughout central and eastern Europe. As table 2 suggests, however, several countries in the former Soviet Union regressed in 1994–95 (as compared with their status in 1991–92, when the surveys there began); most did not change at all; a few advanced.

The leaders, according to Freedom House, are thus the Czech Republic and Hungary, followed by Poland, Bulgaria (partly because of its treatment of the Turkish minority), and Lithuania. The losers, assigned the worst ratings available, are the Central Asian dictatorships of Tajikistan, Turkmenistan, and Uzbekistan, whose performance since 1991–92 has actually deteriorated. Kazakhstan and Georgia are not far behind at the negative end of the spectrum. As for Russia and Ukraine, they are ranked in the middle of the pack, but the survey was completed before the war in Chechnya, which casts a dark shadow on Moscow's record. On the whole, the unsurprising conclusion is that honoring political rights and civil liberties is a function of physical and presumably cultural proximity to western Europe. The minor exceptions are Kyrgyzstan, which should have done worse according to that standard, and Romania, which should have done better.

TABLE 1—FREEDOM HOUSE RATINGS OF POLITICAL RIGHTS AND CIVIL
LIBERTIES IN CENTRAL AND EASTERN EUROPE
(1 = FREE; 7 = NOT FREE)

	Political Rights		*Civil Liberties*	
Country	*1988–89*	*1994–95*	*1988–89*	*1994–95*
Albania	7	3	7	4
Bulgaria	7	2	7	2
Czech Republic	7	1	6	2
Hungary	5	1	4	2
Poland	5	2	5	2
Romania	7	4	7	3
Slovakia	7	2	6	3
AVERAGE (MEAN)	6.4	2.1	6.0	2.5

Source: Freedom House, *Nations in Transit: Civil Society, Democracy and Markets in East Central Europe and the Newly Independent States* (New York: Freedom House, 1995), passim. 1988–89 ratings for the Czech Republic and Slovakia are for Czechoslovakia.

TABLE 2—FREEDOM HOUSE RATINGS OF POLITICAL RIGHTS AND CIVIL
LIBERTIES IN THE FORMER SOVIET UNION
(I = FREE; 7 = NOT FREE)

Country	Political Rights		Civil Liberties	
	1991–92	1994–95	1991–92	1994–95
Armenia	5	3	5	4
Azerbaijan	5	6	5	6
Belarus	4	4	4	4
Estonia	2	3	3	2
Georgia	6	5	5	5
Kazakhstan	5	6	4	5
Kyrgyzstan	5	4	4	3
Latvia	2	3	2	2
Lithuania	2	1	3	3
Moldova	5	4	4	4
Russia	3	3	3	4
Tajikistan	5	7	5	7
Turkmenistan	6	7	5	7
Ukraine	3	3	3	4
Uzbekistan	6	7	5	7
AVERAGE (MEAN)	4.3	4.4	4.0	4.4
AVG. W/OUT ESTONIA, LATVIA, AND LITHUANIA	4.8	4.9	4.3	5.0

Source: Freedom House, *Nations in Transit: Civil Society, Democracy and Markets in East Central Europe and the Newly Independent States,* passim.

Similarly, international observer groups have rated elections since the collapse of communism as freer in countries closer to western Europe.

In central and eastern Europe (including the Baltics), both legislative and presidential elections have been held as scheduled; none has been canceled. It is true, however, that not all parties had full access to television, and minor irregularities were reported in Romania and Bulgaria. Yet, since 1989, every country has experienced at least one and in some cases two or three competitive elections. The legislatures are broadly representative of the people. The rule, adopted from Germany, that keeps small parties with less than four or five percent of the popular vote out of the legislatures has not eliminated discord, but it has added a modicum of cohesion to the region's parliaments. Moreover, Western norms distinguish the new constitutions, although in some cases, as in Poland, political dissension has prevented the adoption of a coherent document. The courts, including constitutional courts, act quite independently of the executive branch of the government. Freedom of religion and assembly too is a fact of life.

In Central Asia—the region farthest from western Europe— no genuine multiparty elections have been held in Tajikistan, Turkmenistan, or Uzbekistan. These three remain politically unreformed dictatorships under strong one-man rule, with Emomili Rakhmanov in charge in Tajikistan, Saparmurad Niyazov in Turkmenistan, and Islam Karimov in Uzbekistan. In Kazakhstan, President Nursultan Nazarbayev, having dissolved parliament in 1995, rules by decree. In a Soviet-style "election," his term of office was extended through 2001.[4] In Kyrgyzstan, charges of ballot-box stuffing and intimidation of certain candidates and of the press followed the 1995 legislative elections. On the other hand, President Askar Akayev, a scholar, is widely regarded as a moderating influence on the frenzied Kyrgyz political scene.

In the three states of the Transcaucasus, few political changes have been introduced, with deadly ethnic conflict a major though not the only factor. In Azerbaijan opposition parties exist in the rump parliament, but effective power is held by President Gaidar Aliyev, a former KGB general and hard-line Communist Party boss, a curious but hardly unique example of the born-again nationalist in the former Soviet Union. In Armenia, the July 1995 elections were described rather generously by foreign observers as "free but not fair." In fact, President Levon Ter-Petrossyan's party won most seats after nine of the 22 opposition parties and groups were banned from participation and from political activity. The ban on at least one party was lifted within a week after the elections. In Georgia the 1992 elections were called quite fair, but in Abkhazia, South Ossetia, and the country's western regions they were postponed because of persistent ethnic fighting. Although President Eduard Shevardnadze—the reformminded former Soviet foreign minister—has accumulated considerable power, he seems mindful of Western opinion.

In the European part of the former Soviet Union, powerful presidents—some favoring gradual economic change—face weak, often emasculated, legislators. President Alyaksandr Lukashenka of Belarus, elected in 1994, is a young, aggressive ex-communist who, while campaigning as a populist in nationalist colors, has returned his country to the Russian fold. As the 1995 elections produced no new parliament (voter turnout was below the required minimum), the communist Soviet-era "legislature" remains in place. In Moldova, competitive elections took place in 1994, won with a large plurality by reform-minded communists who now make up the Democratic Agrarian Party. In mid-1995 President Mircea Snegur left this party because of what he called its attempt "to establish a one-party dictatorship" and because of its pro-Russian orientation.

In Ukraine the country's recent economic reforms are being promoted by President Leonid Kuchma, who was elected in 1994. The 1994 legislative elections, held under a complex and confusing set of rules that were nonetheless generally observed, produced a fragmented and therefore weak parliament. In the most familiar case of Russia, finally, the 1993 legislative elections—regarded as free and fair by foreign observers but not by numerous domestic critics—reflected the country's fragile multiparty system. With the extent of Duma's influence and effectiveness a matter of dispute, President Boris Yeltsin, elected in 1991 before the Soviet Union had collapsed, is Russia's dominant political force—as his successor is expected to be.[5]

The two main conclusions that can be drawn from this brief review of elections and from the Freedom House study on political rights and civil liberties are that (1) political pluralism is now a fact of life in central and eastern Europe, but (2) the former Soviet states east of the Baltics have experienced only modest political change. Specifically, this onetime professor would grade progress toward *political*—rather than both political and economic—reform as of mid-1995 as follows:

A: Czech Republic, Hungary, Poland, Slovenia
B: Albania, Estonia, Latvia, Lithuania
C: Bulgaria, Romania, Russia, Slovakia, Ukraine
D: Armenia, Azerbaijan, Belarus, Georgia, Kazakhstan, Kyrgyzstan, Moldova

F: Tajikistan, Turkmenistan, Uzbekistan
Incomplete: Bosnia-Herzegovina, Croatia, Macedonia,
      Serbia

Alas, even these grudgingly positive estimates of the post-communist political landscape have been roundly dismissed by the people who live there. They consider these assessments as oblivious to the texture of political life, a sign of American grade inflation, for public opinion in the East (as in much of the West) has become decisively and increasingly negative since the end of the Cold War; governments and politicians do not fare well anywhere these days. The single-digit approval rating of Russian President Boris Yeltsin and former Polish President Lech Walesa is matched by the single-digit approval rating of British Prime Minister John Major. Few governments seem able to fulfill popular expectations; the collapse of communism has resulted in neither peace nor prosperity.

Still, despite their apparent similarity to Western sentiments, election and poll results in the postcommunist states must be taken more seriously. There, more often than not, negative attitudes signify not a protest against this party or that politician but a *systemic challenge to the essential features of Western-style democracy*. The choice there is not between liberal democrats and conservative democrats, or between democrats and republicans, but between democrats on one side and authoritarian or semiauthoritarian nationalists, nativists, populists, communists, and demagogues of different color on the other. While in theory most people appreciate such features of democracy as free speech, a just legal system, or the more abstract notion of separation of powers, in practice they reject the way democracy is working and indeed long for a strong, paternalistic leader who would presumably look after their welfare.

In contrast to the situation in the West, then, trend lines of postcommunist public opinion point to rapidly growing majorities rejecting Western-style democratic politics. These trend lines—based on responses to the same questions over a period of four years or more—indicate that whatever popular support there once was for a Western-style democratic political order has all but disappeared (while support for economic reform has also and in most cases significantly declined). There are exceptions, of course, but the trend is unmistakably clear.

Although professional pollsters consider some of its questions too general, the highly regarded *Eurobarometer Survey* of public opinion conducted for the European Union is cited here because it is comparative and because it shows a trend since 1991. Its results are confirmed by countless local polls that are far more comprehensive but less comparative. As it is, complete results are available from 1991 through the fall of 1994 only for Russia and ten countries in central and eastern Europe. The ten countries identified as central and east European in the survey are the six former Warsaw Pact countries of Poland, the Czech Republic, Slovakia, Hungary, Romania, and Bulgaria; the three Baltic states of Estonia, Latvia, and Lithuania; and Albania. The results are reported as *net results*—that is, the percentage of positive responses minus the percentage of negative responses. (For example, a net result of, say, minus 20 percent is obtained when 60 percent of the respondents answer no and 40 percent of them answer yes to a question posed.) The *trend* I calculated then was the difference in net results between 1991 and 1994, expressed as a percentage, while the *trend ranking* indicates each country's relative standing.

The key political question was this: "On the whole, are you very satisfied, fairly satisfied, not very satisfied, or not at all satisfied with the way democracy is developing in your country?" The results, collapsed into two categories of "satisfied" and "not satisfied," were as depicted in table 3.

The survey shows that popular satisfaction with democracy in the countries of central and eastern Europe dropped by a factor of 150 percent between 1991 and 1994 (from minus 16 to minus 40). In 1994, for central and eastern Europe as a whole, more than twice as many people were dissatisfied (66 percent) than satisfied (26 percent), providing the minus 40 percent net result. Support for democratic evolution declined most in Bulgaria and Lithuania. In Russia, meanwhile, the absolute

TABLE 3—SATISFACTION (+) VS. DISSATISFACTION (−) WITH
DEVELOPMENT OF DEMOCRACY
(NET RESULTS IN PERCENT)

Country	1991	1994	Trend	Trend Ranking
Czech Republic	−25	−9	+16	1
Estonia	−21	−26	−5	2
Slovakia	−55	−62	−7	3
Albania	−17	−33	−16	4
Poland	−21	−40	−19	5
Hungary	−19	−43	−24	6
Romania	−11	−36	−25	7
Latvia	−9	−42	−33	8
Lithuania	+23	−31	−54	9
Bulgaria	−6	−87	−81	10
Average (mean)	−16	−40	−24	
European Russia	−51	−75	−24	
Russia	N/A	−75	N/A	

Source: Eurobarometer Survey (Brussels: Commission of the European Communities, 1994), passim.

minus 75 percent figure for 1994 is a product of only 8 percent noting satisfaction with democracy and a stunning 83 percent indicating that they were not satisfied. The table also shows that while in 1991 democracy had more supporters than opponents in one country (Lithuania), by 1994 *every* postcommunist country displayed negative net results, ranging from minus 9 percent in the Czech Republic to minus 87 percent in Bulgaria.

The best relative score was obtained in the Czech Republic— the only country where the trend is still positive; there the number of those saying they are satisfied with democracy has actually increased since 1991. Yet in 1994 even in the Czech Republic only 44 percent said they were satisfied, while 53 percent were dissatisfied (thus the net result of minus 9 percent in 1994).

Although the worst trend lines are Bulgaria's and Lithuania's, the results in (European) Russia and in Slovakia are equally or more disturbing. Together with Bulgaria, Russia and Slovakia displayed the least support for democracy already in 1991, and they remain among the laggards in 1994. In Russia, the proportion of those dissatisfied with democracy and those who are satisfied is a staggering seven to one.

As public opinion in the postcommunist world has soured on democracy, why do Western governments and observers continue to see considerable progress? What are the possible sources of their sanguine observations? They note and appreciate, it seems, that most political laggards of the former Soviet empire are led by nationalists who are moving their countries away from Russia and that some of these political laggards have shown interest in economic experimentation. They appear not to notice, then, that nationalist aspirations and economic experimentation do not necessarily coincide with the practice of political pluralism.

Yet the main reason for the difference between the dominant Western and postcommunist perceptions is that different questions are being asked. The people there ask: What have I gained from the changes that have taken place since 1989 or 1991? The questions asked in the West are these: Do the governments now respect political rights and civil liberties? Are the elections now unfettered and competitive, and is the press free? Is there now a reasonable legal order based on constitutional principles?

What the West wants to know is whether the *processes* of governance have improved since the fall of communism. What people in the former Soviet Union and in central and eastern Europe expect from democracy is security, stability, and prosperity; they expect to benefit from their governments' *substantive* achievements. And that, more than anything else, means economic achievements. This is not to say that they do not want to practice the religion of their choice; that they do not favor freedom of assembly; that they do not want to read different views in their newspapers; or that they do not prefer electoral choice to one-party rule. They do *but. . . .* The "but" means that political rights and civil liberties matter, especially for minorities and intellectuals, but governments must also and above all deliver the economic goods.

This is why the vast majority of the people in the postcommunist world feel cheated. Cynicism about politics and politicians prevails—even more than elsewhere—because of the empty promises made both by the West prior to the collapse of communism and by most vote-hungry politicians after the collapse of communism. The West had encouraged the people of this region to get rid of the communists (and, in central and eastern Europe, of the Russians), saying or implying that once it is done, the good life will follow. Later some of the new parties promised more than they could deliver. In the euphoria that followed the changes of 1989 in central and eastern Europe and the changes of 1991 in the former Soviet Union, most people underestimated the inherent problems of transition and overestimated Western interest in lending a helping hand.

The resulting disillusionment with the performance of democracy and frustration over its tedious processes explain an apparently growing popular willingness, to borrow Erich Fromm's memorable notion, to escape from freedom altogether: unless freedom from excessive political restraints (wherever it has been gained) is coupled with economic well-being that signifies freedom to enjoy the fruits of liberty, the necessities of daily existence will take precedence over the luxuries of political democracy.

Therefore, those mainly on the outside who celebrate gains in countries where the political processes have become more open and more transparent may well be as accurate as those mainly in the inside who—identifying postcommunism with economic decline, with the breakdown of order and security, and with political chaos—keep asking with increasing impatience: Where is the beef?

This is not to suggest that an economic upturn producing higher living standards would transform Tajikistan, Turkmenistan, or Uzbekistan into a pluralistic society. Political democracy does not stem from economic well-being alone; it takes a commitment to elections repeated at regular intervals, a mentality disposed to moderation and tolerance, leaders who have both a vision and the political skills to turn that vision into reality, an understanding of the importance of the Western connection, and so on. But, as a Hungarian saying has it, one cannot sing even the national anthem on an empty stomach. By extension, one cannot sing the praise of political democracy while living standards decline. In short, under conditions of such economic decay, democracy cannot take root.

THE GOAL OF FREE MARKET ECONOMICS

The third goal of transition was to transform the planned, highly centralized, so-called command economies of the communist era by decentralization and privatization into modern, Western-style market economies. That goal enjoyed almost universal support. After all, most communist leaders, including Mikhail S. Gorbachev, had considered the introduction of *some* market mechanisms, if not large-scale privatization, even before the fall of communism. They recognized too that the old command economies had failed, and while a few old-fashioned communist publications still spoke of the sins of capitalism, most people certainly believed otherwise. What they knew of capitalism through Western movies and occasional visits to Western Europe by friends and relatives convinced them that free market economies represented a superior form of economic organization and that they would benefit from adopting it.

In the West, the economic progress made since the fall of communism, and especially since 1994, has received fairly high marks. The received wisdom is that, in many countries, several important economic indicators show signs of improvement. Although the figures and ratings on privatization by the European Bank for Reconstruction and Development—as reprinted by *The Economist*—should be treated with care, it is indeed the case that the private sector has made impressive gains (see table 4). Throughout the postcommunist world, retail trade and the service sector are now in private hands. When it comes to medium-size and large firms, however, a distinction should be made between genuine privatization (which means the sale of state-owned companies to individuals and groups that raised the necessary capital to buy such properties) and pseudoprivatization (which means the putative transfer—on the cheap—of valuable state-owned firms to "closed stock companies" controlled by the old *nomenklatura* and criminal elements). In any case, the pace of privatization is slowing down because remaining state assets are less attractive to potential buyers; there is no market for the unprofitable plants still for sale. The slower pace is also due to

TABLE 4—SELECTED RATINGS ON MARKET REFORM
(4 = MARKET ECONOMY; 1 = LITTLE PROGRESS)

Country	Private-sector share of GDP, 1994 (%)	Large	Small	Restructuring of companies	Prices	Trade, foreign exchange	Banks
	Privatization				*Competition*		
Albania	50	1	3	2	3	4	2
Bulgaria	40	2	3	2	3	4	2
Croatia	40	3	4	2	3	4	3
Czech Rep.	65	4	4	3	3	4	3
Estonia	55	3	2	3	3	4	3
Hungary	55	2	4	3	3	4	3
Latvia	55	2	4	2	3	4	3
Lithuania	50	3	4	2	3	4	2
Macedonia	35	2	4	2	3	4	2
Poland	55	3	4	3	3	4	3
Romania	35	2	3	2	3	4	2
Slovakia	30	3	4	3	3	4	3
Slovenia	30	2	4	3	3	4	2
Armenia	40	1	3	1	3	2	1
Azerbaijan	20	1	1	1	3	1	1
Belarus	15	2	2	2	2	1	1
Georgia	20	1	4	1	2	1	1
Kazakhstan	20	2	4	1	2	2	1
Kyrgyzstan	30	3	3	2	3	3	2
Moldova	20	2	2	2	3	2	2
Russia	50	3	3	2	3	3	2
Tajikistan	15	2	2	1	3	1	1
Turkmenistan	15	1	1	1	2	1	1
Ukraine	30	1	2	1	2	1	1
Uzbekistan	20	2	3	1	3	2	1

Source: The Economist, December 3, 1994, p. 27.

the growing appeal of populist agitation against capitalism, especially foreign investments.

Taking into account not only the scope but the quality of privatization, then, the leaders are the central European states of the Czech Republic, Estonia, Hungary, Latvia, Poland, and Slovakia. In the middle of the pack, Russia—a case of both genuine and pseudoprivatization—has rid itself of about half of its assets, and it has done so in less time than was available to the central Europeans, while Ukraine has improved its position since the ratings in table 4 were prepared. Having done little or nothing, in addition to Belarus and Moldova, are the eight states of Central Asia and the Transcaucasus (Armenia, Azerbaijan, Kazakhstan, Kyrgyzstan, Tajikistan, Turkmenistan, Uzbekistan, and to a lesser extent Georgia). Some of them, as *The Economist* pointed out, "regarded themselves as rich or potentially rich countries, and succumbed to the temptation of behaving accordingly, deferring reform by living off present or anticipated resource wealth (as Uzbekistan has done by selling gold to pay its bills)."[6]

Another important indicator—economic growth—began to show signs of improvement in central and eastern Europe in 1994; until then the figures were thoroughly discouraging even there.

In 1990 Kazakhstan, Kyrgyzstan, and Moldova still reported positive growth figures. In 1991 no country did. In 1992 only Poland moved ahead. In 1993 Poland was joined by Albania, Romania, and Turkmenistan, and the average for central and eastern Europe as a whole was once again in the plus column (showing a modest gain of 0.8 percent). In 1994 growth resumed in all of the states of central and eastern Europe for which data were available, with Poland leading the way, but comparable data about the Soviet successor states remained very negative. In the states of the former Soviet Union the precipitous decline of previous years (an average of minus 8.1 percent in 1991, minus 23.2 percent in 1992, and minus 10.8 percent in 1993) continued in 1994 (when the average was minus 14.3 percent) despite favorable trends in the three Baltic states (see table 5).

When all is said and done, then, *the postcommunist economies have shrunk by at least a third since the collapse of communism.* Even if some of them indeed "bottomed out" or "turned the corner" in 1994–95, as several Western specialists maintain, it will be long before they reach 1989 or 1991 levels. (And neither, of course, was a very good year.) Moreover, the consequences and by-products of negative growth include high unemployment, an often dramatic drop in living standards for most, and inflation. Irrespective of whether the changes have been fast (as in Poland) or gradual (as most everywhere else), the transition from the command economies to market mechanisms has benefited only the enterprising few.

TABLE 5—ECONOMIC GROWTH RATES
(PERCENTAGE CHANGE IN REAL GDP FROM PREVIOUS YEAR)

Country	1989	1990	1991	1992	1993	1994
Albania	N/A	N/A	−35	−10	11	N/A
Bulgaria	−1.8	−10.9	−22	−7.7	−4	1.4
Czech Rep.	N/A	N/A	N/A	−5	0	2.6
Hungary	2.2	−6.7	−11.9	−5	−1	2.3
Poland	−1.6	−9.6	−5	2	4.1	5.5
Romania	−3.3	−12.1	−12	−15	1	3.5
Slovakia	N/A	N/A	N/A	−7	−5	4.8
Slovenia	N/A	N/A	−10	−10	0	N/A
AVERAGE (MEAN)	−.8	−4.9	−12	−7.2	0.8	2.5
Armenia	11.8*	−5.5*	−10	−34	−8.9	−2
Azerbaijan	−4.4*	−11.7*	−0.7	−25	−13.3	−22
Belarus	8.9*	−6.9*	−2	−13	−9	−20
Estonia	3.3	−3.6	−11	−30	−5	3
Georgia	−4.8*	−12.4*	−23	−35	−35	−30
Kazakhstan	2.2	5.6	−7	−15	−13	−25
Kyrgyzstan	3.8	4.0	−5	−25	−13.4	−26
Latvia	5.7	−1.2	−8	−30	−5	2
Lithuania	1.1	−9.7	−13	−30	−10	0
Moldova	9.1*	4.7*	−12	−26	−4	−30
Russia	2.5*	−2.0	−9	−19	−12	−15
Tajikistan	−5.5	−1.3	−9	−34	−21	−12
Turkmenistan	0.5	−2.5	−0.6	−10	7.8	N/A
Ukraine	3.6*	−1.5*	−10	−13	−16	−19
Uzbekistan	3.7	−0.7	−0.9	−10	−3.5	−4
AVERAGE (MEAN)	2.8	−3.0	−8.1	−23.3	−10.8	−13.3

Sources: For 1989 and 1990: For the countries of the Soviet Union, including the Baltics, information provided by PlanEcon (Washington, D.C.); for the countries of central and eastern Europe, Central Intelligence Agency, *Handbook of International Economic Statistics 1995* (Washington, D.C., 1995), passim. For 1991, 1992, and 1993: Central Intelligence Agency, *The World Handbook 1991, The World Handbook 1992, The World Handbook 1993* (Washington, D.C., 1991, 1992, 1993), passim. For 1994: Central Intelligence Agency, *Handbook of International Economic Statistics 1995* (Washington, D.C., 1995), passim.

*Percentage change in real GNP from previous year.

Considering the available economic data as of mid-1995, then, progress toward *economic* reform in the various countries of the postcommunist world may be graded as follows:

A: Czech Republic, Poland

B: Estonia, Hungary, Latvia, Lithuania, Slovakia, Slovenia

C: Albania, Bulgaria, Romania, Russia

D: Armenia, Kyrgyzstan, Moldova, Ukraine

F: Azerbaijan, Belarus, Georgia, Kazakhstan, Tajikistan, Turkmenistan, Uzbekistan

Incomplete: Bosnia-Hezegovina, Croatia, Macedonia, Serbia

Alas, as in the political realm, the people who live in the post-communist world regard these estimates as unduly positive. Indeed, as seen by the results of the *Eurobarometer Survey*, the market economy is rapidly losing its once-considerable popular appeal. The key economic question—one that prompted very positive responses already in 1991 everywhere except in Romania—was this: "Do you personally feel that the creation of a market economy that is largely free of state control is right or wrong for your country's future?" As table 6 shows, the market economy as an ideal still attracts more supporters than opponents in most though no longer all of the central and east European countries, but in Russia (and presumably most everywhere else in the former Soviet Union), the trend points to a substantial decline in popular acceptance of the capitalist experiment. The 1994 (European)

TABLE 6—MARKET ECONOMY: RIGHT (+) OR WRONG (–)?
(NET RESULTS IN PERCENT)

Country	1991	1994	Trend	Trend Ranking
Romania	–5	50	55	1
Albania	45	41	–4	2
Estonia	32	14	–18	3
Poland	47	26	–21	4
Czech Republic	39	11	–28	5
Slovakia	29	0	–29	6
Hungary	52	20	–32	7
Lithuania	55	9	–46	8
Bulgaria	45	–2	–47	9
Latvia	43	–5	–48	10
AVERAGE (MEAN)	38	16	–22	
European Russia	8	–44	–52	
Russia	N/A	–41	N/A	

Source: Eurobarometer Survey (1994), passim.

Russian response, showing 44 percent of the population disapproving of the changes that have been introduced, suggests little public concurrence with, and thus a very dubious future for, further Russian market reform. The pain being felt exceeds the gains being promised and once expected.

Although the goal of full economic transformation is losing much of its early appeal even in central and eastern Europe, the old-fashioned command economies of the past have few champions left either (except, perhaps, in the least developed states of the former Soviet Union). The dilemma of choice is acute. How can these countries cope with the strong egalitarian backlash against private ownership and with the growing resentment toward foreign businessmen who are seen to be looking for a quick buck by taking advantage of poor, inexperienced natives? Under the circumstances, many postcommunist regimes, parties, and politicians find it politically expedient to advocate a middle ground between the "excesses" of capitalism and socialism, and between free trade and protectionism. Indeed, mixing the economic tenets of west European social democracy with a small dose of nationalist semiprotectionism is the course most postcommunist leaders have come to promote these days.

The popular appeal of such a neo-egalitarian course is beyond dispute; social democracy is an appealing formula for transitional economies. In theory, it combines the dynamism of free enterprise with the values of fairness and justice—with efforts to ease the pain of change for pensioners, teachers, state employees, and indeed all others on fixed income. In practice, however, the problem is that poor countries in particular cannot afford to pay the high cost of social support structures; even the rich countries of Scandinavia, western Europe, and North America have had to cut social expenditures in recent years. As for the incipient protectionist impulse, it can only produce stagnation because of the lack of sufficient domestic resources, including capital, for investment.

Unfortunately, the alternative to the neo-egalitarian welfare state has proved to be unacceptable. That alternative is comprehensive, even drastic, reform that entails a vigorous program of privatization, strict control over the money supply, full convertibility, toleration of unemployment. This is what the radical, pro-reform economists used to advocate—but because it was too painful, it lost whatever political support it had once enjoyed.

What most politicians now prefer is what most people want: an economic policy, any policy, that avoids the pitfalls of both the market and the command economy—a policy, in any case, that does not lower the majority's living standards. This is why the original west European ideal of the social-democratic welfare state that permits private enterprise to function but does not do away with social support structures is the preferred compromise of the moment between the "radical" experts who know economics and the political types who think they know what it takes to stay in power or get elected. That this alternative is economically undesirable (because it may buy time but does not offer a way out) is another question.

The absence of good alternatives has paved the way for a very varied lot of former communists to become the dominant force in the postcommunist world, except in the Czech Republic. Ex-communist parties and politicians—appearing as social democrats, socialists, reform communists, populist-nationalist demagogues, or unreformed *apparatchiki*—have returned to join those who never left. In most Soviet successor states, some have managed to stay on all along; others, who initially supported extensive reform, have since become advocates of the "social market"—a code word for neo-egalitarianism. Still others stand on the disingenous platform of gain without pain. On the whole, however, most ex-communists see market reform as a necessary evil to be pursued in a perfunctory fashion. Their lack of enthusiasm for the "chaotic" market—combined with the lack of an appealing alternative to it—reflects the popular mood and indeed the postcommunist reality.

Yet the basic *economic* feature of that reality is that the remaining problems are too serious and too pressing to be put off. Something must be done about the power of economic lobbies and trade unions, which waste no effort to defend their old turf. The same applies to the huge state bureaucracies that are unwilling to give up their old prerogatives. While a few of the region's parliaments are beginning to pass bankruptcy laws, their implementation—even in the case of clearly insolvent and unsalvagable firms—cannot be, as it is now, subject to interminable delays. How long can state-owned enterprises continue to produce goods no one needs or buys and keep their storage facilities full of unsold products? How long will the prevailing concern about unemployment, however understandable, stand in the way of the structural overhaul of not only individual companies but the postcommunist economies as a whole?

Moreover, inflation and monetary indulgence remain among the whole region's unresolved problems. Hyperinflation is no longer as rampant as it was in 1992 (when consumer prices were reported to have increased by more than 1,400 percent in both Russia and Ukraine), or in 1993 (when the increase was a stunning 4,790 percent in Ukraine), or in 1994 (when it was still 3,500 percent in Belarus). Double-digit inflation remains, however, because most of the reasons for inflation still exist. Prominent among them is the practice of printing money in an effort to pretend that living standards have not plunged as much as they have. Relatedly, several postcommunist governments make things worse by excessive borrowing, thus reinforcing inflationary pressures and indeed mortgaging the future. Of course, widespread monetary indulgence recalls the case of Mexico.

Meanwhile, the essential *political* feature of postcommunist reality is that no government can stay in power for long if it fails to be indulgent: if it takes no account of the social consequences of its economic policies. Indeed, all postcommunist governments must try to square the circle by steering a course between what should be done economically to move ahead and what can be done politically to maintain a modicum of domestic stability. Leaders of the less open and less pluralistic regimes, especially those in Central Asia and the Transcaucasus, shy away from market reform because they expect income differentiation and other features of capitalism to foment social tension and provoke public defiance. Leaders of the more open and pluralistic regimes, such as those in central and eastern Europe where elections are now taken for granted, delay austerity measures because their choice is between easing the burden of market reform and turning into critics of the next government. (In these countries, as in the West, pensioners vote in great numbers. And although they suffered longer than the young under communist dictatorships, they are now among the most tenacious advocates of neo-egalitarianism.)

Given the political needs of the moment, which call for minimal or no further reform, and the magnitude of economic problems, which call for radical measures, what is in store for economic reform? Because economics *is* politics in the postcommunist world too, and because politics, attuned to the public mood, is dominated by ex-communists, chances are that few of the economic problems on the agenda will be resolved or even mitigated in the foreseeable future. The parameters of the course ahead are, and will continue to be, defined by two seemingly contradictory tendencies: the popular rejection of radical transformation and the popular rejection of full economic and political retrenchment. This is why the transition in most countries will produce neither a retreat to the totalitarian past nor a great leap forward to Western-style free market democracies. Instead, both the logic of the situation and prevailing sentiments point to the prospective imposition of gradual economic reforms, undaring and probably ineffective, by strong leaders claiming to act on behalf of the public interest.

THE ARGUMENT: TRANSITION TO WHAT?

Consider the replies to the third question posed in the *Eurobarometer Survey*: "In general, do you feel things in your country are going in the right or wrong direction?" The results are reported in table 7.

Consider too the results of a *Eurobarometer Survey* of five former Soviet states, including Russia, supplied for 1994 *only* (which is why comparison with 1991 and thus a trend line cannot be established). They show that negative views about democracy, the market, and the country's "direction" in 1994 were far more dominant in these states than in central and eastern Europe, and that prevailing perceptions were even more negative in Russia—except among completely dejected Armenians—than in

TABLE 7—DIRECTION OF THE COUNTRY: RIGHT (+) OR WRONG (–)?
(NET RESULTS IN PERCENT)

Country	*1991*	*1994*	*Trend*	*Trend Ranking*
Albania	45	41	–4	1
Czech Republic	37	25	–12	2
Estonia	30	17	–13	3
Hungary	–19	–34	–15	4
Romania	26	–6	–32	5
Poland	13	–29	–42	6
Slovakia	13	–39	–52	7
Latvia	47	–9	–56	8
Bulgaria	38	–39	–77	9
Lithuania	28	–49	–77	9
AVERAGE (MEAN)	26	–12	–38	
European Russia	–12	–51	–73	
Russia	N/A	–52	N/A	

Source: Eurobarometer Survey, passim.

these other post-Soviet countries. (Responses to the same three questions reported in this chapter are given in table 8, together with the total of the three numbers. For the sake of easy comparison, the Russian numbers and the average for central and eastern Europe are also added here.)

Taken as a whole, these polls (which accurately anticipated the return of ex-communists) reflect more than "unhappiness" over the "expected problems" of transition, more than "uncertainty" about "initial dislocations" caused by economic change, more than "disappointment" in the present performance of the region's "fledgling democracies." They certainly reflect far more than opposition only to specific policies enacted since the collapse of communism or to some of the politicians who advocated them.

What these polls indicate is discontent so acute and so pervasive as to invite comparison with public sentiments that prevailed prior to the fall of communism. As vast majorities consider the post-communist course to be a failure, they are bent on checking its direction and arresting its development. Fueled by demagogues appearing in different political colors, the angry voices

TABLE 8—EUROBAROMETER NET RESULTS, 1994
(IN PERCENT)

Country	Democracy	Market Economy	Direction	Total
Georgia	−56	−24	−39	−119
Belarus	−62	−29	−32	−123
Kazakhstan	−62	−30	−33	−125
Ukraine	−53	−18	−55	−126
Armenia	−77	−45	−60	−182
Russia	−75	−41	−52	−168
AVERAGE FOR CENTRAL AND EASTERN EUROPE	−40	16	−12	−36

Source: Eurobarometer Survey, passim.

seeking retrenchment express the new consensus that sees the present to be worse than the past—and expects the course being followed to produce a future that would be worse than the present.

Under similar circumstances, equally critical publics in the established Western democracies would call for a change of parties and leaders; in the postcommunist world, by contrast, the publics must challenge the basic elements of the system itself because the only alternative they know to rule by the many is rule by the few, and the only alternative they know to a private economy is the state-run economy. While retrenchment need not go all the way, of course, the prevailing nostalgia about the past and skepticism about the future point to a fundamental correction ahead.

A few important distinctions should be made at this point:

1. Within the prevailing general trend of retrenchment, the evidence points to less progress in Central Asia than in the Transcaucasus, less in the Transcaucasus than in the European parts of the Soviet Union, less in the European parts of the Soviet Union than in the Balkans, less in the Balkans than in the Baltics, and less in the Baltics than in central Europe.

2. Making further distinctions among the leaders, laggards, and losers of the postcommunist world would serve to highlight existing differences among the 27 states and identify their relative positions:

(a) The seven leaders of the pack are the still-promising *democratic states* of central Europe (the Czech Republic, Poland, Hungary, and Slovenia) and the Baltics (Estonia, Latvia, and Lithuania), an area where despite popular backlash, both political and economic reforms continue to be carried on for now.

(b) The 12 laggards, placed far behind the leaders, are the *semiauthoritarian regimes* of Slovakia in central Europe, seven countries in the Balkans (Albania, Bulgaria, Romania, Croatia, Serbia, Bosnia-Herzegovina, and Macedonia), Russia and the three countries of the European parts of the former Soviet Union (Ukraine, Moldova, and Belarus), an area where reorganization and retrenchment coexist in countries that reluctantly pursue modest market reforms, tolerate a press that is partly free, and legitimate their rule by seemingly fair, if manipulated, elections.

(c) The eight losers, which are failing, are the *authoritarian though no longer totalitarian dictatorships* of Central Asia (Uzbekistan, Turkmenistan, Tajikistan, Kazakhstan, and Kyrgyzstan) and the Transcaucasus (Azerbaijan, Georgia, and Armenia), an area that is essentially unreformed and oppressive.

3. Even within each of these three groups, certain differences can be discerned. Examples include those between the Czech Republic and Lithuania among the leaders, between Slovakia and Romania on the one hand and Belarus on the other among the laggards, and between Georgia and Uzbekistan among the losers.

Because uneven development will surely persist in so diverse a region that includes the likes of the Czech Republic and Uzbekistan, the reluctance to identify a general pattern and especially a future trend is understandable. After all, what will weigh more heavily in Russia's future: the first signs of the economy "bottoming out" or the almost universal belief that the country is on the wrong track? What awaits Russian politics after the initially democratic "Yeltsin I" and the increasingly authoritarian "Yeltsin II"? What can be expected of Ukraine, which, doing so little under President Leonid Kravchuk, has been inching ahead in a more positive direction since 1994 under President Leonid Kuchma? What is in store for Poland, whose economic success is due to the pathbreaking "shock therapy" enacted by brave governments that have since been replaced by a coalition of former communists and their erstwhile agrarian supporters? And what matters more when assessing Hungary's future: austerity measures promised to the International Monetary Fund or the country's persistent habit of monetary indulgence?

While existing differences must be neither ignored nor disavowed, and uncertainties about the future must be frankly acknowledged, generalizations must still be made. And there is a general, pervasive, underlying trend that can be discerned: the trend of retrenchment. The momentum of reform has simply dissipated. Radicals have yielded to minimalists, the liberal impulse has yielded to a quest for egalitarianism, demands for freedom have yielded to demands for order. The postcommunist transition has crossed the Rubicon. Given the evidence presented in this chapter, the question is not whether such retrenchment is taking place, but how far back it will take the postcommunist world. Indeed, what is a likely outcome of the transition? If it is neither something akin to a Western-style political democracy and free market economics nor a totalitarian political order combined with a centralized command economy, what? If neither Sakharov nor Stalin, who?

There is reason to suppose that the postcommunist world finds a suitable option in a semiauthoritarian order—one that incorporates features of tsarist Russia, the so-called petty dictatorships of interwar Eastern Europe, and the Third World's "guided democracies." With a strong executive at the helm, the restraints constitutional democracy imposes on central authority could be circumvented. With only limited freedom granted to elect new leaders, the proprietors of power could stay in office by claiming that they need time to pursue long-term objectives in the national interest. With a greater sense of order and discipline injected into the body politic, the right to criticize the state's highest authorities could be curtailed by popular demand. With respect for the police firmly established, both criminals and would-be criminals would behave—or else. With the state owning part of the economy and firmly regulating the rest, the gap between the rich and the poor could diminish.

In such a *semi*authoritarian order, moreover, the authorities would get their way by intimidation, not by massive terror. Several parties would compete for power, though only those that accept the self-styled rules of the game could win. Legislatures would function, though the critical decisions of state would be made by the chief executive and his acolytes. The press would be free, though it would apply self-censorship to forestall state censorship. Private enterprise would be tolerated, even encouraged, but through taxation, control over the banking system, and strict regulations the government would make sure its priorities are observed. Trade unions would be allowed to organize, though their right to strike would be circumscribed. And if massive popular discontent should still surface—as it would—a few cabinet ministers might resign, but the system would remain in place.

By so manipulating rather than fully controlling the levers of power, the semiauthoritarian regime would try to cultivate a tolerant and benevolent, if somewhat paternalistic, image. It would extend the state's domain to public affairs while leaving people alone to practice their religion, attend the schools of their choice, or even travel abroad. Its leaders would be at pains to confide in Western interlocutors how difficult it is to make their "democracy" work and how much they would prefer to have it the way it is in Switzerland. ("Our people are not quite ready for that yet, you know; we're not like the Swiss," they would whisper.) Indeed, they would desperately seek acceptance by the West, particularly the United States, because Western recognition of their "fledgling democracy" would help legitimate their authority at home. If they are accepted by the West, what is left for the domestic opposition to say?

International circumstances in particular argue against the establishment of a full-fledged dictatorship. If elections were *obviously* fraudulent and human rights *blatantly* violated, Western governments would undoubtedly protest. If there was *conspicuous* state intervention in the economy, the issue of membership in the European Union might be removed from the agenda. If transparency was *completely* absent from the budget and the decision-making process, NATO membership would be given no further consideration. If the press was *flagrantly* suppressed, Western reporters would file only unfavorable stories.

It may be more devious but definitely more advantageous, therefore, to adopt a semiauthoritarian pattern—one that observes some of the formalities of democracy, concedes a limited private sphere at home, courts Western opinion abroad, and so on. Would the West notice—would it want to notice—that this is not democracy but a mirage? Many Western groups and individuals would notice, and they also would try to do what they can to make a difference. But they will find few supporters because the semiauthoritarian regimes—Janus-faced—would always present their best side to the outside world and conceal the rest. After all, the Potemkin village was a Russian invention.

The evidence that would expose the ugly side of the semiauthoritarian facade is bound to be inconclusive because it is hard to substantiate elusive processes of domination of the public arena by clever manipulation. In any case, Western "realists" and geopolitical minimalists would ask: Isn't a semiauthoritarian regime also semidemocratic? If so, isn't it unreasonable to expect Romania to behave like Switzerland? Besides, is "domination of the public arena by clever manipulation" really so bad? With concern for promoting humane and democratic values on the wane, Western governments will prefer to believe things are not so bad and look the other way. Noting the nationalist foundation of the semiauthoritarian order, they will proceed on the assumption that, by resisting Russian expansionist designs, these regimes will contribute to Western security. Weren't Franco's Spain and Salazar's Portugal useful allies once?

The case of Russia, however, is different. The future of postcommunist transition there is obviously a foreign policy concern for the West. This is so because a semiauthoritarian Russia would be more widely recognized to be not only a challenge to Western values but a threat to Western security interests as well. Russia would be compared with Weimar Germany, another erstwhile great power, a country confused about its past, uncertain of its future, shocked by its lost status, haunted by a sense of humiliation, full of resentments, and itching for revenge. Still, it is unclear as yet what outlet such a Russia is going to find for the political passions its humiliated condition has unleashed. Who will be blamed for the country's blight? Will it be foreign or domestic scapegoats, or both? All that can be said for now is that the example of Weimar Germany does not bode well for Russia's future.

While Western foreign policies can certainly shape Russian behavior abroad, they cannot counter those almost elemental political passions clamoring for retrenchment at home. The received wisdom in the West notwithstanding, no Western money or investment, no summit meetings or conciliatory gestures, no invocation of the common struggle in World War II, no joint space exploration, no arms-control treaties or cultural agreements, and no catering to its so-called legitimate security interests in the Baltics, the Balkans, or central Europe can make Russia a democracy or even help it become one—unless and until the passions in Russia itself subside. Paradoxically, however, they may subside only when order is perceived to have been restored.

Needless to say, agreements and deals that are fair to both sides, and thus take no undue advantage of Moscow's weak hand at this juncture, should be pursued. Individually and collectively, they can help improve Western relations with Russia. Trade-offs can be particularly useful; in exchange for something Russia wants from the West, it may do something the West wants from it. The problem in the mid-1990s is that many Western Russophiles seem to assume that the West can even influence Russia's most basic *domestic* political choices by, say, canceling NATO's plan to admit new members (but not Russia) to its ranks. In making that assumption, they overestimate both Western influence and the popular appeal of Russian democracy, and they vastly underestimate the appeal of a semiauthoritarian resolution of Russia's current time of troubles. While it is, to repeat, necessary to negotiate in good faith and conclude fair agreements—and to try to keep hope alive—it is simply naive to believe that fancy Western hopes for democracy can take precedence over harsh Russian realities.

If the West chooses to do so, the place where it *can* make a difference in advancing democratic values is among the seven "leaders" of postcommunist transition, all in central Europe and the Baltics, all relatively small. Although their trials are certainly not over either—they are also under pressure to retrench—their democracy and especially their market economies are still in place. Closest to western Europe both physically and culturally, and thus both more exposed and more receptive to Western influences, this is the area where with some luck the promise of 1989—the promise of extending freedom's frontiers—may yet be won.

NOTES

1. The opposite view should be noted here. A few Western skeptics, understanding the seriousness of the problems but overestimating the scope and extent of retrenchment, anticipate the return of something similar to the totalitarian past in most, if not all, of the postcommunist world.
2. Although it is premature to anticipate the precise qualities of such semi-authoritarian regimes, they will, of course, all center on a dominant executive. The countries of the former Soviet Union can be expected to develop somewhat milder and less centralized political practices than those that once characterized totalitarian states, while the countries of central and eastern Europe may embrace somewhat harsher and more centralized political practices than can be found in Western democracies.
3. Richard Schifter, "Is There a Democracy Gene?," *Washington Quarterly* 17, no. 3 (Summer 1994), pp. 121–27.
4. Viktor Chernyshov—a former Kazakh legislator who went on a hunger strike to protest the dissolution of parliament but apparently did not lose his sense of humor—said in March 1995 that Nazarbayev's constitution consists of two articles: "Article 1: The President is always right. Article 2: When in doubt, see Article 1." President Nazarbayev's comment? "We hear cries that there will be a dictatorship. Yes, dictatorship will come, but a dictatorship of the constitution and of the law. There will be a real dictatorship if, under democratic slogans, chaos and anarchy are created. Then the people will call for a firm hand." *Caravan*, an independent daily whose newsprint was destroyed in a mysterious fire, printed this response by a reader: "It's understood by everyone that Nazarbayev won't give up power." However, during a visit to Almaty in April 1995, Secretary of Defense William Perry reported what he was told: "The President has reaffirmed to me ... that he is committed to moving Kazakhstan toward democracy." Sure. All quotations are from Bruce Pannier, "Kazakhstan: A Step Back for Democracy," *Transition* 1, no. 2 (June 30, 1995), pp. 62–66.
5. The legislative elections of December 1995, which took place months after this chapter was written, produced a new Duma packed with strong opponents of domestic reform. Old-fashioned communists and their allies—agrarians and communists parading as "independents"—obtained a majority of the seats. While the vote only confirmed widespread popular support for retrenchment on all fronts, the prompt dismissal of all remaining pro-western cabinet-members—Yeltsin's post-Christmas massacre—indicated that the president was no longer the reformer he used to be.
6. *The Economist*, December 3, 1994, p. 27.

Index

Albania, 194; satisfaction with development of democracy in (table), 180; direction of (table), 192; economic growth rates in (table), 186; feelings toward market economy in (table), 187; ratings on market reform (table), 184; political rights and civil liberties in (table), 174

Aliyev, Gaidar, 176

Antall, Joszef, 33

Appel, Joseph, 134–35

Armenia, 194; economic growth rates in (table), 186; ratings on market reform (table), 184; political rights and civil liberties in (table), 175
public discontent in (table), 193

Asland, Anders, 122, 145

Assembly, freedom of in postcommunist countries, 106–108

Austrian school of economics, 79

Azerbaijan, 176, 194; economic growth rates in (table), 186; ratings on market reform (table), 184

Baltics, partial retrenchment in, 170

Banfield, Edward, 131

Barnum, P.T., 125–26, 127, 128, 130, 137

Belarus, 194; economic growth rates in (table), 186; ratings on market reform (table), 184; political changes in, 177; political rights and civil liberties in (table), 175; public discontent in (table), 193

Bellah, Robert, 112

Berlin, Isaiah, 28

Better Business Bureau, 124, 125, 135

Bismarck, Prince Otto Edward Leopold von, 114

Bosnia-Herzegovina, 194

Bosnian Serbs, 113

Braun, Aurel, 12

Breeden, James, 127

Brezhnev, Leonid, 120

Brown, J.F., 51

Bulgaria, 194; satisfaction with development of democracy in (table), 180; support for democratic evolution in, 180; direction of (table), 192; economic growth rates in (table), 186; feelings toward market economy in (table), 187; ratings on market reform (table), 184; political rights and civil liberties in (table), 174; treatment of Turkish minorities, 174

Bush, George, 114

Capitalism, 121; democracy and, 140–52; and connections between, 140–41; crime in, 143–45; and relevance of legal system in, 144–45; and role of NATO in,

About the Authors

Charles Gati is senior vice president at Interinvest, a global money-management firm with offices in Boston, Montreal, Toronto, Bermuda, and Zurich. Dr. Gati is also a fellow at the Foreign Policy Institute of the Paul H. Nitze School of Advanced International Studies of the Johns Hopkins University. Dr. Gati served as a senior adviser on the Department of State's Policy Planning Staff in 1993–94 and was a part-time consultant there from 1989 to 1993. Dr. Gati has taught at Union College and at Columbia University. He is the author of several books, including *Hungary and the Soviet Bloc* (1986) and *The Bloc that Failed* (1990).

Stephen Holmes is professor of political science and law at the University of Chicago and research director of the Constitutional and Legislative Policy Institute in Budapest. Professor Holmes received an M.A., M. Phil., and Ph.D. from Yale University. He has taught at Harvard, Yale, and Wesleyan universities. He is the author of numerous books and articles, including *The Anatomy of Antiliberalism* (1993) and *Passions and Constraint: On the Political Theory of Liberal Democracy* (1995).

Michael Mandelbaum is director of the Project on East-West Relations at the Council on Foreign Relations and the Christian A. Herter Professor of American Foreign Policy at the Paul H. Nitze School of Advanced International Studies of the Johns Hopkins University. He is also the associate director of the Aspen Institute's Project on American Relations with Central and

Eastern Europe. Professor Mandelbaum received an M.A. from King's College, Cambridge, and a Ph.D. from Harvard University. He has taught at Harvard and Columbia Universities and at the United States Naval Academy. He is the author of six books and the editor of six volumes published by the Council on Foreign Relations Press, including *Central Asia and the World* (1994) and *The Strategic Quadrangle* (1995).

John Mueller is professor of political science at the University of Rochester, where he is a member of the advisory board of the Center for Polish and Central European Studies. He is also the director of the Watson Center for the Study of International Peace and Cooperation. Professor Mueller received his M.A. and Ph.D. from the University of California, Los Angeles. His most recent books are *Policy and Opinion in the Gulf War* (1994) and *Quiet Cataclysm: Reflections on the Recent Transformation of World Politics* (1995).

Robert Skidelsky is professor of political economy at Warwick University, England, and chairman of the Social Market Foundation in London. A fellow of the British Academy, Lord Skidelsky is the author of *John Maynard Keynes* (vols. 1 & 2, 1986 and 1994) and *The World After Communism* (1995), published in the United States as *The Road From Serfdom* (1996).

Edcassells@aol.com
718-798-5352